THE
Fashion Designer
SURVIVAL GUIDE

THIRD EDITION

START AND RUN YOUR OWN FASHION BUSINESS

Mary Gehlhar

Foreword by CHRISTIAN SIRIANO

Published by Kaplan, Inc., d/b/a Barron's Educational Series
750 Third Avenue
New York, NY 10017
www.barronseduc.com

ISBN: 978-1-5062-6560-5

10 9 8 7 6 5 4 3 2 1

Kaplan, Inc., d/b/a Barron's Educational Series print books are available at special quantity discounts to use for sales promotions, employee premiums, or educational purposes. For more information or to purchase books, please call the Simon & Schuster special sales department at 866-506-1949.

Praise for

"Lest fashion's neophytes get too dreamy, Gehlhar is there to ground them . . ."
—Women's Wear Daily

"With insider perspective and industry experience, Mary addresses real-life expectations for creatives launching into the marketplace with guidance, resources and advice throughout the book."
—Maryanne Grisz, President and CEO, The Fashion Group International

"Must read . . . find out from a pro who has worked with up-and-coming designers."
—New York Daily News

"Every aspiring designer needs this book. Mary Gehlhar wrote an invaluable, step-by-step guide to succeeding on Seventh Avenue and beyond."
—Nancy MacDonell, Wall Street Journal columnist
and author of Lilly Pulitzer and The Shoe Book

"For anyone who's ever aspired to be an independent designer, this is the book to pick up."
—The Daily

"This book encourages all aspiring designers ready to embark on an independent career within the industry."
—Rebecca Taylor, designer

"A must-read for anyone in the world of fashion. Gehlhar offers practical tips and strategies to increase chances of success."
—Soma Magazine

Contents

Foreword

If you are reading this page, it means you must be a creative, passionate individual with the exciting dream of starting your own fashion business. Congratulations—you are on your way!

When I am asked "What is your advice to designers who are launching their own fashion label?" my answer is first you should be open to every opportunity. The fashion business is exciting—and tough. Each day you have to wake up ready to work hard and be prepared to open new doors and see the possibilities. It's important to take risks and to push yourself. Fortunately, Mary Gehlhar provides a valuable tool to help you. *The Fashion Designer Survival Guide* is packed with essential knowledge and advice from industry experts and experienced designers to set you on the right path. These insights will give you the solid foundation to create a plan and make smart decisions along the way.

Second, always follow your own instincts. There is no single path to success and there are so many levels of success. It's just important to be true to what you love and are passionate about. I started my career maybe in an unconventional way, but it helped me understand my customer more than most, and that helped me stay on track to success. I wanted to champion people and diversity in fashion, so I made sure, no matter what, my brand would always represent all different walks of life.

As you face each new challenge, trust in your creative ideas and focus on your unique vision. If you stay true to that, it will be your greatest tool ever!

Good luck on the journey. I can't wait to see what you create.

Christian Siriano

Preface

This book was originally published in 2005 and updated in 2008. Now, it's 2021 and we are entering a new reality where the dream of being an independent fashion designer is as exciting, but perhaps more uncharted, than ever. The fashion industry has faced total disruption with changes in technology, shifts in consumer mindset, and a sobering realization of its impact on the environment. In the midst of all this change, a global pandemic stunned the world, forever changing the ways in which we live, work, dress, and buy.

On top of it all, the world has too much fashion product. And because corporate design chases the trends and makes safe bets, too much of it looks the same. As a result, consumers are craving something special. There is a need and a desire for a unique point of view, something with meaning, and a connection to the maker and the community that shares the same values.

The answer of course lies in the creativity and innovation of the independent designers in the small ateliers—the designers who can hone in on unique and creative visions and respond to the specific taste and values of their individual customers. They can cultivate relationships across the globe and build community as they share their story, listen to feedback, and react quickly to new opportunities and ideas.

Of course it's one thing to have vision and ideas, it's another thing to run a business. Design school will teach you about sketching and patterns and prepare you for a career as head designer, but it will not prepare you for the responsibilities and decisions that face an entrepreneur.

This book will help designers understand all of the issues involved in launching a fashion label. It will help you plan and create a foundation for the business and anticipate and prepare for the unique challenges and opportunities that come your way. With insights from experienced designers who are doing this every day, these pages provide the knowledge and resources to forge your own path.

This third edition is extensively updated for a changing world. It includes a new chapter on sustainability, new sections on developing your brand story, and tips to navigate economic crisis. There are expanded sections on direct to consumer selling, as well as the many aspects of marketing, including social media, content creation, email, influencers, and collaborations. There is new advice from dozens of designers who are in the trenches running their own businesses, as well as from the lawyers, financiers, sales reps, buyers, and production experts who are rooting for the next generation.

These pages will demystify the world of fashion. They are a collective summary of what it takes to not only survive, but to thrive. The advice is not sugarcoated, and it's not always what you want to hear. But knowledge is power and it should not discourage you.

This book is intended to help designers in their first few years and to share perspectives with those who have been operating for much longer. It was written to increase the odds of success.

Good luck and enjoy the journey. I can't wait to see what you do!

www.fashiondesignersurvivalguide.com

One Piece of Advice

If you could give today's young designers one piece of advice what would it be?

John Bartlett

"If you want to start your own line I would do one of two things . . . I would commit myself to working for another designer company for at least four years to really learn from their mistakes . . . or I would concentrate on one product category, like T-shirts or shoes, and focus all of my energy developing the best possible product. Too many designers get caught up in doing a whole collection and doing shows. Shows are for ego, product is for survival."

Tommy Hilfiger

"Being a successful fashion designer is about more than just making great clothes. It's about running a business, and that means having a combination of diverse skills—you need creativity, business acumen, social skills, management skills, and most importantly, you need dedication. I started out in this business with $150 and a dream. There were many years, challenges, and lessons learned before getting to where I am today. The best piece of advice I'd give to a young designer is to first dream big and believe in yourself, and then approach fashion from a holistic point of view. You have to start with a great product, but you also need the right vehicle to get that great product into your customer's hands. That means planning, researching, merchandising, building great relationships, having a great marketing plan, and being able to execute all of those things in a carefully thought out way."

Donna Karan

"There are three things you absolutely must keep in mind: Realize that in the end, it's all about the customer—your customer. You need to decide who she is and then really get to know what she's about. That single-minded focus is the way you create a strong, consistent message. Make sure the people behind you are better than you and that you're all on the same page. Lastly, never believe the good press because that means you have to believe the bad. Be true to yourself."

Steven Kolb, CEO of the Council of Fashion Designers of America (CFDA)

"Be yourself. There is so much noise in fashion—there's the history of what happened before, there's what is happening parallel to you—and you should be aware of that. But at the end of the day, you have to go with what you believe."

Richard Lambertson of Lambertson Truex

"Stay true to your design ethics and try to be different, but don't follow the trends. You can't be everything to everybody. I also can't stress enough that the more practical experience you have, the better. Everyone wants to work for the big names, but you can get even more experience working for a small house."

Christian Louboutin

"As a supposedly established designer, I regret to say that I have very few words of advice to give to the emerging talent. The reality is that I continue to learn every day about my work. But, if I may give one word of advice, it would be this: Leave, and always leave, your imagination above everything else; technique should always serve imagination, and not the opposite. To be a good technician is only a help, but should never be a priority. Why? Because technique can shrink your creation, and creation is everything, and the rest should gravitate around this. The more you are free, the more your design will reflect this sense of liberty, which is after all one of the essences of fashion. Fashion tends to represent different points of view and meaning and at its best should reflect individuality, eccentricity, and wit."

Cynthia Rowley

"Coming from a free-thinking art school that encouraged creativity, I very quickly learned about the constant battle between art and commerce and had to find the balance to survive. There are many ways to find your own balance and to learn both sides of the business. Once you learn the rules, I think it is very important to take chances and push the envelope as a designer—sometimes ideas work, sometimes they don't, but the most important thing is that you roll the dice. The fashion industry is forever evolving, and so much of being successful is changing and adapting while remaining true to your vision and maintaining your integrity."

Richard Tyler

"I started when I was 18 by opening my own store. There's nothing like it for finding your own niche, and it ensures your survival. You show your clothing to the world the way you envision it. It's healthy to see what people admire and what they can truly wear. When you get to know your client, they keep you balanced between designing what drives and interests you and designing for the person who is wearing your clothes."

Diane Von Furstenberg

"The important thing is to believe in what you do. Have a big dream and take small steps."

1 BEFORE YOU START

It's up to you. The world is evolving and customers are craving creativity and something new. It has never been so easy to quickly set up a business and reach people around the world. There is real opportunity to build your brand and establish a global customer base for your designs.

The world doesn't need *more*, but it does need *better*. In the face of fast fashion and tech-driven start-ups, small companies cannot compete on price, reach, or speed. But they can compete through their creativity and unique point of view, keeping in mind a few core principles to fuel success.

Be focused. You need a clear point of view and purpose. Do not be distracted by others; stay clear on your unique role in the industry and how you will fulfill it. This doesn't mean you can be rigid. It's important to continually adapt and evolve, but to do so while remaining true to yourself and what you stand for.

Be special. You can't do anything basic. The independent designer's role is to offer something that stands out from the thousands of other dresses, handbags, and shoes. It's the ability to satisfy and delight through your unique story, the product quality, and the customers' experience.

Be customer obsessed. At the end of the day, you aren't making things for yourself. You are making things to satisfy and serve your special segment of customers. It's your job to understand their needs and values and become a part of their lives. Their loyalty is your reward.

As you move forward, the important thing is to know what you are doing, why you are doing it, and who you are doing it for. Your path may include wholesale markets in Paris, made-to-measure fittings for Nashville stars, or relationship building with artisans. It is your unique path and that's what makes the journey so interesting.

The Reality

To help you succeed, right up front we have to strip away the glamorous facade of celebrities and red carpets, fashion week in Paris, and luxurious sourcing trips to Marrakech. I don't want to rain on the parade, but fashion is a business. It's the business of making and selling clothing and accessories for your customers.

Aspiring designers enter the fashion world to be creative, but regardless of creative genius, fashion is nothing without commerce. Even designer Karl Lagerfeld once said, "Fashion is something you wear. It's not something you put on the runway to show how creative you are. There's nothing bad about selling dresses."[1]

Designers need to balance the business and creative sides—one allows the other to live. To say you are a creative person who can't do the other side is nonsense. Surviving day to day in the business is creative in itself. Designers are problem solvers, and every day they find unique ways to satisfy demand and promote their product even without the proper resources or experience. As Andy Warhol said, "Good business is the best art."

Where's the Glamour?

If you are doing this just to be famous, forget it. The fashion world requires hard work, discipline, perseverance, and passion. There is no magic formula or secret to success, and while designers can learn from others, they each must find their own path.

It's easy to romanticize the freedom of having your own business, but it's not as easy as it looks. According to the Small Business Administration, 50 percent of small businesses fail within five years.[2] John Galliano, Yohji Yamamoto, Betsey Johnson, and Michael Kors are just a few of many designers who had to start over after bankruptcy.

Don't be discouraged, but realize entrepreneurship is the hard road, not the easy one. Be honest with yourself and assess whether self-employment is the right path for you. Not everyone is happy as an entrepreneur, and there are realities to brace yourself for up front.

> **It takes more money than you think**. When asked, "What is the hardest part of running your own business?" the majority of designers answered "the money." In fact, Keanan Duffty, Founding Director for the Masters in Professional Studies in Fashion Management at Parsons School of Fashion, says, "No matter how much you think it will cost, multiply that by ten."[3] Up front, you must determine if you can afford to start your own business and whether you are willing and able to work potentially for several years, stretching cash and juggling resources to pay everyone but yourself.

> **You will live, eat, and breathe your business**. Designers work seven days a week, twelve or more hours per day, and have little time for friends, exercise, or vacation. Designer Daniel Silver of Duckie Brown confirms, "It has to become a lifestyle."[4] A designer needs physical and mental stamina and must be absolutely, passionately in love with what they are doing.

It could take years. As many say in the business world, "It takes years to become an overnight success." Getting your fashion label on its feet can easily take five years or more. Many designers who get significant press attention, land celebrity clients, grow their accounts each season, and win the awards are in fact still not making money. Ralph Lauren did not go from tie salesman to fashion emperor overnight.

You will design less than 10 percent of the time. A designer takes on many roles and spends significant time on administrative work, managing people, shipping, overseeing factories, servicing customers, managing social media, and chasing money. Most young designers do everything themselves, and many learn to love these aspects of the business, but they generally spend only 5 to 10 percent of their time designing.

In fact, designer Christine Alcalay advises, "Start now—design. Design like there is no tomorrow because once the business starts to roll, you'll find yourself dealing with contractors, stores, and handling problems long before you have any time to be creative with your pencil and paper. Most of the creativity that follows in the business is how to survive."[5]

It demands militant self-discipline. When you work for yourself, no one is there to make you get out of bed each morning, meet your deadlines, or prioritize your time. An entrepreneur must create her own structure and set daily goals to stay focused and ensure everything is organized and on schedule. The buck stops with you, and when problems arise, you can't run and hide.

You need to be tough and assertive. This is business, and a designer can't be timid or take things personally. Business owners must deal firmly with factory supervisors, store owners, and collections people who may bully, intimidate, and try to take advantage of you. You will have to call people who owe you money, make tough decisions that upset others, and learn to say no.

You are on your own. Being independent means facing the daily stress of not having a steady income, benefits, or any guarantees. Despite how nice it sounds to not have a boss, working alone can be lonely. Independent designers often spend hours by themselves and may feel isolated.

It's not always fair. People may steal from you, stores won't pay, and others will copy your designs. One well-known young designer saw his $1,500 dress in a store on the same floor as the store's own $300 polyester knockoff. Unfortunately, this is part of any creative business. At times, you have to fight for yourself, but at other times, you have to just make the best of it like the designer who walked into the offices of a large, well-known clothing brand and saw photos of his collection on their mood board. Rather than explode with anger, he offered to consult for them and ended up making enough money to fund his next collection.

You Could Be Karl Lagerfeld

Having your own business is not the only way to go. Too many designers get hung up on the idea of being independent and lose sight of other amazing opportunities. Tom Ford, Olivier Rousteing, and Phoebe Philo each made their name designing for well-funded luxury labels, without having to manage the business issues. Even Karl Lagerfeld, though he had his own label, was most famous for designing Chanel.

As Steven Kolb, CEO of the Council of Fashion Designers of America (CFDA) observes, "Opportunity in fashion now for designers isn't necessarily a designer label with your name on it. The tech people or Harvard MBAs with business ideas hire designers to work with those ideas. Initially, those companies are not necessarily driven by design, but they know that the growth of the company will always come back to design. That kind of company is a really valid place for a creative person to be."[6]

There Is No Rush

Many young designers launch too soon before they have a clear vision and without the resources to survive their mistakes or the experience to avoid them. Be patient and realize there is no rush. Take the time to learn, plan, and make connections. As showroom owner Denise Williamson said, "Too many designers want immediate gratification. You have to build it over time and be smart about it."[7] Putting yourself out there too early, building up debt, and making mistakes will slow you down rather than get you there faster. Don't strike until you are ready. Build your resume and put in the time. If you aren't ready now, you can be later. If you have talent, that will never leave you.

The Most Important Advice in This Book

Work for someone else first. Regardless of how many times I say it, or quote others who agree, it won't be said enough. Designers need to work for other designers, and work for them for years, before heading out on their own. This is the single most consistent advice I am given for designers from experts and veterans in all areas of the industry. The fashion business has a history of apprenticeship, and the solid experience attained while working for someone else is critical to survive.

Steven Kolb, CEO of the Council of Fashion Designers of America (CFDA) advises, "Work for a brand whether it's big or small, and just be a sponge and absorb as much as you can. Understand who are the factories and the suppliers and who delivers on time. Find out who are the social media people and the human resources people. Take advantage of the opportunity to learn that information."[8]

Although you are anxious to get out on your own, if you fail, you will end up working for someone else anyway. Do it now and increase your chance of success. Donna Karan worked for Anne Klein; Marc Jacobs for Perry Ellis; Karl Lagerfeld at Balmain, House of Patou, Chloe, and Fendi; and Stella McCartney for Chloe. Alexander McQueen learned tailoring on Savile Row before designing for Romeo Gigli. At a *Teen Vogue* Fashion U event, designer Vera Wang advised attendees, "Get a job! When you get a job, you are getting paid to learn." She was a design director at Ralph Lauren before launching her own bridal line.[9]

Working for a designer is not the only experience that can be critical to your success. Retail experience is vital to understanding the sales environment, hearing customer feedback, understanding how sales people are motivated, and witnessing the cycle of product from presentation to markdown. While attending Parsons, designer Althea Simons of GRAMMAR worked in retail sales at Issey Miyake. She says, "It is so useful to have a retail background as a designer. The sale is the ultimate relationship between the product and the end customer, who is the one who will actually use it. Understanding how people feel in the clothes and how they integrate them with their life is so valuable. Designers can get detached from that."[10]

There are multiple benefits of working in the industry before you launch.

Knowledge. When working for someone else, take advantage of opportunities to visit factories, attend fabric shows, and work with sample makers and patternmakers. This is an important time to acquire technique and perfect your skills. Be an active spectator and witness what makes your employer a success. Designer Derek Lam has said of his four years as vice president of design for Michael Kors, "Michael taught me the importance of identifying with your customer, the importance of quality fabrics, and above all else, to enjoy the business and have fun with it."[11]

Even a bad experience is a great education and shows you what not to do. As Jie Yee Ni of Kordal says, "The things you learn on the job are so different than what you learn in school—it's less conceptual and more hands on. It lets you try things and figure out what you don't want."[12]

Money. Working for someone else helps build the start-up capital you need. Too many people start without enough funds and burn out too soon. When you are new, you will make mistakes, and they can be very costly. Better to learn from them while working for someone else, who can pay the damages.

Connections. Working for another company will lead you to important resources, help you determine whom to trust, and even unearth a potential business partner. You can travel to markets, factories, and fabric and trade shows. When Derek Lam worked for Michael Kors, the buyers, editors, and manufacturers knew him there. Those connections paid off when he set out on his own. Many designers receive support from the factories with whom they create relationships while working for other companies. Their past jobs open doors and give contractors faith in them.

This leads us to a few more important observations about the fashion industry.

It's all about relationships. Business is based on relationships. The interactions you have with financial people, factory owners, fabric suppliers, stylists, sales reps, and editors will largely determine your success. Fashion is a small industry. Everyone talks to everyone else, and word travels fast. In any interaction, there is opportunity.

It's best to be nice. The fashion diva is a fool—a boring stereotype in a busy and competitive field. Bad behavior will come back to haunt you. Ultimately, patternmakers, retail buyers, production managers, and fabric agents all prefer to work with kind, reasonable people, and they are more likely to offer them valuable advice, introductions, and better terms. A few industry contractors even confessed to adding a "pain in the ass" surcharge to their services for designers who are difficult or rude. Fashionably late is also a misnomer. If you are late to meet a factory owner, buyer, or last maker, you simply look unprofessional.

Learn from everyone. The patternmakers, salespeople, contractors, and buyers have a wealth of valuable knowledge and experience that can help you. Ask questions, and listen to advice and criticism with an open mind. Then make the decisions that are right for your brand.

Keep the door open. Learn to say no politely. If you aren't interested in working with someone now—a stylist, sponsor, influencer, or supplier—there is always a chance you will want to later. Youthful pride shuts doors that designers often wish they could reopen. Unfortunately, the most in-demand designer one season may find he is virtually forgotten the next. If you have a dispute or end a relationship, do it as professionally and amicably as possible. Be flexible and learn to compromise, but also be prudent on your own behalf. If someone asks for $10,000, come back and offer $5,000. Business demands constant negotiation.

Friend not foe. Obviously, there is competition in the emerging designer community, but you'll find no better support group than other designers who are struggling with the same issues and understand your highs and lows. Take advantage of the plentiful opportunities to meet each other—waiting at the factory, sourcing at fabric shows, or sitting across the aisle at trade shows. Designers can share resources and knowledge of store credibility, and barter for each other's expertise and skills. You can work together to meet minimums, sell together during market week, hire legal help, stage a pop-up, or just learn from each other's mistakes.

Focus on your own strengths. Some designers have strong advantages—celebrity friends, a huge social media following, fluency in Mandarin, a family-owned factory, an influential husband, rich parents, or even pull with Anna Wintour. Others have the looks or charm to melt icebergs. Get over it. The success of others does not determine your failure. Insecurity is distracting, and jealousy is unproductive. Use the advantages you have—maybe its time management, math skills, a cultural tradition, or beautiful illustrations. Stay focused on your vision and make your own luck.

Failure is part of success. One designer told me the hardest part of the business is how it affects the ego. It hurts if the product doesn't sell, the media ignores it, and the buyers say no. And everyone makes mistakes. But designers survive bad experiences with stores, social media, and business partners. They take time off and come back stronger. As Angela Luna of ADIFF says, "I get told 'no' more than 'yes.' Success is finding your way around that 'no,' whether it's with that person or if it's moving forward and finding another way."[13]

You Survived the Bad News

Now it's time to pave your own way. Everyone has their own unique vision, and as designer Angela Luna of ADIFF says, "The one thing I learned when trying to figure out how to start a business is there is no right way to start. Every person I met with when I was trying to find the first step told me different first steps. Everyone has a different approach."[14] And as designer Steven Cox of Duckie Brown says, "There are more highs than lows, and no matter the problem, there's always an answer." If you are 100 percent committed, believe in yourself, and have a heavy dose of raw determination, it's time to move forward.[15] As designer and educator Keanan Duffty states, "If you are a creative person, you will find a way."[16]

2 THE FUNDAMENTALS

Start with the Mission

Your mission is what drives you and defines your success. It is critical to think about WHY you are launching this business and be clear on your intentions and what you want to achieve. It's different for everyone and there is no wrong answer.

What do you want your life to look like? How does this business and your definition of success fit into that vision? Perhaps success for you is a small, profitable business where you retain total control and creative freedom. Perhaps you are driven by the satisfaction of seeing millions of people wearing your logo. Maybe your end goal is attracting investment to scale and eventually sell the brand. Designers often are driven to identify and solve problems, whereas others may want to build a loyal customer base to support an artisanal handcraft. Whatever they are, you need clarity at the outset as all of your decisions should be driven by these objectives.

What does success mean to you?

"Having a healthy business where everyone involved—our customers, suppliers and manufacturers, and buyers—all feel good about what we are doing."
—MANDY KORDAL, KORDAL

"Success to me means living your purpose. When you come from a place of authenticity and live your truth, that is success. There is so much freedom in doing what lights you up; even the messy stuff becomes part of the adventure." —PAIGE NOVICK

"Doing well and doing good." —Angela Luna, ADIFF

"Sales are really important. But we feel our happiest and that we've done our job when we get a customer email that says, 'I've never felt this way before, I finally feel like myself and that someone is recognizing me.'"
—LAURA MOFFAT, KIRRIN FINCH

"Success is about owning your own time." —LINDSEY THORNBURG

"Having a financially viable business, which means meeting and connecting with enough people who love the brand and the product that they are willing to put their money into it." —Althea Simons, Grammar

"Personally, it means being able to be myself in any situation. Professionally, it will be when the business model we've activated with CANAVA becomes widely duplicated and there are more and more impact-focused, profit-for-purpose brands in the marketplace." —Geren Lockhart, Canava

"I believe success in the fashion business is longevity, stamina, and no debt. As long as I can keep the brand alive and relevant, then that is major success. I'm so happy I'm still at this. It's my passion and I don't see myself quitting anytime soon. Just developing and creating." —Karelle Levy, Krelwear

"To be free to do what I love, to be in the flow of the moment, to have time and space to spend with the people I love, and to learn and gain new experiences in the work I do and the life I live." —Helena Fredriksson, H Fredriksson

The Plan

Before you start your own fashion business, you need to know where you are going and how you will get there. Showroom owner Greg Mills says, "You really have to have passion and a plan. Think about what you are bringing to the game and how to get from point A to B, then to K and Z."[1]

A business plan keeps you focused in the face of fashion fantasy. It defines short-term and long-term goals along with the actionable steps to achieve them. It provides insight into the market opportunity, determines which resources you need, sets up goals and guidelines to make decisions, and proves the legitimacy of your business to potential suppliers, contractors, and investors.

Write It Yourself

In exchange for a few thousand dollars, there are people who will write your business plan for you. While it is tempting to hand off what appears to be an overwhelming task—don't. No one can make a plan for your company better than you, and you will learn much in the process. Thinking through each element of the business is invaluable to creating the company you want and preparing it to succeed. The process is even more important than the final document. It will point out your strengths and weaknesses, helping you anticipate and avoid problems.

While you should not outsource the plan, there are many resources that can help you. Classes and workshops are offered by the Small Business Administration, at colleges, and most cities have local economic development agencies with small business resources. The Pace University

Small Business Development Center in New York offers business plan development and free one-on-one business advisement, training, and research services. You can also find hundreds of courses, resources, and templates online.

Business plans average 15 to 20 pages, but they can be any length and as simple, formal, or involved as you want. Have someone review your plan once you are done. Bounce it off people in the fashion industry, as well as small business owners in non-fashion fields. The Service Corp of Retired Executives (SCORE), a division of the SBA, has more than 10,000 volunteer advisors nationwide who have decades of experience running businesses, including many who were in the fashion industry. The advisors counsel small business owners on a variety of business problems and review business plans, and their assistance is free. Their website has free templates for business plans, sales projections, financial statements, bank loan requests, and more.

Take Your Time

It's not all work. The business plan is part of the creative process, and the time you spend now will result in a plan that you will rely on and continue to evolve for years. Designer and FiftyTwo Showroom owner Ana Lerario advises designers to go slowly and take a long time to plan before they start. "Think through the entire process as if you had a label already. Know how much you will spend, research and choose your patternmakers and factories, plan all the sales steps before you even launch so that when you get the moment to hit, you will be ready."[2]

Review the Plan Often

The business plan is a working document and should be reviewed regularly as your business grows and changes. Spend time each quarter comparing your plan to your current situation to include unexpected opportunities as well as to stay focused and realistic about where you stand in respect to your goals.

Elements of the Business Plan

Executive Summary

The executive summary is at the beginning of the plan, but you should write it last. It is a short summary of the entire plan and outlines your objectives for the next one to five years. The summary should refer to the major points of the plan and clearly state your mission and value proposition, any resources you need, and how they would be used to make the business profitable. Make the summary as interesting and engaging as possible. This is the key section to share with potential partners to capture their initial interest in your business in hopes that they will want to learn more.

Company Overview

The overview is a general explanation of your business and product. Start with your background, your company mission, and the potential for your product in the market. Explain the structure of the business as a wholesale, direct-to-consumer, or made-to-order operation. Describe what you design and whether it is an item- or collection-based business. Specify if the business targets high-end, mass, or niche markets and if it fits an important lifestyle trend. Include the attributes that make your product unique and set it apart from the competition. Briefly describe your customers along with the top-line marketing strategy to reach them in terms of email, websites, brick-and-mortar stores, and social media platforms. Finish this section with a top-line review of the finances involved, the factors that will make you profitable, and the related time frame.

The Marketing and Sales Plan

This is one of the most interesting parts of the plan where you deeply explore the market and opportunities for your product.

The market. Research the size of your specific market both in terms of number of customers and in dollars, as well as how the market is growing. If you design men's hats, research how much men spend annually on hats and what months of the year or geographic areas have the most sales. If you are starting a luxury women's shoe label, identify the number of shoes sold in the luxury price range, where customers are buying them, and what percent of those sales you expect to secure.

Each market is unique and evolving. When researching any market, identify the broad lifestyle trends that relate to your product. The demand for extended size ranges, gender-neutral clothing, or the growing market for eco-friendly and fair-trade materials may be tied to the success of your line. Don't forget the other forces that influence demand for your product. The weather plays a major role in the success of a coat business, and swimwear designers should be aware of both seasonal markets as well as places where swimwear is purchased year round.

Customer profile. This section should reveal a clear and detailed understanding of your customers' demographics, as well as their mindset. How old are they? What is their income? Where do they live, work, and vacation? Include where they shop, how often, and whether they look for bargains or spend freely. What do they care about? A customer may be particular about function, comfort, glamour, fitting in, or supporting a cause. They might be motivated by influencers, innovation, or luxury materials. Be able to picture your customer, and keep that mental image with you at all times. For more in-depth information on knowing your customer, see Chapter 8: Marketing and Branding.

The value proposition and USP. You must define the value you are offering to your customers. Are you filling a specific need, solving a problem, or offering a unique alternative? What is different about your design, approach to dressing, or quality? Explain the USP (unique selling proposition) that makes your product stand out and gives it an advantage over the competition.

Sales strategy. The sales goals should outline the amount of product to be sold each year and where it will sell. Explain your pricing strategy, and include actual numbers for expected sales and projected growth rate each year, as well as details on how you developed these projections. Describe the distribution strategy between online and wholesale accounts and your timeline for seasonal deliveries or new product drops. Decide which markets to focus on domestically and abroad. Outline your plan to hire a showroom or sales rep, to attend trade shows, or to invest in an online sales system. Include customer relationship strategies and promotional plans for paid advertising, social media strategy, pop-ups, and events.

Competitive Analysis

Name your top five to seven direct competitors. These are other designers who make a similar product for the same market. Then name your top three indirect competitors who own a large share of the market (such as Everlane or Moncler). Research how long each has been in business, their annual sales, where they sell, their best sellers, and how they market themselves. Compare the style, price, and quality of their product to yours, and identify their business advantages and disadvantages. Observe the ways they serve customers well and where they do not meet customer needs.

Operations Plan

The operations plan covers the resources needed to run the business from day to day. It should outline details such as staffing requirements, the production plan, technology needs, and the support system for sales and distribution.

Include how many product lines you will produce each year, a production time line for each, and a strategy for managing quality control. Cover as many specifics as possible regarding the contractors and suppliers you will use. Obviously, this will take time and research, but it will be invaluable in helping you fully understand how to get your product made, which is vital to know before you begin sales.

Financial Analysis and Projections

Managing cash flow and planning finances is key to survival. The financial statements illustrate your ability to manage income and expenses and eventually earn a profit. They specify the amount of money you have, the amount you need, and where it will be spent. When creating the financials for your business plan, you may need an accountant or financial professional to help. Actual numbers are difficult to pin down, but it's extremely important to use real figures to illustrate what it will take to set up your business and keep it going on a monthly basis. Several financial statements can be included in a business plan, but below are the big three:

1. **Income statement.** This is a summary of all projected income and expenses by month. Income includes sales and other revenue sources, such as consulting or commissions. Expenses include the fixed and variable costs of producing and selling

your product. Fixed costs are those that do not vary depending on production or sales, such as equipment, licenses, and rent. Variable costs change based on sales and production quantities and include materials, samples, production, shipping, taxes, and sales expenses. The difference between income and expenses is the gross margin.

2. **Cash flow statement.** This statement is EXTREMELY important to a small business, because it shows exactly when and how cash will flow in and out of the business each month. The statement projects when specific expenses are due and where you will get the cash to cover them. The cash flow statement should be created for an entire year and be carefully monitored each month.

3. **Balance sheet.** This draws from the income and cash flow statements to report assets and liabilities at the end of a year. Assets include cash, accounts receivable (money owed to you), inventory and supplies on hand, and equipment. Liabilities include accounts payable (money you owe to suppliers, contractors, and rent), debt to banks, other loans, and taxes.

Setting Up the Business

Choosing the Business Name

The company name should identify the label, support the image, and appeal to your target customer. This is a name that will last for years (hopefully!), so it should give an appropriate impression without being too confusing or random. Choose a memorable and interesting word that reflects the attitude of the collection while setting you apart from others in the market. Don't choose a word that relates too specifically to a current trend or moment in time.

Using your own name for your business is a common option, but one you might want to avoid especially when first starting out. While many famous American and European brands are named for the designer who launched them, realize that you will make many mistakes in your first few seasons. As designer Nanette Lapore explained at a CFDA/Gen Art business seminar, there is a huge advantage to staying under the radar and not putting yourself out there too soon. She started her company and made her mistakes under another name and then was able to start fresh with her own name and identity.[3] Comme Des Garcons, Costume National, and Rag & Bone are examples of well-known brands that are not named for their designers.

A logo is a symbol or specific way that a name is presented to represent a brand and product. For many designers, their logo is simply their name, but the font, color, and shape used to display it create an image for the company. Ralph Lauren's polo player, Chanel's double Cs, and the red box of Supreme each represent an attitude and lifestyle. If your label is minimal, your logo should be simple and clean; if your collection is fun and girly, your logo should reflect that.

You will need to register your business name with your state and obtain federal and state tax ID numbers. In the United States, each state has various requirements for licenses and permits to operate your business, sell your goods, and buy materials for resale.

Don't Use Your Name

"Don't put your name on the label! Emerging designers are often tempted to name their lines after themselves—it's a fashion tradition, a marketing strategy, and a reflection of artists' pride in their work. Once you turn your name into a trademark, however, it becomes your company's primary asset. Any savvy investor interested in backing you will also want that trademark to be part of the deal. When eventually you and your financial backer split, you will likely lose the rights to your name—and see it on the work of strangers." —Susan Scafidi, Professor and Founder, Fashion Law Institute

Establishing Your Trademark

A trademark protects the name, logo, and/or slogan (such as Nike's JUST DO IT) that represents your brand. You need to register your trademark with the U.S. Patent and Trademark Office right away to ensure that you have the exclusive right to use it. Do a preliminary trademark search on Trademarkia to see if your trademark is available and that there is nothing too similar that could be confusing or even damaging to your brand.

Protect Your Trademark

"Retain a trademark lawyer to ensure your trademark name/design is clear and free from any similar marks that could lead to conflict later on. They will help you determine which product category and wording you should use on your application to avoid a big problem down the line. If you are looking to sell or manufacture overseas, your lawyer will also have foreign associates capable of registering your trademark in those jurisdictions you choose. The lawyer should also help you strategize as to the key markets to register."[4] —Attorney Nicholas A. Rozansky, Partner, Brutzkus Gubner

In addition to registering your name and trademark, use a service such as GoDaddy to register your trademark domain with any extensions you may use such as .com or .net, and consider adding additional names that describe your product. For example, if you are a shoe company in New York City called Frankly, you may want to register frankly.com, frankly.nyc, frankly.net, as well as franklyshoes.com. Register your name with your key social media channels too. For more information on how a trademark can protect your business, see Chapter 11: Protecting Creativity.

Creating the Business Structure

The next step is to choose and create the legal structure for your business. Each option comes with different costs, tax implications, and paperwork requirements, which vary from state to state.

Sole proprietorship. Easy to set up, but with this structure you are personally responsible for any losses, debt, or legal actions of the business. This puts your personal assets at risk, and your business income is taxed as personal income.

Partnership. In a partnership, two or more people own a business together. Different structures such as general partnerships and limited liability partnerships define the varying degrees of involvement and responsibility for each partner. Taxes and profits are passed through the partnership as individual income or loss on the partners' personal tax forms. Partners are each responsible for the company's obligations with no protection of personal assets.

Limited liability corporation (LLC). An LLC provides the tax advantages of a corporation, while limiting the personal liability of the business owner, but it is more expensive to set up than a sole proprietorship and requires more paperwork. There are less reporting requirements for an LLC than for a corporation, but you will need to file documents such as an operating agreement and an annual report.

Corporation. Best for fast growing start-ups or businesses with investors. A corporation is a legal entity that is completely separate from the owner. The owners (shareholders) are not liable for financial debt or claims against the corporation. There are two types of corporations—the C corporation and the S corporation. The S corporation has more tax advantages and less paperwork, but both entities require annual meetings, a board of directors, fees, and reports.

Bring in an Expert

"Retain a good CPA (certified public accountant) to assist you in setting up your business correctly for tax purposes and to protect your personal assets. They can explain each option in full and help decide which option is best for you. They will make sure you take advantages of opportunities such as tracking start-up expenses to deduct from your taxes." —Attorney Nicholas A. Rozansky, Partner, Brutzkus Gubner

The Team

Business Partners

Both designers and industry professionals agree that some of the brightest young talents fail because they do not have a good business partner. Designers often struggle with the business aspects of running a fashion label, and even if they have the right skills, it's extremely difficult for one person to handle it all. In other creative industries, such as film and music, the artist is not expected to handle the business side. There is someone dedicated to setting up process and structure and keeping things financially sound.

Most household designer names have a strong business partner behind the scenes. Yves Saint Laurent had Pierre Berge, Calvin Klein had Barry Schwartz, and Philip Lim has Wen Zhou. Having a knowledgeable business partner can help convince retailers, suppliers, and financial people to work with you, and they can also be the "bad cop" to manage the difficult negotiations and payment discussions.

To find a business partner, network in the industry and talk to as many people as you can. Tell lawyers, accountants, suppliers, and customers that you are looking for someone. Many former executives from the fashion industry have an interest in partnering with a new line. They have established credibility in the community and look forward to a new challenge with a less-established name. Nicole Miller's first business partner was her boss from her old job.[5] Someone who currently works for another label, factory, or fabric source may be an ideal partner who knows the business and can provide production expertise and contacts. Another option is to find an MBA student or business school graduate who specialized in fashion and may be interested in working with you. Angela Luna of ADIFF was approached by a young fashion business executive, Loulwa Al Saad, who read about her in the *New School Free Press*. Al Saad was excited by the ADIFF mission and offered her help. They have been working together as business partners for three years.[6]

A partner doesn't have to be a business professional. Many companies are started by two or more creative minds who pool their resources, share the workload, motivate each other, and complement each other's skill sets. However, creative partners may still need to find external people for business expertise.

Be cautious when choosing a partner. You will need to give up some control and work with this person every day. Business pressure can ruin a good relationship with a friend or family member. Most business managers want an ownership stake in the company, and you don't want to give away a percentage of your business without protecting yourself.

Create a Partnership Agreement

"If you start a business with a partner, hire an attorney to create a buy/sell agreement and an operating agreement. In non-complex business formations, this should cost $2,000–$5,000. This will record the value of what each party is bringing to the business—whether it's real money or 'sweat equity' or something else. It will define responsibilities, who makes final decisions, how profits will be shared, and provide an exit plan in case someone wants to leave or be bought out." —Attorney Nicholas A. Rozansky, Partner, Brutzkus Gubner

Building Your Network

Designer entrepreneurs need a strong support group of people, both inside and outside the industry. Get to know other designers, business professionals, and entrepreneurs. Over time, your fashion family will grow to include hair and makeup people, stylists, photographers, suppliers, and others who help uphold your vision. Try to find a mentor and spend time with friends and family who support your dream.

When looking for a mentor, Steven Kolb, CEO of the CFDA advises, "Consider the level of the person you contact. It's not always the CEO or editor in chief who will be the best mentor. Often the person who has only been in the business for ten years may have more firsthand knowledge of what you are going through and can better relate to your experience."[7]

Network your way into the industry and consult with editors and manufacturing and showroom people. Ask established designers if you can meet with them for advice. People can be helpful, but realize they are busy. As Steven Kolb says, "'Can I take you for a cup of coffee?' is the wrong thing to say. If you contact someone on LinkedIn, just be really direct and get to the point."

Designers Ashley Cimone and Moya Annece of ASHYA advise, "Closed mouths don't get fed! Before and since the launch of ASHYA, we have leaned on our community and network for insight, resources, and support. Speaking passionately and openly about our vision for ASHYA and our needs as entrepreneurs has opened many doors along the way. Lean into your strengths, but know your weaknesses and seek support from peers, old and new colleagues, and professionals that you admire. Understand that everyone's time is valuable and limited, so be clear with your ask and know what it is that you have to offer."[8]

At some point, you may assemble a board of advisors who can bring knowledge and cachet to your business and make you more attractive to potential vendors, customers, and investors. Try to include someone who is knowledgeable about the financial world, someone with fashion industry experience, as well as an attorney and an accountant. The people whom you first add to your advisory group will help you grow your network. Designer Bliss Lau teaches the workshop Centering Your Brand and discusses the importance of your *sphere of influence* in finding expertise and advisors amongst the people you already know. As she says, "People love to share their expertise. Everyone knows something and faces similar challenges whether they are in the fashion business or not. These people can be helpful when you need good advice."[9]

Search your area for professional networking organizations and meet-ups designed to help entrepreneurs make valuable business connections. For example, the Athena PowerLink program matches women-owned businesses in various cities with a volunteer panel of local business mentors.

Finding Professional Services

At the root of a successful business is a good team. When hiring legal, accounting, or other services, referrals are best. Don't assume it's okay to work with a relative or friend. Your favorite uncle may have a law degree, but ideally you need someone who has fashion and small business experience and who may have connections in the industry. Ask other designers, accountants, or bankers for recommendations, and then schedule a meeting and spend time with them. This initial meeting should be free. Ask about the professional's background and understanding of fashion. Make sure this person can explain things to you clearly in easy-to-understand language. You need someone with whom you feel comfortable and can communicate freely.

Shop around and compare rates. Most lawyers and consultants charge by the hour, and you should get estimates up front of the time required for each issue. Ask them how to keep the costs down and see if they are open to barter. Product, event invitations, and discounts can be enticing to business professionals. Many firms encourage their attorneys and accountants to do pro bono work. Local bar associations and law schools may offer pro bono legal advice. In New York City, the Fashion Law Institute's Pop-Up Clinics take place monthly and, depending on the issue and the timing, they can set up consultations and provide referrals.

Legal issues. Most people want to avoid hiring a lawyer at first because of the cost. Until you have legal assistance, protect yourself by getting every agreement in writing, and try to communicate important points via email. Keep all paperwork and records in case of disputes. Take notes on important conversations and meetings.

Read all agreements carefully and ask questions if there are terms that don't make sense. A contract should lay out all the responsibilities of both parties. Pay attention to details about dispute resolution and the length of the contract. Always try to resolve disputes without legal action. Lawsuits are expensive and time consuming, and there are no guarantees that you will win. Don't forget to use your intuition. If you have a bad feeling about any agreement, don't do the deal.

Legal advice up front can save you money and help you avoid mistakes in the long run. A lawyer can negotiate leases, obtain licenses and permits, review contracts and agreements, deal with copyright issues, and help resolve disputes. Again, be sure to verify and monitor the fees for legal advice; it adds up quickly.

Bookkeeping and accounting. It's important to keep meticulous records of every financial transaction and to track expenses, cash flow, and inventory diligently. These records are needed for tax purposes, as well as to keep you on budget and to monitor the performance of your business.

Initially, designers usually handle the bookkeeping on their own with good software, such as QuickBooks Pro, Wave, or Kashoo. If you can't keep up, consider bringing in someone for a day or two each week to help. However, even if you have a full-time bookkeeper, it's your responsibility to stay constantly in tune with the finances of your business. The bookkeeper doesn't know what fabric came in and where it went. You have to help allocate each invoice. You should always sign your own checks to stay aware of the inflow and outflow of money. No one wants an unexpected cash flow surprise.

An accountant or CPA should handle big issues such as taxes, payroll, and year-end financial statements. They can also assist with overall business planning, costing, and budgeting. They can help check store credit, obtain financing, make deals, and position your business to appear professional to outsiders.

Insurance. Don't forget to obtain insurance to cover your property and inventory in case of fire, water damage, theft, or business interruption from blackouts or strikes. Liability insurance is also recommended in case your product or place of business causes injury or death.

Employees and Outsourcing

Initially, most designers run the business and handle the major responsibilities themselves, but at some point, they need help. A good place to start is with interns who work for a small stipend, or even for free, in exchange for experience or school credit. Interns can be found by contacting fashion schools in your area. Remember that an internship should be a learning experience for the students and not just cheap labor for you. Make an effort to explain the reason and method for each task to help the interns gain valuable knowledge needed to eventually land a job. Keep in mind that an intern could become a valuable employee or contact after graduation. They are familiar with your brand and you've had ample opportunity to assess their strengths and skills.

Instead of hiring an employee, it often makes sense to outsource certain work to specialists or to bring in freelancers for a period of time so you only have to pay them when you need them. Once the company can financially support part-time or full-time employees, you can expand your staff.

For many designers, the first employee is a general assistant to take on business responsibilities or a production manager to help source and traffic production materials and oversee the factory. It is best to hire to compensate for your own limitations. Know what you are good at and then look for people with the expertise to fill in the gaps.

Ideally, you want to hire people who are recommended by personal or professional acquaintances. Review their experience and skills and check references. In a small company, chemistry is critical. Hire people you like and who fit the culture of your brand. Consider whether you can spend significant time with this person every day. Employees should have a similar work ethic to yours and understand your brand, vision, and business goals.

As a small company, offering a salary that is competitive with larger brands is not realistic. Therefore, it's important to position a job with you as providing more opportunity, diverse responsibilities, and hands-on experience than at a bigger label. Be sure to emphasize the excitement of building a new business from the ground up. If you hire a more senior or experienced person, it may be appropriate to offer profit sharing or even equity in the company. When you do choose someone to hire, make sure you fully understand the legal issues involved, the financial impact on your business and taxes, and insurance needs.

Fashion Organizations and Incubators

The **Council of Fashion Designers of America (CFDA)** is a not-for-profit trade association whose membership consists of America's foremost fashion and accessory designers. It has several initiatives to support the fashion industry in the United States, and a few are especially helpful to emerging designers.

A Common Thread was recently created with Vogue to raise awareness and funds for those in the American fashion community who were impacted by the COVID-19 pandemic. More than $4 million was granted to dozens of businesses that were the most affected. The program took over the CFDA/Vogue Fashion Fund, which was one of the most coveted awards in fashion. For 16 years, the fund annually presented three emerging designers with cash awards and business mentoring from a team of industry experts.

The Elaine Gold Launch Pad is a virtual residency for emerging talent, providing design and business mentorship and a total of up to $175,000 in micro-awards. Participants are encouraged to embed sustainability, technology, and innovation within their businesses.

The Local Production Fund and the Supply Chain Collective are two manufacturing-focused initiatives to help designers find and even fund sourcing and manufacturing. In addition, the Materials Index and the Production Directory list dozens of resources for every step from development through shipping and these directories are available to all.

Membership in the CFDA is by invitation, and each year, several new candidates are voted in by the board of directors. Members have access to professional and business development resources as well as the opportunity to attend numerous functions throughout the year and network with established designers and make important industry contacts.

Regional fashion incubators. Many cities have designated organizations to specifically support local fashion design entrepreneurs. The St. Louis Fashion Fund, the Denver Design Incubator (DDI), the Detroit Garment Group (DGG), the Philadelphia Fashion Incubator, as well as established incubators in Toronto, San Francisco, Portland, and Chicago, each offer a diverse range of resources and opportunities. Financial grants, workspace, mentorship and networking opportunities, introduction to manufacturers, business education, legal assistance, and selling events are all ways in which the cities support the designers who contribute to the local economy by employing the sewers, graphic designers, accountants, and photographers who are also there.

There are many other programs around the world affiliated with universities and colleges. FIT Design Entrepreneurs is an annual program that accepts 25 businesses from NYC to participate in a free "mini-MBA" program. Each business is paired with a mentor to help it complete a business plan, and 12 of the brands advance to "pitch night" where they compete for a financial prize.

If you could hire just one employee or outsource one process, what would it be?

"A freelance, commission-based salesperson with great contacts."
—Angela Luna, ADIFF

"One of your first hires should be a technical designer or production manager to make sure your product is great. If you don't have a good product to sell, the rest doesn't matter." —Tara St James, Study NY

"Ultimately, I would hire someone who comes from the technical/digital world who is also very passionate about the fashion industry. The future for independent fashion brands is direct-to-consumer, and the way to build your brand is through digital marketing and branding. I would look for someone up on all of the latest cutting-edge trends and tools available via social media and e-commerce to connect with consumers." —Ruthie Davis

"We need someone to help with production coordination to free us up to be more involved in business strategy and forming partnerships rather than being in the weeds dealing all day with cut tickets." —Laura Moffat, Kirrin Finch

"A CPA. We are not financial wizards and believe we should outsource what we are not good at." —Thea Grant

"Social media is a challenge for me. I would love to hire an employee dedicated to managing all social media platforms." —Annie Lewis, Lewis Cho

"Customer service. Since my latest venture is a digitally native direct-to-consumer brand, how we interact with our community is of the utmost importance." —Geren Lockhart, CANAVA

"Start by hiring one person that is simply willing to do anything and isn't above getting their hands dirty. When you are just starting, you need a person that can help out in any way possible. But if I could hire one person now, it would be a dedicated money person. Somebody that says, 'Here's how much you have, here's how much you need, and here's how much you make' to set realistic boundaries. It's a buzzkill, I know. But it's not something you personally want to obsess over either—you have other work to do. And you don't want to make a dumb financial decision that will put you out of business."
—Andy Salzer, Hiro Clark

"At this point, I am hand-dyeing all of the fabrics used in my mini-collections. This process, while creatively fulfilling and very fun, is quite time consuming. If I could outsource anything, it would be the garment production. I still construct each piece by hand, a process I enjoy, but you can't put a price on pristine and professional sewing and tailoring, and buyers are always looking for quality." —ALISON KELLY, FLORA OBSCURA

"A financial advisor to review and plan around where I am spending and where I am making, what's working and what isn't. I need to be doing that consistently, and it's the thing I have least time and desire to do." —ALTHEA SIMONS, GRAMMAR

"One person to do all my digital work—outreach, marketing, coordination, and website. I'm the happiest when I spend as little time as possible in front of a screen. When I started my business in 2001, the way to work was very different from today's digital world, I'm still in love with that old way of working directly with people and with my hands, so anyone that could manage the digital part of the brand would be my hero." —HELENA FREDRIKSSON, H FREDRIKSSON

"As my business has fluctuated between the art and fashion world, I've gone through so many variations. I just have myself, my assistant, and my industrial knitting machine. With just this small staff, we've been able to supply boutique clients via wholesale and also do direct to consumer. The one thing I'd love to hire out is the sales and marketing aspect. My favorite part of my business is the creative process, so I'd like to find a way to focus on the creative and production and outsource the in-person and online sales presence." —KARELLE LEVY, KRELWEAR

3 THE MONEY

One of the realities of starting your own design business is that it takes money—money that can be hard to find. In fact, when asked what the hardest part of having your own business is, Andy Salzer of Hiro Clark replied, "Trying not to think about the money every day."[1] Unfortunately, thousands of good designs are never produced because there is not enough money behind them. On the other hand, millions of mediocre, unnecessary products are mass-produced and distributed around the world because the financing is there to back them up.

Once you start your label, you will probably lose money for the first couple of years. The *break-even point*, where you have enough income from the business to equal your expenses, will elude you because as the business grows, costs increase. For example, if a designer sells $100,000 worth of product and has a profit margin of 10 percent, he is making $10,000. At $200,000 in sales, he is making a little more. But then at $300,000, he may suddenly lose money because he had to hire people, rent a larger studio, or invest in equipment. He had to increase his costs in order to manage the increased business.

The reality is that that many designers' fame far exceeds their finances. After five years in business, numerous industry awards, press attention, sales in more than 80 high-profile doors, including Bergdorf Goodman, Proenza Schouler—with wholesale volume estimated at more than $6 million—was not expected to break even for another two or three years.[2]

How Much Do You Need?

One reason designers fail is that they don't start with enough money. Too often, they financially overextend themselves and have to close the business after a year or two to start over, but this time under a burden of debt. You can, and should, delay the launch of your label until you are financially prepared.

How much you need is a difficult question to answer. The economics are different with each designer and depend on the type of business and your goals. The story of Calvin Klein starting his business with $10,000 is a famous one, but that was in 1968. Some industry professionals suggest starting with as much as $1 to $5 million, but most start with much less. Tim Moore, director of business development at Hilldun Corporation, suggests you can start with as little as $25,000.[3] If you have a very focused product, you can start small and grow slowly. Designer Wenlan Chia started her label Twinkle with $900 in yarn and some knitting needles.[4] And Aurora James launched Brother Vellies with $3,500 at a NYC street market. If the response to your line is immediate, it may require more investment soon. Milly started "bare bones" with $100,000, but an additional investment of $350,000 was needed to fill the first year's orders of ten monthly deliveries.[5] From that point on, the business financed itself.

A designer should plan enough funding to cover the initial outlay for setting up the company as well as the operating expenses of production, materials, fabric, patterns, shipping, sales, and rent until cash is flowing back into the business. Creating a business plan should have resulted in a realistic cash flow statement that includes the cost to operate each season. While some advise having cash to last through the first six months, usually it takes at least three seasons to see any money flowing back into the business, and most recommend having enough to get you through the first three years.

As a worst-case scenario, when you start a business, it's good to be realistic and know up front how much money you are willing to risk. Many designers set a threshold for the amount they will invest before they throw in the towel.

Cash Flow: The Two Most Critical Words

Cash flow is the major reason small businesses fail. Each day, money flows out for fabric and samples, rent and utilities, supplies, postage, and more. The cash flows in from online sales, when retailers pay, or when the designer receives some form of financing or payment for a freelance project. Obviously, the goal is to have more money flowing in than flowing out, but this is easier said than done.

To manage cash flow, you need to track the movement of money and regularly project the inflows and outflows several months in advance to know how much cash you need and where you will get it. Even at the large companies, only planning and constant monitoring can prevent crises. As designer Alicia Bell says, "You need access to money at all times."[6]

You Can Only Ship According to Cash Flow

In fashion, cash flow is particularly challenging, because designers must spend significant amounts of money on materials and sampling far in advance of getting paid. As a direct-to-consumer business, unless you are selling made-to-order or working with an on-demand factory, you need to have inventory before you can sell it. Your cash is tied up in that product until it sells. If you wholesale to retailers, you get paid even later. As you see in the following schedule, spending to develop a collection generally begins at least nine months before you get paid, and at that point, you have already spent more on materials and samples for the next collection.

Example of a Wholesale Cash Flow Schedule	
October 2021 December 2021	Purchase sample fabrics for Fall 2022. Pay to create patterns and samples for Fall 2022.
January 2022	Finalize Fall 2022 collection and begin sales.
April 2022	Finalize production quantities and purchase materials.
May 2022	Buy sample materials for Spring 2023. Pay for production Fall 2022.
July 2022 August 2022 September 2022	Begin patterns and samples for Spring 2023. Finalize Spring 2023 collection. Begin shipping Fall 2022 and receive COD payments. Begin to receive Fall 2022 payment on net 30 terms.

Because of the cash flow delay, getting more money is not as simple as increasing your orders. Bigger orders require more cash up front to produce. As a rule of thumb, you can generally produce orders for twice what you have in capital. For example, if you have $50,000, you can take $100,000 in orders. You ship and then wait for the stores to pay before you can produce more. If you get $200,000 in orders, you have to prioritize them. Pick the top $100,000, which are the most important to produce first. Call the other stores and tell them you can't manage their order yet, and ask if they will take the goods at a different delivery date or in a smaller quantity. Once you have the first batch of orders shipped, you can get the money (via factoring, COD terms, or direct-to-consumer sales) to start the next batch.

Negotiate terms. If you have confirmed wholesale orders, try to negotiate the payment terms with your suppliers. Support from vendors and contractors can be a critical contribution to cash flow for a designer. If the mill or factory gives the designer *terms*, then the designer has 30 or 60 days to pay for fabric or production instead of having to pay up front. It's like having an investor in the business. In fact, designers often partner with their factories, designing product for them or even selling a portion of their company to them, in exchange for investment and access to the factory's sourcing and distribution. Good credit opens doors. If you pay fabric and production people on time, they will help you with discounts and terms and will be flexible on minimums.

A designer's policy in collecting from stores also makes a big difference to cash flow each season. Asking for deposits or requiring COD from the stores brings the money in sooner. Demand is power, and if a line receives press coverage, has buzz online, or has a strong sell-through, buyers will be more flexible with payment and may even support production with a deposit. Online sales and pre-order can supplement cash flow throughout the wholesale season.

Discipline Now Pays Off Later

Controlling costs is key to making your resources last. Even a designer with $1 million in sales can be barely surviving if expenses are high. The majority of money that comes in must go back into materials and production, leaving little to cover other costs.

The designers who lose money tend to be the ones who had employees from day one, paid for PR, rented studio space, and spent a significant amount of money on the development of large collections. Designer Wenlan Chia of Twinkle didn't move into a studio space until after four years in business. She had been working from her Manhattan apartment, which her husband referred to as "an office with a bed."[7] When she shipped, the entire place was overrun with product, boxes, shipping materials, and paperwork.

As shoe designer Ruthie Davis says, "You have to be realistic when building a fashion brand. In the beginning, it was fun to be in Neiman's and dress Beyoncé and have my shoes on the runway and the red carpet, but in the end, I have an MBA and I know the real challenge is to run a business that can sustain itself over time. I took away my ego and downsized. I gave up the cool lofty office and worked with freelancers instead of full-time employees; I cut costs and now sell more and more on my own online, and as a result, I am profitable."[8]

Samples can easily turn into a money pit, so be sure to stick to your budget when selecting materials and developing designs. You can create a gorgeous sample line on a tight budget if you keep the collection small and don't order excess fabric or overcut.

Pay Yourself

Your own labor is an important cost factor, just like the cost for sample makers, accountants, and patternmakers. Up front, you should decide how much to charge your company for your own work. Even though you probably won't cut yourself a check for some time, the cost of your labor must be included in your cost of goods and pricing strategy to accurately reflect the work that went into the product and to protect your margin down the road when you decide to outsource some of these responsibilities. Obviously, you can't pay yourself the high salary you would probably earn working for another company, but designers generally allocate a low hourly wage or annual salary to represent their labor in their financial projections.

Where to Find Money

Personal Sources

The first option for financing a label is the designer's own personal resources. In fact, when starting out, this is often the only option, until the business has some sales and can get off the ground enough to attract outside financial support. Many designers and industry experts recommend *bootstrapping*—using personal money and keeping costs very low for as long as possible. Not only does this lessen the risks and costs of working with outside sources, but the reality is, the designers who run the most carefully planned and smart businesses generally are those with their own money at stake.

Personal savings. Your first option is to use savings you have personally built up over the years, hopefully while working for another designer and getting experience.

Don't quit your day job. Most designers, including those who have shipped for several seasons, cannot afford to devote themselves full-time to their new company. They continue to work full-time, or at least part-time, to support their label financially. Ideally, your day job will be at a fashion company where you can continue to learn, make connections, and benefit from the expertise of coworkers.

While a design gig is ideal, any kind of work can help fund your own business. Designer entrepreneurs are funding their lines with graphic design work, writing, illustrating, bartending, visual display, retail sales, decorating Christmas trees, costuming, and interior design. I have even met buzzworthy designers who are shipping their deliveries after a full days work as a software engineer or stock trader.

Freelance and private label. Freelance design work is an ideal way to support your line financially. It provides the flexible schedule you need to manage your own business and keeps you tapped into the industry and its resources. Freelancing is extremely common and doesn't in any way mean you are less serious or dedicated to your own label. Designers who have been shipping their own line for several years freelance regularly, and they frequently run into each other in the design offices at J. Crew or Nike.

Mass manufacturers, tech-driven labels, and high-end brands bring on young designers to design collections or to collaborate on product groups with them for a fee. They hear buzz about the designer's own line and prefer to cash in on that talent rather than hire their own in-house person. Some want to credit the designer publicly and benefit from that person's cachet as a new talent. When Coach hired headwear designer Eugenia Kim to design a collection of hats for the brand, it gained expertise and buzz, while providing cash and a new set of customers to the smaller label.[9]

Freelance jobs can pay very well and provide financial support for a designer's own line. As designer Bliss Lau states, "Designing private label collections can bring in the necessary investment I need to infuse capital into my business. Ideas are my currency, and I can choose to sell my ideas to finance the growth of my business." The best way to find freelance work is through word of mouth. Let people in the industry know you are available, and reach out to job placement services that focus on fashion.[10]

Private clients and sales. A loyal private clientele can provide reliable income that pays up front. On occasion, private customers have even become financial backers. Designers also create excess samples for the purpose of selling at sample sales and shopping events when they need cash. If you can successfully spread the word about a private sale in your studio or showroom, you will receive payment for product on the spot to help fuel the next season. Just be wary of tying up money on extra product that may not sell.

Personal loans. If you don't have enough of your own money, the next most common source of funding is from friends and family. Mothers, fathers, uncles, wives, and close friends have invested a great deal of money in fashion. While it's wonderful to have the support of people you love, it's important to be aware of the emotional issues involved in taking money from family and friends. Money can put pressure on a relationship, and even the closest friends usually expect to be repaid. There is always a risk that you will fail and Grandma's money will be lost. Money from family and friends may also come with strong opinions and regular doses of advice. Sometimes this can be helpful, but at other times it is a source of conflict. When you take money from people close to you, be up front with them regarding their role in the company. Unless you want them to be a major player in the business, be clear that you can consider their opinions, but final decisions remain with you.

Credit cards. Credit card financing is another common route young designers take, but it is the most expensive and, therefore, dangerous. If you do use credit cards, be careful! Credit cards have extremely high interest rates, and it is easy to get caught in an overwhelming cycle of owing so much interest each month that you can't afford to pay off the principal. In fact, if you have credit card debt and are paying a typical interest rate of 15 percent, it would be better to take out a small bank loan at 6 percent to pay off the credit card immediately.

Paying off credit card balances regularly and on time can build the credit rating you need to qualify for other financing options later. When using cards, find one with the lowest possible interest rate. Look for new cards with promotional offers such as "zero APR for six months," and stay mindful of when the promotional rate expires or you will be paying 18 percent before you know it. You can transfer balances from card to card to continue taking advantage of promotional rates, but this requires attention and time and, if you slip up, may result in a bad credit rating.

Outside Financing

At some point, as your business expands, you will probably need outside financing to support increased production. Before you seek outside funds, plan ahead to know how much you will need, when you will need it, and exactly how it will be used. Searching for funding at the last minute is expensive and risky, and you may not make the best decisions when under pressure.

Understand that most of the financial world sees fashion as very high risk. It's a creative industry subject to trends, consumer whims, and even unpredictable forces such as weather. It will take significant effort to convince anyone to hand money over to you—especially if you have little experience and limited proof of success. Anyone who gives money wants something (generally a lot more money) in return.

Don't hesitate to tell people you are looking for funding. If you don't, they may assume that you are financially set. And you never know who can help. It's possible to meet potential investors at parties and meetings, in the factory, on an airplane, or even in the grocery store. While your business plan will include extensive information about your company and goals, be ready to describe your brand and its potential in person quickly and concisely—in 30 seconds—at any time. The financial world calls this the "elevator pitch." It's what you would say if you met a potential investor in the elevator at the top floor and only had until you arrived at the first floor to gain the individual's interest in your company. The purpose of this pitch is to attract a person's interest enough to want to learn more.

A sample elevator pitch may sound like this:

> *"I design a line of high-end silk and organic cotton dresses, which are inspired by the ancient embroidery techniques of the artisans in Merida, Mexico, who make them. I have $1 million in sales on my website and also sell to Neiman Marcus, Net-a-Porter, and eight other small boutiques. The line has been featured in Vogue and photographed on Selena Gomez, and it has 90,000 followers on Instagram. I'm seeking financing to expand my distribution and production to service more stores, as well as to develop bags, hats, and other accessories per the request of my current and potential customers."*

What money people want. Whether it's a loan officer or a potential investor, no one will look at your design portfolio, declare you a genius, and write a big fat check. People work with you based on the belief that you can sell your product in increasing quantity over time, while managing your cash flow well enough to pay them back—plus a profit.

New businesses don't have a long track record. Therefore, investors and bankers look at a multitude of factors to decide whether or not the business is a good investment or just a risk. They want to see a realistic plan and the facts and data to back it up. They need to see projected cash flow, growth strategy, and a realistic ability to repay them on time. They mostly want to see proof of concept—which means *sales*. They will also look closely at your personal track record with money—your credit history, payment history, and current debts and assets. A designer must get used to opening the books and showing everyone the numbers. While it may be uncomfortable, it comes with the territory.

Investors will also judge your character and professionalism and ask for references. Show your passion and tell them about your industry training and experience and ability to manage people, budgets, and processes. Include a strong list of references from professionals in the fashion industry, your supply chain, and anyone in the business world who believes in your potential and will add to your credibility.

As you seek funding, be sure to ask questions, and if you are turned down, find out why. Don't forget the golden rule: *Everything is negotiable.*

Read the fine print. With any financial arrangement, a designer should make sure he thoroughly understands all the terms. Confirm the interest rate, the length of the loan or partnership, the back-out clauses, the repayment terms and deadlines, the payment amounts, and any additional fees or requirements.

Small amounts of money are easier to get, but with small amounts, it is even more important to evaluate whether the loan is worth the risk and cost. Before you accept any deal, plug the numbers into a cash flow statement to see when the money will come in, when you will need to pay it back, and if it will really be enough to help you grow and make a profit.

Generally, in terms of expense, bank loans are the cheapest method of financing, followed by factoring, invoice or purchase financing, and finally equity financing, which usually costs a percentage of ownership in the company.

Lenders

Bank loans. Bank loans are the most common type of outside financing and, while loans can be the least expensive option, they are often the hardest to get. When you take out a loan, you receive a certain amount of money and then pay it back, with interest, over a set period of time. Banks offer loans with both fixed and variable rates of interest. With a fixed rate, you pay the same percentage of interest throughout the life of the loan. A variable rate will fluctuate as federal interest rates change.

Shop around and compare loan rates and fees at several banks. Some designers have had success with small banks that deal with small customers and small loans, yet others find that the big banks can be the easiest places to get a loan of up to $50,000 because it is such a small amount of money to them.

Banks don't like risk, and some insist a business be at least three years old before they will consider it. Banks carefully check the creditworthiness of the business owner, and most require security—something of value that will become theirs if the owner defaults on the payments. The bank could ask for business collateral, such as equipment, inventory, or accounts receivable, or it might require personal collateral, such as your condo. While you should try to avoid giving personal guarantees for a loan, this may be the only choice you have.

A bank may require a cosigner for the loan. A cosigner is held liable if the person with the loan fails to pay. The lender can go after the cosigner and her assets to recover the loan amount. Consider this seriously. You don't want Grandma to lose her house because you didn't manage your cash flow. When you choose a bank, find someone there whom you like and who understands small business and even fashion. Your lender should be someone with whom you can readily communicate and who could even become an important resource and advocate for your business.

Other loans. Some other types of loans for small business owners are worth exploring.

U.S. Small Business Administration (SBA). The SBA will not only direct business owners to numerous loans, but can often guarantee a loan for them if they don't qualify on their own at a bank. The SBA can help fill out loan applications and shop business owners around to different lenders. Some SBA-acquired loans are expensive, but they may offer a longer maturity, providing you more time to pay them back.

Minority and women business owner loans. Associations such as the National Federation of Business and Professional Women's Club and the Association of Black Women Entrepreneurs direct small business owners to financial resources and loans. Hello Alice offers loans and business support for all underrepresented business owners, including women, people of color, the military community, LGBTQ+ people, and people with disabilities. The Tory Burch Foundation is a fantastic resource for women entrepreneurs offering business advice, mentorship, low cost loans, and the opportunity for female entrepreneurs to apply for a one-year fellowship.

Local economic development agencies. Local organizations often offer loans for entrepreneurs in their area. Some provide tax incentives or grants to businesses, which create jobs, restore old buildings, or move into specific neighborhoods. Many offer business training and support. For example, the Brooklyn Economic Development Corporation, which created the Fashion Manufacturing Initiative in partnership with the CFDA, holds fashion-specific entrepreneur seminars. Seedco Financial is a national nonprofit that provides loans for small business owners in specific communities in several different states. Menswear designer Andy Salzer says that securing a Seedco loan was key to the growth of his first business.[11]

Online lending marketplaces. Online lending marketplaces enable people to list and bid on loans using an auction platform. Designer Lara Miller's third loan, from Prosper, provided $10,000 to put toward production and sample costs.[12] It takes time and effort to track down and sort through these potential sources, but it is time well spent as you never know where you might find a little pot of gold.

Factoring

by Tim Moore, EVP/Director of Global Business Development, Hilldun Corporation

Factoring is a simple and effective tool used by designers to grow faster and more efficiently. Factors provide a cash advance once goods are shipped and invoiced so companies do not have to wait for the customers to pay. By receiving this advance, a designer can pay his suppliers and contractors, enabling him to ship more product in the same period of time. If a designer comes up with the money required for his first shipment, he will be in business. However, he will begin to feel a cash crunch when he has multiple deliveries in a row and has not been paid for his first delivery, but must begin production for his second and third deliveries.

- **Without factoring.** Designer has $150,000 in orders to ship over a three-month period—$50,000 in June, $50,000 in July, $50,000 in August. She only has the money to pay for the June production of $25,000 (assuming the cost of materials and production is 50 percent of the wholesale amount). She will have to wait to get paid from the stores before she can go back into production for her July and August deliveries.

- **With factoring.** Designer has $150,000 in orders to ship during a three-month period—$50,000 in June, $50,000 in July, $50,000 in August. She only has the money to pay for the June production of $25,000. Upon shipping the June delivery, she forwards a copy of the invoice to her factor and receives a payment advance of 70 percent, or $35,000. This money will allow her to go back into production immediately for the July and August deliveries.

Factoring exists because suppliers and factories need to get paid before the designer is paid by the store. Also, due to the seasonality of fashion, designers ship heavily during certain months, and their need for cash rises quickly during peak seasons.

Designers should understand that the factor's advance should only be used to pay for the production of goods or anything directly related to goods being shipped to stores, such as fabrics, production, trade shows, and sales. If designers use the factor's money to produce a fashion show or buy bigger office space or new technology, their current cash flow will suffer, and they may not have the funds to fill their next orders.

The main advantage of factoring is that designers get their money before being paid by the stores. Besides providing advances to help cash flow, many factors save companies time and protect them from risk by checking credit and handling collections to get paid by the stores faster. Collections are done in a professional, strategic manner that will only enhance a company's relationship with its customers. Who wants to ask for an order one day and call regarding past-due invoices the next? Stores know that if they do not pay the factors, they will damage their credit.

The factoring cost of 2 to 3 percent of sales is not costly, considering companies will be outsourcing a good portion of their receivables management and will have access to additional funds to grow their business. However, factoring costs money, and companies should always be aware of their expenses.

What makes you factorable? Many factors work with start-ups as well as well-established companies. Generally, before you can be considered by a factor, you need to be able to ship up to $75,000 to $100,000 of goods. Some require $1 million per year, yet others will start at much smaller levels, such as $25,000. You can get a factor at any size, but if your sales volume is small the arrangement can be extremely expensive. The cost of factoring, and the way a factor structures its deals, can vary greatly. The cost can range from 1.5 to 7 percent of sales, depending on the size of the business, how long you have been in business, the risky attributes of the company, the capital in the business, customer makeup, and the nature of the business. Generally, the higher your sales volume, the lower your factoring commission.

When choosing a factor, make sure you understand how the factor structures its deal, that it knows your business, and that it has quality systems. Try not to pay more than 3 percent for non-recourse factoring, which means the factor takes the credit risk and pays its client, even when a store defaults on payment. Factoring is not a regulated industry and can provide funding when banks are unable to do so. Some factors are set up for very aggressive lending and charge more for it.

Working with a factor does not end all your problems. You are still responsible for handling disputes with the stores. If a store calls and complains that the merchandise does not fit or is not what it ordered, designers cannot say, "Oh well, deal with my factor."

Basically, when a business decides to look into financing, it will decide whether to work with a bank or asset-based financier. Banks generally look for established companies that can provide a financial statement showing the company is profitable and has solid net worth. Because most new companies do not live up to these standards, asset-based financing/factoring is usually the way to go. However, many companies, which have been around for a while and are in good financial condition, stay with factoring because of the service and flexibility factors provide.

There are different opinions on factors. Some designers compare them to loan sharks, while others swear that factoring is critical for cash flow and for protecting yourself from the stores. It's easy to see the advantages. Factors provide money when you need it most. They eliminate risk by handling credit checks and pay you if a store they approve doesn't pay or goes out of business. When you factor, the stores tend to pay faster, and it is easier to negotiate terms with your suppliers.

The downside really arises from the rates and fees. Be wary of incremental fees for specific services and small volumes, as well as long contractual commitments. Some factors want to lock you into a contract for a certain amount of sales volume and charge the commission for that volume, whether or not you actually reach it. For example, if you commit to $1 million in sales and you pay a 1 percent commission, even if you only hit $500,000 in sales, you still have to pay the 1 percent on $1 million. You shouldn't commit to a specific sales volume unless you are certain that you will hit it. It is better to pay a higher percent on a lower sales volume if you are unsure.

One other reality of factoring is that factors only cover orders from stores that they approve. They often deny approval of the small boutiques, which are most supportive of new designers. In the end, each factoring service has different agreements and terms, some more favorable than others. You need to do due diligence and calculate the net cost to you before making an agreement.

Purchase order financing. Purchase order financing lends money based on confirmed orders from stores. These are expensive loans because of the risk involved. The order doesn't guarantee that a retailer will accept the goods on delivery and pay. It's very difficult to obtain purchase order financing when you only have a small amount of sales. Some require as much as $1 million in orders. For large orders, purchase order financing can be found at a variety of banks, factories, and companies that specialize in this type of financing.

Line of credit. A line of credit can be obtained from a bank, and unlike a lump sum loan, it lets you borrow with more flexibility. For example, if you have a $50,000 line of credit, you can borrow $1,000 or $5,000 simply by writing a check. You only pay interest on the amount you actually borrow. If you never tap in to the line of credit, you never owe anything. While most lines of credit are based on assets such as receivables and inventory, they can be secured with personal assets.

Letter of credit. A written commitment from your bank guaranteeing that you will pay a specific amount to the seller once they meet the delivery deadline and conditions. These are generally used by designers to pay for production or by stores to pay the designer. The bank will charge a fee or commission based on the amount of the commitment.

Many designers use a combination of the above just to get through each season. For example, designer Alicia Bell started with a bank loan and arranges purchase order financing to cover her until the clothes are shipped and the invoices are turned over to the factor. The factor gives her the money to pay back the purchase order financing—and she starts again.

The Right Financing Depends on Your Individual Business
by Tim Moore, EVP/Director of Global Business Development, Hilldun Corporation

I often get asked, "How much money do you need to start a fashion business?" The real answer depends on your terms with your supply chain and customers, your company overhead and sales volume, and the structure of your business.

Financing is needed when you have to pay your suppliers before you receive payments from your customers and you don't have funds to meet these obligations. You want to leverage every relationship along your path. The more support (*support* meaning payment terms) you get from your supply chain and manufacturers, as well as customers—whether wholesale or direct to consumer—the less financing you need to fund your growth. Here are a few scenarios:

Designers with great relationships all around. Let's say you spent years designing for other designers and worked in all aspects of the business. During this time, you built relationships with good suppliers and contractors. Now it's your turn to launch a brand. You immediately call on these relationships. Your production house is willing to make your samples and defer the payment. Then you contact the top 50 stores that are already familiar with your work and get orders from a good portion of them. Your suppliers and contractors are willing to supply the materials and produce the product for the orders, and they expect payment after they deliver the goods. Your stores pay upon shipment so you can pay your suppliers immediately after you ship. In this example, you need minimal funds to start and grow your brand.

Most of the time, designers are unable to get this much support at the beginning, so they need financing to fix the snag in the chain.

Designers with some good relationships, plus factoring. A designer launches a brand and gets support from all their suppliers and contractors; however, when they sell the product, the stores want terms of 30 or 60 days to pay. This creates a snag. The designer can get everything made and shipped, but the suppliers expect payment before the stores will pay. In this case, the designer can factor the invoices to get an advance and pay their suppliers/contractors. The suppliers will continue to support them for seasons to come because they know they will get paid.

Designers without relationships, but strong sales plus letter of credit. If a designer launches their brand, but they don't have relationships yet with their supply chain, they will need to produce a sample collection and pay for it up front. Sample collections can cost from $15,000 to $50,000 during the early stages. A full package contractor will buy the piece goods and produce the product, but they require a deposit of 30 percent when the order is placed and the remaining payment before the goods are released. Providing a letter of credit to the contractor would enable them to buy the piece goods, make the product, and receive payment once the goods are released. Factors and purchase order funding companies open letters of credit based on orders from high-quality stores. They generally want to see orders of at least $100,000 to $200,000. Once the goods are shipped and the stores pay, the payment received from the stores pays back the funds from the letter of credit. Letters of credit backed by purchase orders typically cost between 1 to 3 percent per month. Letters of credit also contain clauses protecting the lender and designer against late shipment or bad quality.

Designers with steady direct-to-consumer sales plus merchant cash advance. A designer launching a direct-to-consumer brand needs to pay for a sample collection and purchase inventory to hold and ship as the sales come in. Then they need to build up enough sales to provide the cash to go back into production to make more goods. A merchant cash advance (MCA) looks at a brand's history to determine how much of a loan it will provide. A designer needs to have at least 6 to 12 months of a good sales track record to qualify for an MCA. If a designer is shipping monthly e-commerce sales of $25,000 to $50,000 and growing, an MCA company would provide a loan of $100,000, payable over the next six months, with a repayment amount of $130,000. As you can see, this is a large amount to pay for a $100,000 short-term loan. However, if that designer can use the loan to build inventory of $100,000 and sell it for $300,000 perhaps twice during the six month period for a total of $600,000, they would have a gross profit of $400,000 minus $30,000 to the MCA for the use of the funds. MCAs are expensive and should be used with caution and only when they are the best option for a growing brand.

Designers with small volume plus a bank loan or line of credit. Banks can provide small lines of credit secured by the SBA and by business or personal assets. However, these types of loans are limiting and inflexible. A designer may secure a $50,000 to $100,000 line of credit with a bank when their sales volume is small, and this may feel like a lot of money. However, their business can grow quickly, and since there isn't an automatic repayment plan (or mechanism) in place, they end up owing the bank the full amount of the loan when they still need additional funds to grow. They are unable to use receivables, inventory, or purchase orders to obtain additional funding since the bank holds a first lien on all assets, and other lenders are unwilling to provide funding until the bank is paid off. This is a very common dilemma for many growing fashion brands.

Ultimately, the different types of financing can work together to support the production and sales cycles of your company—at different stages of your growth.

Investors

While designers often feel an investor is the answer to their problems, many experts advise that looking for investors in fashion is a waste of time that would be better spent buckling down and growing their business themselves. Investment is not a quick cash infusion to carry a brand to the next season. Investment should only be sought once the business has been carefully refined to a level of consistent success and set up for the next stage of growth.

For investors, fashion is very risky, especially with a new, unknown name. They want businesses with a solid base that are steadily growing and have the potential to expand to new channels and global markets. They want to know that your product is in a growing category, that you have significant market demand, and that your line has unique attributes to differentiate it from others. They want *proof of concept* with repeat customers and a minimum of $5 to $25 million in sales.

Too many designers look for investment without really understanding the risk. Investors provide you with financing in exchange for *equity*—this is actual *ownership* of your company. Investors buy a percentage of the company and generally want some control over the business to help ensure the growth that will guarantee a profit.

As designer and educator, Keanan Duffty says, "Be careful what you wish for. Getting an investor was the worst thing that happened to us."[13] Investors put pressure on the company to scale and become profitable and often will make decisions that alter the core of the business without consideration of your vision. It's best to avoid selling even a tiny percentage of your business until that funding is the only option for the next stage of growth.

How to Find Investors

At the end of one of his Spring runway shows, designer Miguel Adrover followed the last of his models onto the runway wearing a T-shirt that read: Anyone seen a backer? While this may not be the most effective way to find financial investment, it doesn't hurt to be creative in your approach.

Investment is not just about money. The best investor is a *strategic partner* who believes in your vision and can provide critical business advice, industry expertise, marketing knowledge, and access to technology and systems. They have strong connections with factories and suppliers and can negotiate on your behalf. Fortunately, many of the private equity funds that are focused on fashion have managers with extensive industry experience. They understand the value of a good designer and are realistic about the time frame needed for success and growth.

Investors who do not come from the fashion world can pose serious risks. They don't understand the industry or how to value the intellectual property of the designer. They expect high returns in just three to five years, so they may push a company to scale too quickly and make changes that jeopardize the unique selling point of the line. When things don't work out, they back out, leaving the designer with extensive debt, damaged supplier relationships, and a confusing, overextended brand.

The best way to meet a potential investor is through personal introductions from other businesspeople, lawyers, accountants, or—ideally—your retail, supply, or production contacts in the industry. Connections are vital, and you should cast the net wide. Ask for advice from others who have gone through the fundraising process. Industry associations can help you find executives who may be interested in supporting a designer with potential. Don't forget to spend some time reviewing potential connections on LinkedIn.

Angel investors. Angel investors are wealthy individuals who invest their own money in small businesses and usually are found through word of mouth or family and friends. There are "angel networks" that focus on specific areas of business; geographic areas; or on businesses started by women, minorities, or other groups. Be warned that some networks charge a fee to review companies on behalf of investors. If the network is not focused on fashion, it is unlikely to provide results. The majority of fashion backers come from within the industry.

Factories and suppliers. As said previously, if there is a supplier or factory with which you conduct a lot of business, ask it to partner with you. In addition to negotiating good terms, partnering with the factories and mills can mean receiving your fabric and production earlier, allowing earlier delivery to the stores, and having more time to sell at full price. Better pricing helps you control your costs, and a strong relationship can eventually lead to greater financial support. Ralph Lauren's first investment of $50,000 came from Norman Hilton, his suit manufacturer.

WS & Company, a Canadian manufacturer and supplier of jersey and fleece garments, bought a 50 percent controlling interest in Andy Salzer's label, Yoko Devereaux. WS & Company is a vertically integrated manufacturer that handles sourcing, cutting, sampling, screen printing, and inspection. Andy was working with WS & Company for four years before he approached the firm with a formal presentation, asking it to become a full production partner to help with shipping, bookkeeping, and providing capital to grow. They adopted a shared resource model and created a new company, with Andy staying on as creative director while licensing his name to the new company. Although Andy gave up a controlling interest in his own company, it was worth it for him to turn over many of the time-consuming aspects of running a label and free himself up for new projects to grow the company to the next level. Andy had pitched to many others outside of the industry for capital interest, but says it was impossible to secure commitment from "suits" who didn't know him or the business. It's very difficult to sell yourself to a group of strangers who want to know what guarantees your staying power in an industry where there is a new name every week. But WS & Company knew him, had worked with him, had seen the growth of the business, and, therefore, believed in the investment.[14]

Fashion and retail brands. Large fashion brands, department store chains, and holding companies occasionally invest in or buy smaller brands that fit well into their mix. Vince purchased Rebecca Taylor, and cashmere label Naadam invested in Thakoon. Large companies such as LVMH and Kering hold several brands of different sizes within their groups. These are strategic investors who choose companies with growth potential that will benefit specifically from their retail channels, international distribution, marketing abilities, and supply chain ownership. Generally backed by private equity, they tend to purchase a controlling share of the company, but are focused on long-term growth.

Former fashion executives. Former executives of more established companies in the fashion and garment industry often invest in young designers. Andrew Rosen, who cofounded Theory, has backed several smaller labels that benefit from his extensive contacts and expertise. These investors want to be involved in the running of the business and often seek personal fulfillment in addition to their financial goals. Even if they don't invest, they can point you to other sources and become valuable mentors and advisors. A few of the retired executives at the Service Corps of Retired Executives (SCORE) said that they would personally invest in a designer if the right one came along.

Venture capital (VC) funding. While you may hear about a lot of VC funding in fashion, this funding is focused on businesses that are generally technology and data driven. They usually focus on a specific product that was developed in response to market analytics and that can be scaled quickly for huge returns in just five to ten years.

Vanity investors. Vanity investors are interested in the glamour and social industries of bars, clubs, restaurants, and fashion. They may put up $200,000 just for the thrill of being involved in the fashion world and ask for little involvement or control. Their goal is to have access, to sit front row at your show, wear designer clothing, have glamorous photos for their social media feed, and see behind the scenes. If you can provide that without compromising your brand or giving up a percentage of the company, go ahead and consider it.

Crowdfunding. Many designers successfully use crowdfunding platforms including Kickstarter, Indiegogo, and GoFundMe to raise money. It can secure cash needed for production, and the pre-orders can boost quantities to help meet factory minimums. Even more importantly, it is a great way to test product, measure consumer interest, and introduce your brand to people you might not otherwise reach.

You need to make a compelling video to show the unique aspects of your product and capture attention with your story. Most designers offer investors a good discount on pre-order of the product. Be clear about the materials, sizing, and any options you offer for color or design. Make your financial target realistic. Once your campaign hits, spread the word on social media and email to all your contacts and press. You may want to offer an extra discount for people who donate first to get things going. Send updates to your investors during production, and make sure you deliver on time and with great service to turn them into loyal customers and advocates.

Losing Control

Giving up control can be dangerous. Lawyer Steven Hahn states, "An investor would most likely insist on receiving majority control of the entity with veto ability on any major (and sometimes any minor) business decisions. You should consider what this actually means. The designer is now relegated to the status of employee."[15] Designer Christine Alcalay agrees, "I didn't go into this to answer to someone else; you don't open your own business and work this hard to just become an employee."[16]

Try not to give too much equity away. Outline who will be responsible for decisions on production, hiring, and sourcing, and make sure you maintain control for the creative aspects of the brand. Investors may make decisions without consulting you and may pressure you to do things that aren't part of your agreement, such as design their cheaper lines. Investment from a factory means you have to use that factory, even if you aren't happy with its production.

Tim Moore of Hilldun Corporation warns that "nine times out of ten investors don't understand your business, have expectations that are too high, and can cause your business harm."[17] Some large manufacturing companies buy small companies as a tax write-off against their successful businesses. They don't really believe in the growth potential of the small line and are even counting on it to lose money.

Many designers—including Halston, Jil Sander, and Ralph Rucci—actually lost the use of their name for periods of time. Designers should negotiate to keep control of their name by licensing rather than selling the name to a partner. If you can't license the name, partner with the investor under a new name to protect yourself.

A designer must believe that the investor has the business acumen and knowledge to make not just good business decisions, but decisions that are in the designer's best interest. Make sure the investors are aligned with your mission and will support it. For example, if you are committed to guidelines for sustainability, they need to know that you will not sacrifice those guidelines for greater profit.

Always Get Outside Counsel

Surround yourself with good advisors. Have a good attorney review the deal and help you negotiate terms, percentages, and control over decision making and your name before you sign. Solicit second opinions from both inside and outside of the industry to help you think clearly. Designers have been approached to give up 50 percent of their company in exchange for only $100,000, and in a designer's desperation for cash, it takes a good friend or counselor to talk them out of it. When you are desperate to pay a contractor or supplier, $100,000 can sound like salvation, but that amount will only float you through a season or two, and when it's gone, you may not even own your own company.

Business involves calculated risk. Keep your head on straight, ask lots of questions, research other deals involving the investor, and check references.

Back on Your Own

Often, investor situations don't work out because the business doesn't grow fast enough or there are creative differences about the direction of the line. Investors may want to take the line to a mass market, altering the design and the quality of materials as they seek to cut costs. Investors always build an exit strategy into their deals in case the company doesn't hit its goals and they want to get out before losing more money. Designers have lost backers in the middle of production and had to cancel their orders with stores. Chanel invested in Isaac Mizrahi, giving him the opportunity to grow and operate on a large scale, but when Chanel pulled out, he was out of business.[18] Once a backer leaves, the designer may need to refocus and start over from the beginning.

If you were given $100,000 to spend on your business right now, what would you do with it?

"We would scale our production operations in Greece with higher quality machines and hire people so we can take on more collaborations there. Oh, and I would finally pay myself." —ANGELA LUNA, ADIFF

"Hire a production manager, invest in marketing to drive traffic to the website, and fund my wholesale production for next season." —AUTUMN ADEIGBO

"Get to know everything about my customer. Who are they and what do they want? If I had $100,000 today: analytics, site enhancements, digital ads, and strategic gifting. It doesn't sound sexy (to me), but you've got the creative and design under control." —ANDY SALZER, HIRO CLARK

"I would analyze my business and make a strategy over six months. Then invest some of the money into product and some into smart, divergent marketing to support it. All in all, I would use the money to precisely plan a long-term strategy so that I could not only make something highly creative, but make it as successful as possible. But sorry Mary, I need $150K please!" —BLISS LAU

"Invest in inventory. We have so much impact built into our business model that if we have more product, we can do more good both environmentally and socially." —GEREN LOCKHART, CANAVA

"First, I would put a down payment on a house with a back house for KREL. That way I can work like an artist in the middle of the night and not waste time on commuting or waste money on rent. I would also use the money towards online marketing and a full-time website manager and in-house inventory photographer. Many of the styles we make are one of a kind, and since I love playing with color and fiber, I'll make the same style in so many fabric variations and they all act completely different. I would also love to add more knitting machines, either a full garment machine or a fine gauge knitting machine, but that's more than $100,000. Again, can I get more?" —KARELLE LEVY, KRELWEAR

Navigating an Economic Crisis

The COVID-19 pandemic has had a devastating effect on the world, impacting every aspect of life and business. It permanently changed consumer habits, shifted ways of working throughout the fashion industry, and was particularly difficult for small business. Independent brands do not have the large cash reserves to get them through months without sales, and many designers lost an entire season. Stores canceled orders, customers stopped shopping, and manufacturing was globally shut down. Many brands were unable to sell the current product they had, but also unable to produce and fill orders for the next collection. It is impossible to be prepared for such an unprecedented, unimaginable situation, and, as with 9/11 and the 2008 economic crisis, many small fashion brands were unable to survive.

In times of crisis, designers are forced to be flexible in how they produce and sell and need to pivot in response to changes in how people shop, work, and dress. However, the things that don't change are the core values and POV of your brand. The businesses that best weather the storms usually have a strong brand message, a tightly edited selection of core product, a low overhead, and a loyal customer base.

The First Priority Is Cash Flow

Sell what you can. Do what you can to move the in-season product you already have to increase cash flow and reduce inventory. Focus on e-commerce with the best-selling products and items that are most relevant to the time—such as the "work from home" loungewear that carried many brands through the COVID-19 quarantines. You want to avoid excessive discounting, but short-term flash sales, a percentage off specific products, or a donation of sales to a crisis-related cause can motivate customers. Archive sales or online sample sales can unload older merchandise, and you may want to reach out to off-price retailers or sample sale platforms to see if they can take any goods. Reach out to private clientele and offer pre-order on items in production to contribute to immediate cash flow. During COVID-19, many designers created revenue by selling gift cards, shifting production to make masks and other PPE, or even selling illustrations and handmade items.

Cut costs. Evaluate every expense and cut all nonessential spending. Immediately slash marketing expenses, such as digital ads, travel, or plans for new equipment or staff. Reduce the budget for photo shoots and sample development, and consider shipping by sea instead of by air. The biggest expenses for many small businesses are rent and employees. Talk to your landlord immediately about an abatement, and consider closing the office or letting go of studio space to work from home. You can try to avoid layoffs by asking your team to take a temporary pay cut or reduce their hours.

Negotiate. During a crisis, everyone in the supply chain is facing challenges. The retailers suffer from a lack of sales, the factories struggle to fill orders, and no one is getting paid. It is important to get on the phone with all of your partners to communicate your situation and create solutions.

Supply chain. To preserve cash, ask suppliers and factories to extend payment terms so you can survive and pay later. Review what is already in production. Focus on moving forward with less seasonal merchandise, and consider reducing or even canceling production orders to avoid excess inventory that may not sell.

Wholesale. Call all of your wholesale accounts to confirm orders and negotiate terms. If they want to cancel orders that are already in production, remind them that you have already made and paid for the goods and they need to accept them. Offer a discount, a different assortment, or staggered delivery dates to make it work. Inform them of any delivery delays you anticipate as a result of problems with production to avoid chargebacks. Look through your agreements and ask for new arrangements regarding sell-through, unsold inventory, and markdowns for this season. Confirm orders that have not yet been produced. It's better to not make the goods if they are unlikely to sell, and it's best to avoid shipping to retailers who may not survive. This is a good time to reevaluate which relationships really work for your brand and focus on fewer, stronger partnerships.

Other creditors. Try to negotiate new agreements with everyone you owe. Bankruptcy is only necessary if creditors refuse to negotiate or create a payment plan. Remember, bankruptcy doesn't give you money; it just provides time to restructure your debt, and you could lose any assets you put up as collateral when you launched.

Look for financial assistance. Research financial programs that support small business and local economies, such as low or zero interest loans through the Small Business Administration (SBA) or the federal or local government. Apply for grants and industry-related relief initiatives, such as the CFDA/Vogue Fashion Fund's A Common Thread.

Stay Close to Your Customers

The way you communicate with consumers during a crisis is essential to that relationship when things resolve. Often, the usual messages meant to drive sales are inappropriate to both the mood and reality of the time, but it is important to stay close to your community and offer a regular variety of positive and inspiring content. During COVID-19, designers shared everything from mood boards, playlists, movie reviews, DYI projects, coloring pages, and inspirational messages for their audiences who were stuck at home and spending a lot of time online. Some designers took the time to deep dive into their customer research, even reaching out personally to top customers to thank them for their business and ask what they like best and want in the future from the brand. Many designers became more experimental, testing new formats such as Instagram Live or TikTok for the first time.

Moving Forward

Stay cautious and creative. In developing new product, it is crucial to stay close to the values and core products that define your brand and to focus on fewer, better things. Trans-seasonal items with unique, special elements are less vulnerable to discounting and more appealing to consumers who are reluctant to spend. Cut back your amount of SKUs, don't oversample, and eliminate any product that is unlikely to do well. Make use of deadstock fabric and re-offer past unsold "classics" to keep costs and inventory risk low. A focus on local production can help you control time lines and processes as the recovery unfolds.

Adapt. Technology continually opens the door to new ways of communicating and selling, and it presents opportunities for designers to increase their efficiencies and even lower costs. The cancellation of fashion weeks and trade shows shifted wholesale and PR strategies to presenting collections via video through virtual showrooms and events. Digital wholesale buying platforms such as Joor enabled brands to upload imagery of their product for buyers to remotely review and place orders. Developments in 3D imaging and fit technology are making up for some of the disadvantages of viewing product from afar. It's likely that many press days and editor meetings will continue to take place in private Instagram accounts and on Zoom.

Review and plan. During crisis, businesses must face the difficult question of whether they can actually survive. The answer requires a review of finances and a critical look at the business strategy. Create a realistic plan for future sales versus expenses, and decide how you may have to shift your business in the future to achieve profit. If you can see a clear path, you should do what you can to hang on. Don't borrow funds without a realistic plan to pay them back, and do not resort to high interest rate credit card loans in a panic to survive. Sometimes the smartest thing for long-term survival is to pause and protect the cash you have while you plan for a later relaunch.

Designer Geren Lockhart, who designs her own direct-to-consumer brand Canava, says that after the 2008 financial crisis she realized, "There is no failure anymore. The economic crisis, 9/11, COVID-19, or other circumstances are not only beyond your control, but can allow you to reevaluate things you were already wondering about. When I closed my label Geren Ford, I was already moving away from wholesale because I didn't believe in the business structure anymore."[19]

Work together. Stay close to your community and reach out to other designers and industry contacts to see how you can work together, support each other, and share resources. You can collaborate to solve problems and create opportunities, such as the 20 independent designers/makers who formed the Better Together Shop during COVID-19 to cross promote to each other's audiences and sell as a group.

4   PRODUCT DEVELOPMENT

Product is king. It needs to be the most important focus for any entrepreneurial designer. There is already so much in the marketplace, and it is impossible to compete with fast fashion on speed, quantity, or price. Despite the size of your following, the buzz from the press or the amount of your funding, if the product isn't great—it will fail.

As designer Althea Simons of GRAMMAR says, "The product binds me and my customers together. The product is the thing that makes a difference in their lives. I put all my love, passion, and energy into making it the best I possibly can; someone feeling that and paying for it brings us together and gives the brand relevance."[1]

The development of your product is an integral and interesting part of design. It requires a careful balance between maintaining creative expression and point of view as a designer and resonating with a customer so they will buy. Successful designers stay aware of the marketplace as they develop each collection. They have a deep understanding of their customer and what need or desire their product will fulfill. As designer and educator Keanan Duffty says, "You have to consider both creativity and commerce and find the intersection of those two. Commerce is not a dirty word."[2]

It Takes Time

Product development can and should take time. This is the stage when you are creating the core of your company and identity as a designer. The bag that becomes an overnight success usually took at least two full years to develop. Taking the time to get it right now will pay off later when you are occupied with the many aspects of production and sales.

GRAMMAR

GRAMMAR was born out of misfortune when designer Althea Simons's apartment building burned down and she lost all of her belongings. The difficulty she felt trying to replace her wardrobe led her to apply her eye for detail to the challenge of creating the perfect white shirt. She worked for over a year to create branding and find partners for her business before launching with a Kickstarter campaign. She met with several patternmakers to create test samples, and many suppliers to source the organic long-staple cotton she uses. "You're only as good as the people you work with," she says. "You have to find people who believe in you and think what you are doing is going to work."

Focus On Your Customer

In a world of so much choice, it is critical to have your specific target customer in mind as you develop the line. Focus on their lifestyle and mindset—do they cook or eat out, live in a house or apartment, travel for work or sit at a desk all day? Maybe they go directly from a corporate office to meditation class or from teaching children to performing in an orchestra at night. What is their emotional need around dressing? Do they want to look sophisticated, show off their body, or stand out from the crowd? What do they value and how does your product fit into their life and fulfill their aspirations?

"Who is your customer?" is one of the first questions a retail buyer, investor, or editor will ask you, and you need a quick and concise answer. In press releases, designer Michael Kors described his line MICHAEL by Michael Kors as "carpool couture." The line focused on fashion-conscious soccer moms who spend much of their life in the car. The clothes were practical yet chic and more affordable than his signature collection. Alexander Wang famously coined MOD—"model off duty"—as the customer for his line of casual downtown-cool clothing. Some designers worry that specifically designing for one customer type will limit their market, but in today's crowded and competitive industry, the more you can narrow your definition to a tightly focused niche, the more you will resonate with that customer. You cannot offer something for everyone.

Legendary designers often have muses—Yves Saint Laurent and Loulou de la Falaise, Marc Jacobs and Sofia Coppola—who inspire the designers and help them stay focused when creating the line. A muse can be someone you know or a celebrity or public figure who represents the ideal customer for your line. Many designers are their own muse, inspired to create items that fit their lifestyle and taste. Keep a mood board of photos and other visual reminders of your inspiration, your customer, and their lifestyle and values in your studio to help you stay focused.

Have a Point of View

A designer needs a signature point of view to differentiate his line from others and make it special. Each season, work to establish what the marketing world calls "the DNA of the brand." This is the overall style and aesthetic customers think of when they hear your name. It's what enables a shopper to say, "That looks like Chanel" or "She is so Gucci."

The POV of your label can be based on a lifestyle, a feeling, a time in history or even a tradition—using materials and techniques from your culture to make a modern product. Developing the point of view takes time. When designer Reed Krakoff redesigned Coach, he said he spent "a year and a half or two years of really flailing around and being too contemporary or too European."[3] It took a lot of trial and error before landing on the acclaimed signature style of "accessible luxury." He knew when he hit it. It doesn't happen overnight.

Your point of view can center on filling a hole in the market. Designer Geren Lockhart noticed an opportunity for sustainable, high-quality leisure and intimates for the people she knew who were buying basic intimates at the GAP because they didn't want to spend $40 on underwear.[4] And designers Moya Annece and Ashley Cimone launched their brand ASHYA when they discovered a void in the market for a functional but sophisticated belt bag, which was instrumental to their lifestyle of travel and cultural exploration.[5]

Once the point of view is defined, capture that essence and make it integral to all of the designs. The identity of a label can encompass the fit, fabrication, and appeal to a particular lifestyle. Even among the dozens of brands of jeans, whether it's the weight of the denim, the curve of the waist band, or the use of natural indigo dye, each brand has defining characteristics.

Put your product identity into words and test each item against that definition. If your signature is sexy, flirtatious, and fun, each product must meet those criteria. At first blush, point of view may sound creatively limiting, but in reality, it refines and focuses your brand.

Inspiration or Appropriation?
by Susan Scafidi, Professor and Founder, Fashion Law Institute

Fashion designers find inspiration in many places, including other cultures' closets. While cultural exchange adds richness to life, and culture itself is continually evolving, many fashion houses have been called out in recent years for engaging in offensive cultural appropriation. Think Victoria's Secret sending a model down the runway in a feathered Native American–style headdress and not much else or Valentino pairing an African-inspired collection with traditional braided hairstyles on mostly white models.

Where's the line between fashionable inspiration and potentially harmful misappropriation? Only a source community can say for sure, and even then members of a culture may not always speak with one voice. However, the research behind the book *Who Owns Culture? Appropriation and Authenticity in American Law* suggests a rule of three S's:

1. **Source:** When borrowing from another culture, consider the source. Is the community one that is still affected by historical oppression or ongoing discrimination?

2. **Significance:** Think about the significance of the cultural product to which you're attracted. Does it hold great meaning, or is it perhaps sacred or even secret?

3. **Similarity:** Is your use merely a slavish copy of the original, without significant transformation?

If the answer to any of these S's is yes, then your otherwise well-intentioned use may result in offense or economic harm to the source community—not to mention a social media storm.

Looking for an alternative route? Instead of copying, consider collaboration with a designer from the source community or local artisans, which can result in a win for everyone.

Be Consistent

A buyer for Saks Fifth Avenue told me that the key to a small designer's success is a strong POV, bolstered by creativity that is consistent from season to season. Yet consistency is cited by buyers as one of the biggest problems with new lines. Each new item may have unique influences, but overall the point of view must remain consistent over time to meet the expectations of retailers, editors, and consumers. Take time to look at designer collections and study the consistency from item to item and year to year. Consistency across all products can allow you to extend your brand to new areas, such as beauty, shoes, and housewares. Ralph Lauren has been the master of consistently telling the same story with each product for more than 50 years—whether it's a bomber jacket, a polo shirt, handbags, or bed sheets. He represents a specific all-American, upper-class lifestyle, and everything created, at every price level, fits that image.

Gustavo Cadile: Design What You Love

When Gustavo Cadile started his signature label, he decided to focus on the ready-to-wear market, as this seemed to be the market with the most opportunity. Although his passion was for eveningwear, he observed that the eveningwear collections in the stores were very small, while ready-to-wear collections were larger and had the majority of the promotional support.

He continued to make the eveningwear he loved for private clients and soon designed a wedding dress that would change his career. The dress was worn on Friday, and on Sunday, he received a call from Joan Kaner, the fashion director of Neiman Marcus. Ms. Kaner's friend had attended the wedding and forwarded a photo of the dress to her. Joan met with Gustavo, loved his work, and pronounced him ready to sell in the eveningwear salon at Neiman Marcus. She said he had to have a showroom first and made several recommendations. Gustavo signed with Michael Atchison, the well-respected eveningwear representative for brands including Monique L'huillier.

Now Gustavo sells his exquisite beaded gowns to socialites and well-dressed women for $3,000 to $5,000; the evening wear collection is sold at Saks 5th Avenue and the bridal line at Bergdorf Goodman. He creates special-order dresses sold at trunk shows and retails at more than 25 high-end boutiques nationwide. Gustavo travels throughout the year for more than 30 personal appearances. His celebrity clientele includes Eva Longoria and Catherine Zeta Jones. Gustavo plans to add a less expensive secondary line of cocktail dresses catering to businesswomen. He says that you can start with higher-end, expensive product and later add a less expensive line, but you can't start with a cheaper product and add the higher end. He lives for the glamour of seeing women in his dresses, and his advice is that you must focus on what you really love to do—not what you see in the street or in the market.[6]

Design from the Gustavo Cadile collection
Photo: Toto Cullen, Art Direction: Sofia Sanchez de Betak, Model: Pau Bertolini

The Quality Standard

I once stepped into a Los Angeles store where the owner was fuming about the skirts she had just unpacked in a shipment from a new designer. Touted as being made with the highest-quality couture technique, hand sewn, and very expensive, the skirts were a mess. The inside of each was a tangle of loose threads, frayed edges, and crooked seams. It was a complete embarrassment, and the buyer will never place an order with that designer again.

Quality is a combination of the craftsmanship, materials, and finishing. Designers should study quality by looking at a wide range of garments from designers they admire. Look at vintage garments from the 1940s and 1950s—when garments were made with great care—as well as mass-produced items. You'll learn that great fabric does not guarantee great quality. Beautiful leathers are often wasted on poorly constructed garments, and beautiful construction is wasted on cheap synthetic blends. Price is not always an indicator either. One can find $800 wool skirts that aren't lined and $30 white cotton shirts that are beautifully made.

It Must Look the Price

When developing your line, aim for the highest quality possible for your price. Once you set this standard, it is vital to stay consistent to meet customer and buyer expectations. Successful brands, ranging from high-end Louis Vuitton to the less expensive Everlane, carefully maintain the same quality standard from season to season.

Price should be kept in mind throughout the design and development process because it affects the materials you can use, how intricate the design can be, and who will be able to buy it. A crucial part of the design puzzle is figuring out how to make the product great within its price point—while still maintaining your profit margin.

The Trends

Many designers say they don't look at fashion week or other collections because they don't want to be influenced. But designers should be generally aware of the major fashion movements and what is on the streets as buyers, editors, and many customers do think in those terms.

As a small company, it's impossible to keep up with trends and compete with fast fashion. If you try, it can dilute your identity and make it difficult for anyone to know what to expect from you. Stay focused on your customer and POV. Faux fur bags may be flying out of the stores, but if your customer won't wear them, they shouldn't be in your line.

Sometimes you can benefit from trends that fit your unique point of view. Robert Burke, consultant and former senior vice president of the fashion office and public relations of Bergdorf Goodman, said that they first picked up menswear designer Thom Browne because they noticed a trend in young men wanting to dress up and wear a jacket—but not look like their father. Thom had a line that fit that, was very specific, and yet was unlike anything else they were seeing in the industry.[7]

More important than seasonal fashion trends are the overall lifestyle trends that affect fashion. When people started wearing their gym clothes on the street, the athleisure category was born. Entire e-commerce sites focus on the demand for modest dressing, and many labels are cutting a broader range of sizes. Consumers are demanding fair trade, sustainable products, and luxury increasingly incorporates items made by craftspeople using traditional techniques. It helps to be aware of changing mindsets and how they affect what people buy and wear. Staying in touch with what is going on around you may open up new business opportunities to which you can respond in your own unique way.

Product Range

Donna Karan famously launched her brand with a legendary collection of "seven easy pieces"—a group of skirts, tops, and bodysuits that all worked together and communicated the message of easy dressing, comfort, and style from day to night. Here are a few principles to guide you in creating a tight product range.

Focus. Shoppers don't need more; they need something that resonates specifically for them. Focusing on a single product category, value system, or aesthetic can establish a strong and loyal relationship with your customers. It's better to do one thing well or shine in one or two categories than to take on too much.

Designer Lindsey Thornburg has been collaborating with Pendleton home since 2011, making cloaks from their signature blankets. As she says, "There is so much fashion in the world and this product fits into a very specific realm of 'fashion forward heritage.' I focus on opening this silhouette up to new markets versus always creating something else. Every year we modify it bit—maybe the iPhone gets bigger so we change a pocket—but we try to refine the silhouette versus just designing more things."[8]

Start small. It used to be standard for designers to create full collections of 50 or more styles or SKUs (stock keeping units) for the stores. Fortunately, bigger is no longer better, and when you are new and have limited resources, it's best to start with a small number of pieces with limited color options and grow over time. Recently, designer Thakoon Panichgul relaunched his business with a collection of just 12 styles.[9]

Many brands launch with a single "hero" product. An item that excites consumers, sells well, and establishes a following for the brand. One product can put you on the map and then you can expand in a steady, focused manner, adding new items that build on that original aesthetic and concept. Mansur Gavriel launched with their hugely successful bucket bag and then built out their offerings with shoes and ready to wear. A simple nylon Kate Spade bag launched an entire lifestyle brand.

Edit. Too many ideas are confusing, and without careful editing, a line can look directionless and immature. *Quality is more important than quantity*, and the goal is to leave in only the strongest pieces for a tight, balanced collection. Product needs to look good when photographed and have "hanger appeal" to make it attractive in the store. Ask professionals you trust, such as a stylist or sales representative, to help you merchandise the line and eliminate items that don't work.

Balance. A collection is not a random selection of great items. It must have an overall direction, and the pieces should work together as a group. Unless you focus on a single classification, carefully review the collection to identify gaps and establish a cohesive range of items that tell a similar color and fabrication story. Eventually the ideal range each season will likely combine a few fresh ideas alongside a continuous offering of best selling shapes and silhouettes updated with new colors, patterns, or details.

Core Product

The 80/20 rule states the 20 percent of products bring in 80 percent of sales. Many labels have built their business on a strong demand for one signature item. The Burberry trench, the Diane Von Furstenberg wrap dress, and the Ralph Lauren Polo shirt are all examples of the core product of successful brands.

Core product is great for business. The styles can be carried over from year to year by keeping them fresh through subtle changes in color, fabric, or design. Because development and pattern costs are already covered, these items have a higher margin and it is easier to predict future expenses and inventory needs. Your suppliers and manufacturers are already on board—they understand the product and are happy with consistent orders and increasing quantities.

To develop core product, you need to find something you do well that consumers love and do it again and again. Sometimes core product is the "hero" product that launched the brand. Other times, certain best sellers naturally evolve into core product. Designer Mandy Kordal re-creates her Lived In Collection of best-selling staples each season in her signature natural colors.[10]

Even more than other product, the core product must clearly represent your brand vision to stand out from others and it must stay consistent in quality and fit from season to season so customers get what they expect.

Keep It Fresh

Be careful not to rely too heavily on core product. You need a regular offering of fresh and distinctive items to attract new audience, uphold the brand story, and keep customers interested. LA shoe line Labucq generated a lot of clicks to their website with their distinctive Page Wedge in orange, where more customers ultimately bought it in black.[11]

Creative "image" pieces reinforce the brand magic, but items that go viral on social media may or may not lead to big sales. The unique specialized items that build buzz are also often difficult or expensive to produce, so don't go overboard. These items are ideal to offer in limited edition quantities designed to sell out.

The unique designs that grab attention are often adjusted for sales. Menswear designer Thom Browne put himself on the map by creating a short, shrunken silhouette for his suits. But while the men who worked in his store wore their suit pants hemmed high above the shoe, they sold pants with unfinished hems so the customer could choose a more traditional length.

Patterns and Samples

One of the first steps in producing a design is to create the patterns from which your samples will be made. It is critical to find good talent at this stage. A great patternmaker can elevate the product and pinpoint problems in the design, construction process, and materials.

An expert pattern is the foundation of a good product. Most important, it determines fit, which is one of the most common reasons that items don't sell. Signature fit is what put many designers on the map. The Veda jacket and the Malia Mills swimsuit are the results of great patterns.

Who should make the patterns? Many designers learn patternmaking in design school and some even teach themselves. A basic knowledge of patternmaking will help you better understand construction and fit, communicate clearly with patternmakers and other contractors, and pinpoint problems. However, while making your own patterns will save substantial money and give you control, it's critical that you really have the skills to do an expert job. Factory managers have told many designers they won't work with their self-made patterns anymore because the mistakes cause time delays at the factory. Even if you are extremely deft at patterns, they are time consuming, and as your company grows, you may have to outsource this task to focus on other aspects of the business.

Where to find a patternmaker. The best way to find a patternmaker is through personal referrals from people in the industry. Ask contractors or factories if they can recommend someone. The CFDA website has a resource section that includes patternmakers in New York and LA. Makers Row has extensive resources for all production services and suppliers. We Connect Fashion and Fashiondex also list patternmakers and other contractors.

A patternmaker should have many photos and examples of their work, as well as actual garments made from their patterns. Ask who else they work with and inspect the quality and fit of the samples. Look for photos of their work on their website or social media.

You get what you pay for. Good patternmakers are expensive, but money spent here can save considerable money later on. Most designers are willing to spend whatever is necessary for good patterns and will make their budget cutbacks elsewhere.

Generally, patternmakers charge by the piece and the price is determined by the complexity and amount of detail in the garment. Some charge an hourly rate and will provide an estimate of the number of hours required once they understand the garment. The more complex the pattern or garment, the more time it takes and the more it will cost. Pricing can vary widely among different patternmakers and services. Generally, jackets fit into one price range, from $300 to $500, while skirt patterns cost closer to $200. Typically, a patternmaker will require a 50 percent deposit before beginning work.

Most often the pattern price includes the pattern, a muslin prototype made from the pattern, and one round of revisions based on a fitting. A full development package, including pattern, technical drawings, muslin, and first sample, will cost around $1,200 to $2,000 per style depending on the design. If you subsequently make more changes to the design, you will have to pay for the adjustments.

Communicate clearly. Before the patternmaker can begin, the designer must be very clear on how they want the finished garment to look, including the details of shape and fit, right down to pocket placement. Both patternmakers and factories cite stories of designers with ideas that are impossible to make, and designers are often frustrated when shown a sample that is nothing like what they envisioned.

Sketches of the front and back of the garment, technical drawings, and detailed specification sheets are valuable tools to communicate the overall look of the garment as well as measurements for the sample size and details such as the width of the pant leg or the size of pockets. Swatches are helpful to understand how the fabric will affect the garment, and a mood board can help the patternmaker understand the overall aesthetic of your brand.

Many designers use reference garments to demonstrate a certain fit, style detail, or assembly detail. Patternmaker Jené Stefaniak, owner of StitchLuxe, recommends you avoid providing low-quality fast fashion garments as references as they are often poorly constructed and can even be asymmetric and not an ideal base for new designs. She says, "The most important thing is to have a clear conversation with the patternmaker after you have your designs and product goals finalized."[12] She spends time with each designer discussing their line prior to starting development. She likes to find out who their target customer is, what brands they see their line hanging next to, and their target cost and end price for each style. These are all factors that will determine how the patterns are drafted and how samples and production are finished.

Be sure to listen to the patternmakers' advice and feedback. They are experts in construction and fabric and how certain details affect the hang or the fit. They can suggest improvements and help you avoid problems and save money in production. Jené also recommends, if you have a hard deadline such as a photo shoot, pop-up, or presentation, be clear about your dates from the start of the development process and most patternmakers/sample makers are happy to accommodate. If you have a more flexible deadline, this is also appreciated.

Choosing and Working with a Patternmaker
by Anna McCraney of Blank Canvas Development

Do not hire a patternmaker right out of design school. While most fashion design students learn the basics of patternmaking, the intricacies of form and fit, notches and darts, stretch and drape are lost on someone with only a couple of years of experience. Look for a patternmaker with decades of experience and the portfolio to prove it. Simply getting a sleeve cap or a collar to lay correctly is a skill unto itself, and unless you have done it 100 times, 100 different ways, you don't know how to do it yet.

Start with one style to test the partnership. You have no idea how you and your patternmaker will work TOGETHER. Even if they have made amazing things for other people, your communication styles may not jive.

Give them as much information as you can to visually explain what you want to create. This can be simple drawings, photos of details you like, or inspiration garments. Make clear notes and give clear direction. Have them make a pattern, and then a muslin. This way, you are both working together to get the design right.

Be clear about your time lines. If they say that they will deliver by a certain date, expect that. If they don't, hold them accountable and look for someone who can meet deadlines. There is nothing fashionable about being late when you have deadlines to meet.

Do not overvalue claims by any company providing "digital patterns only." A good patternmaker will work directly on a dress form and do fittings directly on a person. There is no true standard body, and each pattern should be unique. A good patternmaker will make their patterns by hand, and then the perfected patterns can be digitized when you mark and grade for production.

Work with a patternmaker who regularly works directly with their sample sewer. Patterns are a language and you need all of your service providers to speak the same way.

Work with someone domestically. Even though a lot of production and development is done overseas, there is so much that can get lost in translation. You need someone who understands your aesthetic, fit, and vision. Time differences will wear on you, and unclear emails will bog down the process. A weekend in New York for a fitting will cost you a lot less than the mistakes that come from the back and forth during an approval process with someone you have never met.

Source your fabric yourself! You are the designer and should already have your idea for the fabric even if you haven't found the perfect vendor for it. It is important for your patternmaker to know whether they are working with a knit or a woven, and if it is a lightweight or a heavier fabric. You can attend trade shows or connect with domestic and overseas fabric mills to order swatches and choose what you want. Blank Canvas has a great list of mills and fabric agents. Ultimately, what you choose will factor into the end cost of your product, so you need firsthand knowledge of where it is coming from, what it costs per yard, and what the mill's minimums and lead times are. Look for agents and vendors who stay true to their promises.

Start small and take your time. Blank Canvas gives a lead time for development of six to eight weeks, but we suggest you allow a lot more time. Once you have what you perceive to be the perfect product, you can do a test run of 10–20 pieces and share them with editors, influencers, and potential clients for feedback. At that point, you have the opportunity to refine your product before you sink tens of thousands of dollars into large production runs. You can also figure out your margins and lead times and get an idea of what your demand will be in this very competitive market. Be flexible and patient. You want to know that what you are providing is good quality for the right price.

Blank Canvas Development offers pattern making, sample making, and a full menu of product development and production services to take your designs from sketch through final production. Founder and designer Anna McCraney, a graduate of The Rhode Island School of Design, perfected her development skills making patterns for her own line, Annabelle, and as a head designer at Dolce Vita and Amanda Uprichard. In 2009 she won Bravo's *The Fashion Show*, hosted by Isaac Mizrahi. Her 20 years of experience and relationships with factories allow her to negotiate fair prices and fast turnaround while encouraging sustainability, and American manufacturing.

First Samples

The samples are the most critical tool for sales and require time and effort to perfect. Each sample can easily cost $1,000. Most young designers have a bad habit of oversampling. Keep your eye on the budget and limit the number of styles in the collection.

Who should make the samples? A designer does not need to sew. Many of the biggest names in the fashion business would be lost behind a sewing machine. However, basic sewing skills are vital to understanding construction and fit and will help you pinpoint problems in a sample that doesn't look right and communicate better with the factory.

Making your own samples will save you money and allow more control over the product and production schedule. While some designers are extremely talented with a sewing machine, it's usually easy to spot samples made by a designer because they lack the quality and expert finish of a professional. Whether it's an issue of skill or just equipment, be honest with yourself. If your in-house samples aren't as good as they could be, outsource.

Ideally your patternmaker will work with a sample maker for the first samples. If you are hiring the sample maker, make sure they have expertise in the type of product you design, look at examples of past work, and ask about turnaround time. Sample price is affected by the number of pattern pieces, the complexity of the garment, and the extra details of lining, topstitching, buttonholes, and finishing.

The factory you use for production may offer sample-making services. If the factory makes the first sample, it will better understand the garment and give a more accurate estimate of production lead time and cost. However, the cost of that first sample may be quite high. Sometimes a factory will inflate the sample price considerably because it is concerned that after the designer receives the sample, it will be given, along with the entire production job, to a cheap factory overseas. To counter this, the factory prices the sample high and then makes up for it in a cheaper production price as an incentive for the designer to keep the work there. Many overseas factories produce samples as part of their production package and then ship them to you for approval. Some even travel to large cities around the world each season to create and review samples in person with designers.

Be a perfectionist. When working with new designers, retail buyers say the biggest problem is usually the fit. And poor fit is one of the biggest reasons for e-commerce returns. Test each sample on a fit model who accurately represents your target customer. The fit model will give movement to a garment and show whether it hangs correctly or if it pulls or sags. A model can also tell you about comfort and ease and if there are issues in putting the garment on, taking it off, sitting down, or reaching. Most likely, at least one round of alterations will be needed after trying the sample on the model, and the sample should be redone until it's right.

Some designers act as their own fit model, but with clothing it's very difficult to get a full perspective of a garment on your own body and to pinpoint where it needs alteration. Before you finalize the collection, try the samples on a few "real" people to hear feedback and see how the samples hang on different bodies. I have seen shock on designers' faces when, after creating all their samples and perfecting them on a model, they realize how different the garment looks on a "real" body.

In addition to fit, check the sewing and construction details of the item. For clothing, do a wash test of the first sample to alert you to any shrinkage, fading, and stretching that result from care and cleaning.

The final collection. When the first samples are complete, edit the line to remove samples that should not go to market. Some will need to be eliminated because they are too expensive, take too long to produce, or simply don't fit the collection. Create a SKU plan for the number of pieces per category that you are planning to produce. A collection of ten pieces may include five tops, three bottoms, and two jackets. Each size, color, and style will need a different SKU number. You should have this prepared to create line sheets and when approaching factories for accurate quotes and schedules.

Once the line is finalized, you can use this set of samples for photography for your lookbook and website. If you want to sell wholesale, you may need duplicate samples for the selling process. For example, you may need one set of samples for a Paris showroom, one for a West Coast sales representative, and another for use at the trade shows.

Shoe Development
by Shoe Girls Studio

The cost of prototyping footwear designs can range from low to high depending on many factors, including location, the complexity of the design, materials chosen, hardware, and embellishments. Assuming you have a European factory, this process can range from €2,000 to €8,000+ per style. For example:

- **Custom Last:** €200–€500 per pair

- **Custom Heel Mold**: €700–€900 per size

- **Prototype:** €2,000–€4,000+ each style

A small capsule collection of four styles, using two custom lasts and two custom heels, would cost at least €10,000 just for the samples (production is additional).

Usually, the development process takes six to eight months. This includes the time for shipping the samples back and forth to review and edit. You will go through at least three rounds of sampling during the prototyping phase:

1. Technical: Perfect the fit and pattern

2. Material: Improve designs through color and material exploration

3. Sales: Finalize design, color, and material choices

Note: Samples are usually done by the half pair until you get to the sales sample.

TIPS

- Develop multiple styles on the same last. You will be able to use the same components across many styles, plus your product will have sizing continuity.

- Use what is available. Try to design around or find matching components from open market materials for your design.

- Remember colorways! For a single style do two to three colorways; varying your materials in a single style can make a one style feel like three separate designs.

- Don't do half sizing unless half sizes are key for your product's consumer. This will help minimize the number or lasts, molds, and components that you will need to pay for.

Shoe Girls Studio is a footwear and accessories design and development agency with global production in many countries, including Italy, China, and Mexico.

Costing

Throughout the entire design and development process, it's important to keep track of every single cost associated with each sample and be aware of how these costs of production will affect the final retail price. You don't want to create a product that no one can afford to buy nor a product that won't provide a profit.

The first sample will allow you to create the first production cost estimate for your design and to verify that you can actually afford to produce and sell it at the appropriate price point. Designers roughly guess that the production cost per item will be half the cost of the sample, but as you price out different quantities with suppliers and factories, your estimate will become more accurate.

Production costs will change based how much you produce. The larger the order quantity, the lower the cost per item because of volume discounts for materials and sewing. Small orders can lead to production and material surcharges.

Cost of goods sold (COGS) includes all the materials and labor specifically required to produce the actual items. It covers materials such as fabric, trims, zippers and buttons, handles, lining, fusing, thread, labels, and hangtags, as well as the labor costs for production patterns, marking, grading, cutting, sewing, and packing. Don't forget the costs of any specific hangers, ticketing, and shipping required by retailers. Create a cost sheet to track the costs for each new item.

The final price of your product will depend on many additional variables, including the product category, the target market and customer, and whether you are selling wholesale or direct to consumer. If the actual cost of each sample is too high to result in a realistic and profitable price, the design will need to be altered. A great trouser with beautiful buttons and embellishments may need to be pared down if the production quantities are small and the cost of those elements result in an unreasonable price.

Sample Cost of Goods Worksheet

Style #		Season:		
Description:				
Piece Goods	**Width/Style**	**Cost per Yard**	**Yardage**	**Cost**
Fabric 1				
Fabric 2				
Lining				
Interfacing				
Other				
Allowance				
		Sub Total Piece Goods Costs		

Notions	**Style/Size**	**Unit Cost**	**# of Units**	**Cost**
Buttons				
Zippers				
Thread				
Labels				
Trim 1				
Trim 2				
		Sub Total Notions Costs		

Labor				**Cost**
Production Samplemaker				
Cutting				
Grading				
Sewing				
		Sub Total Labor Costs		

Shipping				**Cost**
Hangers				
Bags/Shipping Boxes				
Hangtags				
Other Costs				
		Sub Total Shipping		

Total Cost of Goods Sold	
Wholesale Markup	
Wholesale Price	
Retail Markup	
Suggested Retail Price	

Fabric Name:	**Sketch**
Content:	
Source:	
Swatch:	

Price

The price of each product must accurately reflect its value and quality, and it should competitively position you in the market and stay consistent each season. Price defines your margin—the difference between costs and sales. If you price the collection too high, it will not sell; if it's too low, you lose your margin, and this will eventually drive you out of business.

Small design companies generally cannot compete on price because of the high costs and required minimums for materials and production. It is better to compete on value with a unique point of differentiation, a higher-quality standard, and a price that provides a better margin to cover your expenses and sustain the brand.

Understand the price range for your market. Research and compare the different items in your line with similar products that target the same customer and marketplace. A higher designer price point range includes labels such as Jacquemus and Proenza Schouler, while the mid-range contemporary price point includes brands such as Ganni or Tibi. While the prices of the different products in one line will vary widely, whether it is leather coats or cotton tank tops, a brand should be consistent within the market range.

Covering your costs. One of the biggest mistakes new designers make is not charging enough to cover all of their costs, much less provide a profit. The price must cover both the cost of goods sold (COGS), which you track in your costing sheet, and the indirect expenses. *Indirect expenses* include design and development costs, marketing and sales expenses, and overhead and administrative costs.

- *Design and development costs* include expenses to develop the collection from hiring the fit model to trips to fabric shows. Remember to account for your own labor if you make the patterns or samples, otherwise the pricing won't cover your costs when you start to outsource this work.

- *Marketing and sales expenses* include photo shoots, website development, trade shows, advertising, packaging, public relations, and showrooms. Markdown allowances, discounts, returns, and canceled orders are also costs of sales.

- *Administrative costs* include rent, bookkeeping, attorneys' fees, telephone, and other costs of running the business.

While COGS is attributed to each product, indirect costs need to be divided up and allocated across the entire collection. The process takes time, and many designers become Excel wizards as they work to allocate costs correctly.

Calculating price is not an exact science and can be complex. Several methodologies exist, but the most common approach is to apply a standard markup of between 2.2 and 2.5 to the cost of goods sold to cover all indirect costs and provide the profit margin. For example, if COGS for a blouse equal $50 and you use a 2.2 markup ($50 x 2.2), your price will be $110.

Pricing must consider whether you sell your product direct to consumer or if you plan to wholesale to stores. If you wholesale, you must consider how the store markup will affect the retail price. Pricing strategies vary by store, but generally, retail markup ranges from 2.2 to 2.8 on top of your wholesale price. Apparel is at the low end of the scale; jewelry and shoes are at the high end. For a retailer with a markup of 2.2, the math works like this:

$$COGS = \$50$$
$$\textit{Wholesale price} = \$110 \ (\$50 \times 2.2)$$
$$\textit{Retail Price} = \$242 \ (\$110 \times 2.2)$$

You can see how products that sell direct to consumer can have a lower price point and higher margin because you are not sharing the markup with a retailer. However, direct to consumer can have higher marketing costs to attract more customers, large technology infrastructure outlays, and significant expenses for packaging, shipping, and returns. Designer and educator Keanan Duffty advises, "If you launch as a direct-to-consumer business, you have to consider whether you eventually want to wholesale. If so, you need to be already working on that margin. If you try to change later, your price will be too high and you will have to source a more cost-effective way to make the product."[13]

Once you apply the markup, return to your research to determine if the resulting retail price makes sense for the market. If it's too high, it means the COGS are too high and you must find a way to simplify the design, use less expensive materials, move your production, or gain efficiencies with larger volume to bring down the costs.

Another pricing strategy that many independent designers employ is to start with the price you believe the target customer will pay and work backward. The qualities of the materials and construction define the costs, but this "value pricing" strategy considers how the unique aspects of your product and brand story affect the perceived value of the product and what the consumer is willing to pay. Once you settle on a number, you subtract your costs and determine your margin.

Protect your margin. Your gross margin is the percentage of the selling price left after COGS. Designers should aim for an average gross margin of 60 percent. The gross margin needs to be sufficient to cover all of your indirect cost and still leave you with a profit. Items that a designer sells in large numbers, such as T-shirts, may be less expensive or more efficient to produce and therefore provide a higher margin.

Ultimately, it's not about the volume of product you sell, it's about the margin, or how much you make. Usually, the goal is for pricing to leave roughly a 15 percent net profit margin after all direct and indirect costs. The only ways to increase your margin are to increase your price or lower your costs. The longer you are in business, the more you will build in efficiencies, and some costs will go down. You will accumulate patterns that can be used again or adjusted by switching out sleeves or collars. You will meet the minimums for cheaper production and discounts in materials. The margin can increase as the business grows. Never underprice your product just to attract customers and build volume. If you do not start out working on the right margin and price point, it is very difficult to adjust later.

5 SUSTAINABILITY

Fashion is one of the most polluting industries in the world, making sustainability a critical issue for fashion companies. The process of making, distributing, and eventually disposing of fashion product has significant environmental and social impact.

Environmental Impact. Fashion production relies on an extraordinary amount of natural resources. Vast quantities of water are required for growing cotton and other raw materials, for washing and dying fabrics, and for processing yarns and textiles. Pesticides and hazardous chemicals from bleaching, printing, stain proofing, stone washing, and tanning are released into the air and into rivers and groundwater, polluting fresh water sources, tainting food crops, and killing wildlife. Plastics and microplastics from synthetic fibers pollute our oceans, and landfills overflow with millions of tons of discarded clothing.

Human impact. Dangerous work conditions, unfair compensation, exposure to toxic chemicals, abuse and overwork, child labor, and even slavery are too common in the global fashion supply chain.

Animal welfare. Animals are exploited in the fashion industry for leather, down, wool, silk, feathers, cashmere, and fur. Cruel methods are used for trapping, skinning, and execution, and animals suffer in crowded, dirty pens and cages. Starvation and abuse are common.

These issues are all significantly worsened by consumer demand for a continuous stream of new product at unrealistically low prices. A simple cotton T-shirt relies on people to plant, grow, harvest, weave, cut, stitch, finish, label, package, and ship. If that T-shirt only costs a few dollars, someone is suffering in the process.

The good news. There is growing awareness and demand for better practices in sourcing and manufacturing, and it is increasingly an expectation from customers. According to a recent study, two-thirds of U.S. consumers consider sustainability when making a purchase and are willing to pay more for sustainable products.[1] As a designer, you have the ability to improve lives through sustainable materials, eco-friendly processes, income for artisans, and attention to animal welfare and the health of the oceans. Business can be a great catalyst for change and consumer education. As designer Eileen Fisher says, "It's okay to produce if you do it in the right way."[2]

What Is Most Important to You?

In facing the overwhelming issues around ecological and ethical production of fashion product, there is no single industrywide standard to follow and no company can address everything. There are choices to make between the environmental benefits of organic cotton, linen, and hemp; or fair trade cotton benefits to growers; or recycled materials that help keep garments out of landfills; or factories that recycle wastewater to protect natural resources.

Take time to think about your values and how sustainability fits into both your brand and the qualities of the product you want to design and deliver to your customer. There are resources to help you choose. According to their website, Danish brand Ganni used the United Nations Sustainable Development Goals (SDGs) as a guide. They picked three—climate change, gender equality, and designing for circularity—as the framework to create their sustainability mission.

Start at the beginning. Define your sustainability values and goals before you launch. Jewelry designer Bliss Lau emphasizes, "It's much harder to transition and improve practices later when you are already working with vendors. At that point, you end up needing to change not just your own practices, but those of the entire supply chain."[3]

"What are you making and why?" Designer and sustainability expert Tara St James recommends designers evaluate their point of view and their product at the outset to make sure there is a need for it in the market. "Understand how it's made, what it's made of, and where. Learn about every aspect of the supply chain to make wise decisions both financially and sustainably."[4]

Make your commitment. Write a *sustainability statement* to clarify your standards for yourself and everyone that works with you. Develop guidelines and restrictions for your materials and supply chain. Even if sustainability isn't part of your brand story, it is important to commit to goals and have them available to share. Allbirds markets its sneakers as "the world's most comfortable shoes," but it's easy to discover that they are made from a sustainably sourced eucalyptus and wool blend.

Good design is sustainable. A large share of produced fashion is never sold and ends up wasted in a landfill or incinerated. Sustainable product is product that sells well and lasts for many uses and even many years. Regardless of how you source and produce, design must come first to ensure a product that has value for the consumer. It should look good, function well, and be available at a price that makes sense. Low price and poor quality result in rapid disposal. While better materials and quality standards result in a higher price, they also increase the life of the product and add value for the buyer.

As designer Geren Lockhart of Canava says, "Sustainability is not just about the fiber, it also considers lifestyle and product use. Robes are already designed with a loop in the back to hang them up between uses. So we put a loop on everything so it can be cared for—hung up rather than just thrown on the floor and unnecessarily washed."[5]

The *slow fashion* movement means taking time to be thoughtful about design and the resources you use and ensuring that each garment is individually made with care to stand the test of time. It focuses on delivering new product when it is needed and available rather than chasing a preset seasonal calendar. The development of strong core product and cross-seasonal best sellers is good for business and for the planet.

Manage inventory. The most sustainable thing you can do is "less." Try to test new product online and launch with small production runs to help you predict future demand. Avoid placing large orders on projection, and say no to retailers who demand excessive quantities, which often result in markdowns and unsold inventory. As emphasized in Chapter 4: Product Development, smart businesses focus on tight product ranges that appeal to a specific target customer.

Don't be afraid to run out. Many of the most sought-after fashion brands operate on a scarcity model to increase excitement around product drops and wait lists. Made-to-order and pre-order business models are increasingly common and acceptable to consumers. The growth of on-demand production will be revolutionary for reducing waste and excess product. Don't forget to consider what will be done with unsold, returned, or excess inventory and materials.

Consider circularity. Also referred to as "cradle-to-cradle" or "closed loop" fashion, circularity considers sustainability at every stage of the life cycle of a product. It starts with product designed and produced without microfibers or other harmful materials and with an emphasis on the quality and longevity of each item. There is focus on an end life for the product, with all materials being either infinitely recyclable or biodegradable. The goal is to design something that is made to last—and when it does wear out, it can be recycled into something new.

Sourcing Sustainable Materials

Sustainable fabrics are increasingly easy to find. Trade shows such as Première Vision dedicate large areas to organic, certified, and newly developed fabrics, many of which are available in small quantities. Just beware of misleading information and greenwashing. Look for certifications and ask questions.

Ask the fabric agents, showroom representatives, and your current suppliers to help find sustainable options. The CFDA Sustainability Resource Guide includes a materials index as well as the very informative *CFDA Guide to Sustainable Strategies*. The Sustainable Angle and Common Objective both list sustainable materials and ethical factories with low minimum order quantities (MOQ).

Tara St James runs the Re:Source library at FIT, which offers consulting and open library days for sourcing the most up-to-date sustainable materials. She explains that accessibility and minimums really vary. "If the mill is already using organic cotton or recycled polyester, then you won't face significant minimums, but if they have to acquire the fiber just for you, they may require an order for thousands of yards. Instead of stating 'here is what I want,' call during your development process and ask what they have available. You can also work with other designers to combine orders to meet minimums."

You will pay a premium to develop a more sustainable and ethical product. The materials are more expensive than their conventional counterparts, and this will be reflected in the end price of your product.

Natural Fibers and Materials

Cotton. When sourcing sustainable materials, nothing is perfect. According to the World Wildlife Fund, it takes 714 gallons of water to make one cotton T-shirt and 1,800 gallons just to grow the cotton for one pair of jeans. The conventional cotton crop uses 7 percent of all pesticides and 16 percent of all insecticides on the planet![6] Organic cotton foregoes these toxins, protecting natural resources and the health of both wildlife and the farmer. However, organic cotton does require the same excessive quantities of water, and it is still often treated with toxic chemicals and dyes to achieve desired finishes and color.

Linen, hemp, and nettles require much less water and pesticides than cotton. However bamboo fiber, often marketed as sustainable, is actually harmful to produce because of the extensive chemicals required to soften the hard wood into fabric.

Wool, down, and cashmere face environmental and ethical issues, and child labor is common in the silk industry. But standards, including the Sustainable Cashmere Standard, Responsible Wool Standard, and Responsible Down Standard, and alternatives such as Peace Silk, protect farmers, grazing lands, and animals.

Leather-related livestock farming contributes to deforestation, water and land overuse, and gas emissions. The tanning process requires vast quantities of toxic chemicals that are dangerous to humans and prevents this "natural" material from biodegrading. Vegan leathers are generally made from petroleum-based PVC and polyurethane plastics.

However, plant-based bio-leathers made of agricultural waste use less water and chemicals. Pinatex from pineapple, mycelium leather from mushrooms, and biodegradable composites such as Mirum™ can be molded, imprinted, tanned, and dyed to create the pattern and texture of leather. Algae, eucalyptus, and natural rubber foams can replace petroleum- and oil-based materials in sneaker production.

Viscose, rayon and the creation of other cellulose-based fibers drives deforestation in the Amazon and are often extremely toxic to process. However, Lenzing™ follows robust environmental policies, harvesting only FSC-certified trees and using less toxic solvents in producing TENCEL® and other products. Exciting alternatives also include Circulose® from discarded cotton clothing, Evrnu® from cotton waste, rose petal silk, and algae- and kelp-based products such as AlgiKnit.

Synthetics

Synthetics come from nonrenewable petroleum. When washed, outerwear and activewear garments of nylon, polyester, and elastics shed millions of plastic microfibers into our water, which runs into our soil and oceans. These materials will not biodegrade, but they can be recycled if they are not blended with other fibers.

Recycled Materials

Tara St James advises, "One of the easiest and most accessible options for small companies is using postindustrial and postconsumer recycled fabrics." Recycled nylon, polyester, and cotton are readily available, and there are many incredible options such as upcycled cotton from the New Denim Project in Guatemala and reclaimed and recycled cashmeres.

Recycled plastic bottles and reclaimed ocean plastics are used to create materials such as sequins, trims, fleece, and fibers like REPREVE® and Eco-Pel, which is an eco-friendly option for faux fur. ECONYL® made from discarded fishing nets, industrial plastic waste, and fabric scraps is a great option for outerwear and swimwear.

Kordal Studio pant sourced from the New Denim Project, Guatemala
Photo: Chloe Horseman

Deadstock

Using materials that are already made is always better than making new ones. Deadstock is fabric left over from factories and mills, which is no longer being manufactured. It has long been an important source for small companies making samples and small quantities. It is easy to obtain and there is a vast variety of fibers, prints, and finishes to be had. Designers can also source from their own archives and bring back materials and prints to update in new silhouettes or with smocking, quilting, and new trims. Zero Waste Daniel is a New York designer who creates his own textiles entirely from scraps from New York's garment industry. Deadstock is covered more in Chapter 6: Fabric and Materials.

Designers can also repurpose, or *upcycle*, unworn or postconsumer items into new product. The Eileen Fisher Resewn Collection is made up of pre-worn Eileen Fisher product that is reconstructed into new designs. Smaller labels including Rentrayage, The Series, jewelry designer Thea Grant, and CFDA award winner Bode each use vintage items, reworked T-shirts, dresses, and even sleeping bags in their collections. If you decide to sell upcycled items, be sure to explain to your customer that items are one of a kind and may have inconsistencies.

Packaging and Trims

Sourcing alternatives to plastic buttons and zip pulls, shipping on cardboard or recycled hangers, and using compostable bags and recycled boxes for shipping are all ways to improve the sustainability of your brand. When ordering a T-shirt from designer Maria Cornejo, I was able to choose an option to receive it in a pre-used box with pre-used packing materials.

Sustainable Production

Being a smaller company usually means you are not sourcing from major factories where the most human rights violations occur. However, there are small factories everywhere, including some in New York and Los Angeles, where workers are subjected to unsafe and unhealthy work conditions and paid shamefully low, illegal wages.

Ask Questions

There are many questions to ask your factory, which are outlined in Chapter 7: Production in this book, but there are specific things to address regarding ethical and environmental practices. If possible, the best approach is to visit the facility and see for yourself.

- Do workers receive a true living wage?
- Do workers receive benefits for their families?
- How does the management ensure safe working conditions?
- Have they conducted any environmental and social assessments or audits?
- Are they fair trade, GOTS certified, or working toward any certifications?
- Will your production involve any subcontractors, and can you contact them as well?
- How do they address sustainability?
- Are the raw materials and fabrics certified and can they be recycled?
- How do they manage excess and waste?
- Do they clean and recycle wastewater?
- What chemicals go into the making of a material?
- Can they use low impact dyes, which are waterless or chemical-free?

Manufacturing locally makes it easier to tour the facility and regularly verify working conditions and sustainable practices by sight. Producing locally also reduces the need for excess transportation fuel and materials. It's important to consider the ways you can reduce the carbon footprint of your supply chain. For example, if you are already sourcing organic linen in Turkey, see if you can cut and sew it there as well to eliminate excess time and resources in transporting it to yet another country.

Be aware that while designers need to negotiate to keep their costs down, when you demand a lower price, the workers are likely paid a lower wage. If you place your orders too close to the shipping date or make late changes to the design, the pressure will be put on the workers to ensure the tight deadline is met. Be mindful of the human impact of your decisions and your ability to influence best practices.

Jewelry and Sustainability

For centuries, jewelry has been associated with circularity as people repeatedly melted and reformed precious metals and reset gems and stones. However, now jewelry is often linked to deplorable mining practices, child labor, the environmental and health hazards of chemicals such as mercury and cyanide, and an excess of cheap, disposable plastic.

There are plenty of options available for ethical and environmentally conscious jewelry designers. Metals can be sourced from fair trade and fair mined sources. An even more sustainable option is recycled metals. Gold, silver, platinum, and base metals and alloys, such as brass and copper, can be repeatedly melted without compromising quality. Nikki Reed, the founder of jewelry brand BaYou with Love uses recycled gold, mostly from used technology recovered and responsibly extracted from Dell's U.S. recycling programs.[7] When purchasing 100 percent recycled metal, ask your suppliers where it comes from and if they have certification to prove it is 100 percent recycled.

For gemstones, recycled, reclaimed, and vintage stones are readily available. For new stones, it is critical to work with suppliers who can fully trace their stones and identify the origin and standards of the mine. Lab grown diamonds are also increasing in popularity with both designers and consumers. RJC certification from the Responsible Jewelry Council is a widely available standard for gold, silver, diamond, and colored gemstone supply chains.

Jewelry designer Bliss Lau says the most important thing to do is to ASK QUESTIONS of your vendors and suppliers. Ask about country of origin, provenance, human rights practices, and even how they handle wastewater. Bliss created a code of conduct for her business and a transparency review document that she sends to vendors asking questions about how the suppliers are sourcing their goods.[8]

In your own studio, try sourcing alternatives to chemicals and establish methods of safe disposal. Pay attention to the content of your workshop materials to avoid cadmium and lead. Jewelry designers should always offer upcycling, redesign, and repair services to their customers.

For further research, groups like Ethical Metalsmiths, the Responsible Jewelry Council, The Alliance for Responsible Mining, and The Ethical Making Resource offer extensive education and referrals to vetted suppliers.

Share Your Commitment

Don't forget to communicate your sustainability practices with your customers. Explain the thought that went into each step of sourcing and production to shed light on your commitment and the specialness of each product and material. Explain why your products cost what they do, be transparent about your supply chain, and share information about the farmers, workers, and processes that were involved.

Label your products with environmentally responsible care instructions such as "cold water wash" and "line dry." "Dry clean only" labels are vastly overused by suppliers for simplicity and by designers who don't understand fabric. A large number of "dry clean" items wash beautifully on the gentle cycle.

Offer repair services and encourage your customers to care for their items, resell their purchases, and recycle old items or even send them back to you for a discount on something new. The brand For Days uses a membership model to encourage customers to recycle. Customers pay a monthly or annual fee and receive a number of recycled cotton T-shirts and other basics in various silhouettes and colors, which they can exchange for new ones at any time, knowing the returned garments are recycled. Designer Mandy Kordal offers sweater repair and mending workshops.

This chapter has barely scratched the surface of the important and complex issue of sustainability. There are exciting developments and new concerns every day. You can find important resources and references to learn more in the Business Resources.

Study New York's garment label includes in-depth information on the origin of the materials and even the name of the sewer who made it.
Photo: Study New York

Standards and Certifications

Different third party certifications exist in the supply chain to verify no harmful substances or practices have been used at the fabric processing or manufacturing level. While certification is reassuring to both designer and consumer, unfortunately there are so many, each with different qualifications and goals, that it can be overwhelming and confusing. Mireia Lopez of Milo Tricot advises, "It is critical to keep in mind that there are many small workshop artisans in rural areas and smaller suppliers who meet all the requirements of ethical and sustainable certification, but they don't have the resources to apply." There are also plenty of "eco-labels" with misleading marketing claims that are not audited or proven.[9]

Asking questions and having industry referrals is a good way to start new vendor relationships. If in doubt, fabrics and final products can be independently tested at labs such as SGS and Intertek. Mireia advises, "It would be valuable to try to do a life cycle assessment (LCA) of your product at the beginning of the design stage to understand its full environmental impact, and then find windows of opportunity to improve and reach your goals."

Here are just a few of the more common certifications and standards:

B Corp Certification B Lab gives this certification to companies with a proven commitment to a wide range of environmental and social goals, including their impact on workers, customers, suppliers, community, and the environment.

Bluesign® is a Swiss certification with strict requirements for manufacturers and brands regarding people, health, and the environment during each step of the sourcing and production process from raw materials to finished product. It includes consideration for water and energy conservation, chemical use, and safe conditions for workers.

Cradle to Cradle™ (C2C) certification focuses on issues of health, renewable energy, water and carbon management, social fairness, and product end life in terms of materials that can decompose or be reused.

Fair Trade Certification™ Fair trade products are made under conditions that prioritize worker safety and fair pay. These businesses also often invest additional money in the local community. Look into groups associated with the Fair Trade Federation or World Fair Trade Organization or certified by Fair Trade USA or Fair Trade International.

Global Organic Textile Standard (GOTS) Certification verifies that a textile was made using at least 70 percent organic materials or that the mill, dyehouse, grower, and other producers used organic practices to create it. GOTS also upholds International Labour Organization (ILO) standards. For a finished product to be GOTS certified, every step of the supply chain has to be certified, which is extremely difficult for small companies. But if you source certified materials for your production, you can state "made of GOTS certified materials" on your label.

Higg Materials Sustainability Index, created by the Sustainable Apparel Coalition, measures the environmental and social impact of brands, manufacturers, and materials with consideration of dye toxicity, carbon footprint, water usage, and the biodegradability of materials.

Leather Working Group certifies tanneries and leather traders with gold, silver, or bronze rankings based on guidelines intended to protect the environment with consideration for waste management, chemical usage, and energy use.

The Nest Seal of Ethical Handcraft focuses on small craft and artisan workshops around the world and ensures that a product has been made under fair and ethical conditions.

Standard 100 by Oeko-Tex® certifies that textiles are free of harmful levels of an identified list of 100 toxins. The Leather Standard by Oeko-Tex® tests for harmful substances used in leather products and production.

The Global Recycled Standard (GRS) verifies that a product really does have the recycled content it claims to have.

Textile Exchange sets multiple standards for raw materials and fibers. The Responsible Down Standard (RDS), and the Responsible Wool Standard (RWS) address animal welfare as well as land management issues from farm to final product.

6 FABRIC AND MATERIALS

Choosing and sourcing fabric, materials, and trim is an exciting and critical part of the design process. A certain ribbon or tweed can inspire an entire collection, and very specific materials are often required to execute the full vision, quality, or function of a design.

Raw materials such as fabric are usually the largest expense for a fashion company, and what you use will have the biggest impact on your costs and pricing. Careful sourcing and management of your supply chain is critical to meet deadlines, maximize your profit margin, and minimize waste.

Learn First

Before you source any materials, learn about fibers, textiles, trims, and finishes. This will help you with the entire development and production process. The content of each material greatly affects the design results, and a designer should understand the attributes of natural versus synthetic fibers and the ways the weave and weight affect the shape and durability of a product. Important details include how a fabric washes, hangs, stretches, or shrinks and how the color or print is dyed. Your knowledge will also help you communicate with suppliers and manufacturers. Ultimately, a designer should be able to feel a fabric and know if it is suitable for a design.

The best way to learn about fabric is through hands-on experience. Internships with other designers as well as working a stint at a fabric store such as Mood is great training. You can also learn by visiting a fabric show and speaking with the representatives when they aren't busy with customers. When they have the time, people love to share their expertise. A designer can volunteer to help a fabric rep in exchange for "fabric lessons." It's well worth packing up a booth or working a few days in an office to acquire this knowledge. Educational events and workshops, such as "Textile Tuesdays" run by Study NY, highlight both materials and suppliers.

The Challenges

There are many sources of fabric, and researching and reviewing the options can be overwhelming at first. As a start-up, your options will be narrowed considerably once you consider price, minimums, and lead times. Choosing the right fabric is as much a business decision as an aesthetic one.

Minimums

Most suppliers of fabric and trim have a minimum order quantity (MOQ), which is the minimum amount of yardage (or meters in Europe) that designers must order. The minimums exist because for the supplier, servicing, producing, and shipping small quantities is time consuming and less profitable. Each supplier has a different threshold of what quantities are worthwhile. Minimums can range from 15 to 5,000 yards, but generally for the designer fabric market, the average is around 300 yards. Different fabrics from the same mill have different minimums, depending on the content of the fabric, the finishes, or the print.

When you are new to the market and your orders are small, meeting minimums can be difficult. Designers should not waste money purchasing excess quantities. When approaching any source for fabric or trim, find out the minimums up front. It's a waste of your time to discuss materials you can't have. You don't want to fall in love with a sample fabric that you can't get for production.

The reality is that new designers frequently cannot meet the minimums required by fabric suppliers. Don't despair—there are several things you can do.

Buy sample yardage. Generally, a supplier has two prices for fabric: the price for sample yardage (a higher price for a small amount of fabric to create a test sample for the design) and the price for production yardage (the lower price charged for the larger quantities needed for production). Sample yardage is expensive, 20 to 50 percent more than production yardage, because the quantities are small. But if you can't meet the required quantity for the production price, you can purchase the entire amount needed at the sample price. However, the cost will be high, and there is a risk that the mill won't work with you next season because you didn't return for a larger production quantity.

Pay more. Sometimes a source will make a MOQ exception if you pay a premium per yard or pay a fee. This is generally a much better deal than paying the full sample yardage price. Many European mills have expensive "couture" lines of fabric. Because the fabric is expensive, the profit margin is higher for the mill, and it will sell that fabric in smaller quantities. You can also negotiate with the supplier to find other ways to get past minimums or keep your price down. Ask them if a major manufacturer is buying the fabric, providing the opportunity to tack your order onto the larger one.

Buy stocked fabric. Ask the mill or supplier what fabric it has in stock. Most places house a selection of fabrics and piece goods in standard sizes, which require smaller minimums. If they don't stock exactly what you want, such as black lace, they may have white lace you can dye. They may also stock greige goods, which are unfinished goods that can be quickly dyed or treated. Ask whether they sell off leftover fabric at the end of the season. If you do buy stocked fabric, find out how much they have in total. If they run out, you may be back to facing a 300-yard minimum to fill orders.

Be creative. Designers find other clever ways to deal with minimums. For example, if you offer a shirt in four colorways and the orders don't meet the minimums to buy the fabric in each color, you could buy the fabric for all of the shirts in white and dye it yourself (just make sure the fabric and thread can actually be dyed).

Lead Time

Another factor that can limit your fabric options is lead time. This is the time it takes to receive the materials once you place the order. Lead times vary. Some fabrics arrive in two weeks, but eight weeks is standard with mills and converters if the materials aren't in stock. The same applies to trims. Basic items such as zippers may be stocked, but a special button or ribbon could take several weeks to arrive. Large orders take precedence, and your small order may be pushed to the end of the queue, causing unanticipated production delays. Many designers claim that one of the biggest challenges to delivering orders on time is the delays in receiving their fabric and materials.

Large, established fashion brands spend massive budgets on "supply chain optimization" technology and systems to save time and money on production. Plan carefully to know exactly how much lead time your production schedule affords, and make sure that you always build in a cushion in case of problems. While you may dream of buying beautiful fabrics from Italy, when starting out, it can be best to purchase domestically. As designer Gary Graham says, "Delivering on time or early is so important when you're first starting out, so working with mills and choosing fabrics you know you'll receive on schedule is very important."[1]

Sit down with the sales agent and ask what you can receive in the least amount of time. Be sure to include shipping time in the schedule. It can take more than a week to get the fabric from the mill and through customs once it's ready.

Cost Considerations

Know your budget and stay within it. Materials and trims range widely in cost, and expenses can escalate quickly if you let your creative side off the leash. Fabric can account for as much as 30 percent of each season's costs, and the cost of each material will affect the final product price.

Know in advance what you can spend while protecting your profit margin and creating items shoppers can afford to buy.

The fabric expense must make sense for the garment. Designer Nicole Miller explained the importance of fabric quality and price making sense to the end consumer. "It has to look like the money. You can buy a plain linen for $25 per yard, or you can buy a beautiful evening fabric for $25 per yard. You can get the money for the evening dress, but you won't for the linen because no one can tell a nice linen from an average linen."[2]

If you use an expensive fabric on an intricate garment with complicated construction, tailoring, or pleating, the high fabric cost will add to the high production cost, potentially resulting in a market price too high to sell to your customer. To keep the cost of the final garment reasonable, expensive fabric should be used for simple designs that cost less to cut and sew. Designer Gary Graham offers options to buyers when using expensive materials. If he is using a $21-per-yard jersey for a dress, he will offer the dress in a $3.50-per-yard cotton ribbing as well. The quality of material must also be consistent throughout the product. Don't line a beautiful silk charmeuse gown with a cheap polyester.

Designing your own prints is very expensive and depending on your print process, each color may add to the cost. To save expense, keep the number of colors per print down and then create the print again in different colors to get more use from it.

Limit yourself to fewer fabrics. For the first few seasons, this will help you keep down expenses and meet minimums. A fabric can be used in multiple designs and still look fresh to the buyer and customer. For example, the same silk chiffon will look completely different in an evening dress versus a playful tank top. It can be lined or unlined; crinkled, pleated, flat, or bias cut; and mixed with different trims.

Don't order excess fabric. Over-ordering is wasteful, ties up your cash, and results in excess inventory that can be difficult to use. In fact, menswear designer Robert Geller recommends that new designers focus on buying only piece goods versus placing fabric orders. He explains that even if a fabric is only $2.50 a yard and you buy 20 yards, you may only get enough orders to use 10 yards, which means your fabric really cost you $5 per yard because you must factor the cost of the excess into your overall expense.[3] Unfortunately, if you try to resell leftover fabric to a jobber, you often receive as little as 1/30th of the price you paid. Of course if you have a strong season and have to repeatedly reorder small quantities of fabric at the higher price to fill orders, you will also be wasting time and money. With experience, you will learn to anticipate reorders for certain items and order the right amount of fabric in advance. But when starting out with limited funds, it's not worth the risk.

Don't order fabric until you are sure. During product development, do everything you can to delay ordering sample fabric until you are sure it will be needed in the final collection. Many designers design their entire collection from swatches and even finalize the silhouettes before ordering fabric.

Always confirm price and payment terms. When you are ready to order, clarify the price for sample fabric, a full roll (generally 60 to 80 yards), and production quantities. Don't be afraid to negotiate to get the best price available for the quantity you need. Read the fine print and work out delivery details and payment terms up front. Most fabric suppliers require prepayment or cash before delivery (CBD), payment in full on a credit card, or at least a deposit with the balance due cash on delivery (COD). Once you establish credit or build a relationship with the vendor, you can ask for net 30 terms, which give you 30 days from when the fabric is shipped before you have to pay. When buying imported fabrics, confirm the price currency. There is a big difference between US$8 per yard and €8 per yard. (Note: Fabric from Europe is sold by the meter, adding yet another variable.) When the U.S. dollar declines in value, U.S. designers should keep an eye on the exchange rate. If the dollar falls by 5 percent, the fabric cost increases that much, and it may be necessary to source your materials elsewhere.

Don't forget shipping cost. Too often, designers are shocked when they receive the final materials bill because of the shipping and duty cost to bring goods into the country. When choosing materials from overseas, find out whether the price includes shipping and insurance and try to anticipate the total cost before you order. You don't want to end up like the menswear designer who had suiting from Italy sitting in customs for weeks as he tried to find cash to pay unexpectedly high duty fees. His production was delayed by each day his fabric sat in port, and to add insult to injury, U.S. Customs charged a daily storage fee for the goods.

Pricing terms specify which party covers the different costs of shipping. If the price is FOB (free on board), it includes only the transportation from the mill to the shipping port, not the shipping, duty, or other costs from that point on. CIF (cost insurance freight) includes shipping to the port nearest you where duty, insurance, and further transportation becomes your responsibility. To avoid surprises, you should ask if the mill will ship LDP (landed duty paid) in which shipping and insurance to the final destination and taxes and duty are included in the quoted price.

According to the Harmonized Duty Tariff Code, there is a different duty charge for each type of material and garment imported. Whereas linen might be charged 3 percent, the wool duty could be 30 percent, radically affecting the total cost. For example, a designer who shipped 600 meters of white cotton from Italy, which cost $1,100, had to pay $1,500 including shipping and duty, an increase of about 36 percent. And a fabric agent shipped fabric that was $7 per yard FOB, but $13.50 per yard LDP. The duty charge almost doubled the price of the fabric. Duty is also affected by country of origin and the fabric's planned use. If you are shipping Italian fabric to India for production, different tariffs will apply and can vary widely, significantly affecting your cost.

A customs broker or freight forwarder can help accurately estimate shipping and duty cost. Brokers are paid a percentage or fee based on the size of your total order. They can also help with tracking orders, managing delays or inspections, and meeting product labeling requirements. Although expensive, UPS or DHL are often best for shipping small quantities under tight time frames. These companies will handle customs, and it shouldn't take more than two to three days to receive fabric from Europe shipped by air.

The Sources

Finding the suppliers who have the product you need and who will help you get your materials on time, in good condition, and for a fair price is challenging. Don't just choose a supplier who has goods you like. Get a sense of the person and their control over the entire process. Know that the agent or sales representative across the table can pick up the phone and get the job done. It takes time to find reliable sources and develop relationships with them. There are several avenues to explore.

Trade Shows

Textile and fabric trade shows take place around the world on a set schedule. Twice a year, dozens of mills and textile manufacturers display their new fabrics at the shows. In addition to being a source of fabric, textiles, and leathers, the shows are a great source for all kinds of trims as well as factories that offer production packages. While you will find many booths that require high minimums, there is usually an area at each show specializing in vendors who offer smaller quantities. Première Vision and Texworld both host large shows in New York and Paris. Spin Expo NY focuses on yarns and knits. Lineapelle is dedicated to leather and components for shoes and bags. LA Textile—the Los Angeles International Textile Show—is a good option for designers on the West Coast.

To place an order at a show, suppliers will ask you to fill out an application detailing how long you have been in business, your resale or tax number, and references to verify creditworthiness. Regardless of where you end up sourcing your materials, it's worthwhile to visit a fabric show at least once. The shows highlight trends, new developments in sustainable sourcing, and high-tech innovation fabric, and they host a variety of educational seminars around sourcing, certifications, importing, and production. To attend, designers must show proof of a legitimate business.

Mills and Agents

The mills are the actual manufacturers of the fabric or textile. They own the goods and control the flow of the beginning yarn through each of the weaving, dyeing, and finishing processes. This "vertical" structure involves fewer outside entities and, therefore, should be very reliable. However, even the mills outsource some products, often to suit the trends. Find out a mill's in-house specialty as these products are more likely to arrive on time and in good condition.

While there are still a few mills left in the United States, there is a wide variety of materials to choose from overseas. European mills are known for high-end quality fabrics, such as Italian cashmeres and leathers, as well as innovative and luxurious fabrics and prints. Japan has high-tech fabric; Korea has outerwear and synthetics; India has embroideries, beading, and silk; and China offers a large variety of inexpensive goods. Most designers work with at least some imported goods. However, extra shipping and duty cost, shipping delays, customs, and vacation times are issues to consider when working with overseas sources. Italian mills are closed for the entire month of August, and Asia has several holidays, some of which result in mills being closed for more than a week at a time. Long lead times can jeopardize delivery and the ability to fill reorders from the stores. For your first few seasons, buying overseas might not be worth the additional stress.

Working directly with the mill generally entails very high minimums and long lead times, especially if you are interested in developing your own fabric. Most mills have showrooms and salespeople around the world who showcase the products, know where the goods are at all times, and can help supervise the process to control quality and stay on time.

Independent sales agents often represent one or several mills and take a commission on their sales. A good agent can source goods from multiple places, help negotiate the best pricing, and help with problems and delays that arise during shipping and at customs. When you meet with an agent, ask how long they have been with the mill. This will indicate the strength of their relationships and ability to help you receive the goods on time.

Converters

Converters buy unfinished fabric or greige goods from mills and finish the material themselves by printing, treating, and/or dyeing it for resale. Converters generally have lower minimums than the mills and offer a wide selection. However, they have less control over the goods because they didn't actually create them. When working with a converter, ask if it stocks any of the fabrics or yarn or if it waits for all of the goods to come from a mill. Get a sense of how closely it works with the mill and what level of control or influence it has over the yarn used, the flow of process, and the lead time.

The Secondary Market

Local jobbers in the secondary market don't actually produce or treat fabric. Instead, they buy unsold and leftover finished goods from mills, manufacturers, and designers. They offer a potentially ideal place to find small amounts of a large variety of unique fabrics without worrying about minimums, lead time, and quality. In many cases, the fabric is at the store where the designer can look it over and take it immediately. Mood Fabrics in both New York and Los Angeles and the fashion district fabric stores and warehouses across the country are examples of the secondary market. When buying from a jobber, there are two key issues to keep in mind:

1. **Quantity.** Because the fabric is left over, the risk is whether you can get enough for production. If you have strong sales for a particular item, the fabric quantity needed may be higher than expected, and unlike a mill or a converter, a jobber can't make it for you. Some jobbers may help you find out which mill originally made the fabric and call to see if there is any more. Most often, you have to try to source it yourself or find a similar replacement. To eliminate some of the risk when you buy sample fabric from a jobber, ask the jobber to hold the remaining stock for a few weeks until you have the sample and know if you need more. Ask up front what can and can't be reordered.

2. **Consistency.** Because jobbers buy goods from all over the world in a wide range of styles and quality, the goods are inconsistent. They may not have accurate information about the fabric content, making it difficult to estimate shrinkage and functionality. The law requires the fiber content of a garment be included on the label when sold, along with the care instructions. A lab such as Vartest can conduct a quality test to identify the fiber content, dye processes, and finishes that affect wear and care.

Some jobbers offer wholesale and may be willing to purchase fabric from a mill on your behalf and help you reach the minimum if you pay for the majority of the order and they believe they can sell the rest at the store.

Deadstock

Deadstock is fabric or materials that are left over and no longer being manufactured. The term can cover product found at jobbers and online sites such as Queen of Raw, as well as materials found at flea markets, antique fairs, or scrap warehouses such as Fab Scrap. While this is a common and affordable approach for small companies, as you grow it may become difficult to find enough of a fabric to fill orders or cut a full size range. The finite quantity of deadstock can have its own appeal for some designers and customers. Emily Bode, who won the CFDA Emerging Designer of the Year award in 2019, started her menswear line Bode making one-of-a-kind garments from antique textiles. Just be clear in communicating to customers if your product is limited edition or even one of a kind.

Online Sourcing

There are hundreds of wholesale material directories online where you can search by fabric type, country, certification, finishes, and more. The CFDA Materials Index includes many sustainable options. Sites such as Swatch On, DigiFair, We Connect Fashion, and Fashiondex include a variety of sources with small minimums. The latter publishes many guidebooks for designers, including *The Small Design Company's Guide to Wholesale Fabrics and Trims*, which specifically lists hundreds of suppliers that work with small design houses. Online platforms such as SynZenBe offer access to custom fabrics as well as in-stock and overstocked materials. Keep in mind, it's important to get swatches before you order online to accurately see the color, pattern, texture, or quality of the material.

Full Package Production (FPP)

Increasingly, factories and manufacturers have vertical operations and are able to source all of your raw materials for you. The factory can negotiate discounts and demand quick and reliable delivery because it orders for multiple clients representing a large amount of business for the mill. They can work with the mills to create fabrics and materials to your specifications and give you access to many different options.

Designers meet with the factory early in the development process or send swatches and samples back and forth to review options for fabrics, skins, trims, hardware such as zippers and buttons, and even labels for finished product. Many overseas factories, such as knitwear manufacturers in China, send packages of yarn options in various colors, fibers, and blends. For designers, it is extremely convenient to have their choices laid out before them, knowing that all the options are accessible and they don't have to spend time running from place to place procuring the raw goods or taking up additional time shipping them from supplier to factory. An FPP factory will also manage delivery and storage and handle any quality issues.

The downsides of this approach are that it can take several weeks to receive your options and go through the approval process. A factory may only work with specific suppliers, actually limiting your choices. You have more control over your time line if you source and ship yourself; but most of all, most designers love the process of researching fabrics, sourcing each detail, and working with the suppliers themselves.

Sewn Goods

Some companies start out as T-shirt brands or graphic-based labels with screen printing on sweatshirts or bags. Most of these designers work with already-sewn "blanks" to avoid sourcing raw materials and production facilities. However, at some point, you may need to step up to a better quality or develop a signature shape or fit for your designer product.

Increasingly, brands are creating upcycled garments from pre-worn items. Rentrayage and CDLM are just two designer brands that remake discarded and vintage clothing into high fashion one-of-a-kind looks. Thrift shops, flea markets, clothing mills, rag yards, and even garage sales can be great sources of clothing that deserves a second life.

The Order

Build Relationships

The fashion industry is built on relationships and the relationships you develop over time with suppliers will be invaluable. Fabric company CEO Wen Zhou put up $750,000 from her business for designer Philip Lim to start his label.[4] And it's not surprising that designers who speak fluent French or Italian often evade the minimums at European mills. A supplier of activewear fabrics at a trade show told me that even though he has a 500-yard production minimum, if he enjoys speaking to a new designer and determines from the conversation that the designer is serious and smart, he may let that person buy small quantities with a credit card.

Some fabric suppliers enthusiastically support new designers. Erich Soldat of Textile Agency said, "Young designers bring energy and creativity to fashion and keep New York fashion from being boring."[5] Jasco Fabrics supports new talent and allows unknown designers to order small quantities of its high-quality, American-made jersey.

To increase the odds of getting fabric from a new supplier, demonstrate some knowledge of fabric, share your vision and plan, and mention interest in your collection from your social media following, the press, or stores. Let the supplier see the potential for increased business, and convince them that you are able to pay.

When a rep gives you an appointment, be prepared and don't waste their time. Agent Erich Soldat emphasizes, "No designing here!" If you start developing your concept in a supplier's office while looking at all the fabrics and asking for random swatches, you won't be invited back. Have your concept and direction for the collection before you meet the fabric agent. Explain exactly what you need so they can help you find it quickly.

Communicate

Communication is key to ensuring you receive exactly what you need, on time and without issues. You must be very clear about the fabric content, weight, quantity, color, and delivery expectation. Be specific about the finishing of the fabric. After testing, one designer realized her entire order of "waterproof" jackets were only "water repellent." She had to donate all of the jackets with the incorrect finish and reproduce them under an extremely tight deadline.

Pantone chips are standard for showing the colors you want, but realize that fiber content and weave can affect the end result. It is best to provide a sample in the same fiber as your fabric to show the target color.

Don't forget to get the care instructions for the fabric to include on your product labels, and test wash a piece of the fabric according to these instructions to check for shrinkage or colorfastness. Garments from new designers often are returned because colors bleed or garments shrink when worn or cleaned. Suppliers should know the shrinkage factor of a fabric, but with a test you will be certain.

Confirm the information you need to meet all labeling requirements regarding fabric content. Be certain that any fabric treatments or finishes meet the environmental standards of where your product will be sold. All apparel items sold in Europe and California must meet tight regulation of chemicals and content.

Exclusives

A new designer fell so in love with a printed fabric she sampled at Première Vision that she planned her entire collection around the print. Then the mill called to tell her the fabric was no longer available because a big brand had bought a large amount of it and demanded an exclusive. Unfortunately, this is one of the hazards of being the little guy. If it happens to you, ask the mill to send you alternatives to help you find a replacement.

Exclusives tend to prevail with more recognizable things such as prints. Keep in mind that when you buy fabric, you do not have an exclusive. Large overseas mills often distribute their goods to many different agents, and they can end up everywhere. Ask the supplier if another designer or manufacturer has bought the same fabric to avoid having your luxury market coat in the same fabric as the hot new item at Anthropologie.

Replacing the Goods

Sometimes you may need to replace materials or supplies, even after you have shown or posted your samples and taken orders. A jobber may run out of the goods, or fabric may arrive too flawed to use.

When replacing materials, try to match the original as closely as possible in terms of quality, look, and feel. Once you find something, you should be open and show it to the buyers and customers who ordered the affected items for approval. There is a risk that they won't approve the replacement and will cancel their orders, but better to be honest and let it happen at this stage than later when the items are already produced and shipped.

When you replace goods, make sure the production bundles don't mix the original fabric with the replacement or you may receive a garment with one fabric on the body and another on the sleeves. Remember to include any cost differences resulting from replacement materials on the cost sheet.

Don't Let It Be Late

Once a material or trim is late, everything is off schedule. The production will be delayed, and you will have to make up time to hit your delivery deadlines. Asking for money back from the supplier won't get your orders shipped on time. The key is not allowing it to be late in the first place.

Don't take anything for granted. Stay on top of the mill or agent at all times to ensure the goods are on schedule. Call and ask where the fabric is in the production process. Have they received the thread, has it been dyed, is it being woven, is it on the truck, and when will it get to the port? If the person on the phone doesn't know, ask him to find out. Many things can push the fabric off schedule, and as a small company you are not a priority. Each mill has a set number of looms. If you need 300 yards of tweed and a rush order from Marc Jacobs comes in for 5,000 yards, your job may be removed from the looms to get them all working for Marc Jacobs. You must stay on top of your order or it will be continually swept aside.

Obnoxious is not effective, so be polite and professional when you check in. Remember you are building relationships that will increase your influence later on. When you work with an agent, ask what mill is working on the fabric. If the agent isn't getting answers to your questions, you could contact the mill directly to track the goods.

Quality Control

Many things can go wrong with fabric production, and you cannot take anything for granted. A good mill should contact you in advance if there are problems and show you the fabric to make sure you still want it. Large manufacturers usually request a sample half yard from the production run of the fabric to check the quality before it even ships. The mills may refuse to do this for small customers, but it doesn't hurt to ask.

It is imperative to inspect all items thoroughly and immediately upon receipt. This may mean a trip to your production factory, assuming you ship the goods directly versus transporting them yourself. Inspect everything carefully *before* it's cut. Once it's cut, you own it, and the supplier is not responsible. Technically, if you contract out the cutting, the contractor is responsible for spotting flaws, but check the goods yourself to be safe.

- Measure to make sure you received the correct yardage.

- Ensure that the fabric is the correct width. If you created the marker and planned quantities based on 60 inches, everything will be off if the fabric is 56 inches.

- Check for flaws or quality issues relating to the color or weave.

- Check the goods against your initial sales sample. If the product differs from what your customers ordered, they might send it back.

If you find a problem, call the supplier immediately to negotiate a solution or replace the fabric as quickly as possible. If possible, the agent should come to look at it and make a settlement before it's cut. While the mill should replace the damaged goods or take them back and refund your money, more often, for the sake of time and shipping, they will offer you a discount on the goods if you keep them and work around the problem. This is generally the best option to keep production from being further delayed.

Keep in mind when negotiating a settlement that flawed fabric may cost more to cut because you have to work around the flaws. When you buy from a supplier, find out the policy for late or flawed fabric. If there is no recourse, you may want to reconsider working with that supplier.

7 PRODUCTION

If you went to fashion school, you probably learned about the production process as it relates to big companies, but it is very challenging to navigate the world of production on your own. Many designers name production as the part of their job that is the most difficult, but despite the frustration, production is where your brilliant ideas become reality.

A critical person in large fashion houses is the *production manager*. For most new labels, this means you. The designer must manage all the steps of production, from initial samples through final shipping, and plan carefully to stay on schedule, meet deadlines, and keep track of every cost from start to finish. Don't take anything for granted—actively oversee it all.

The Production Plan

In general, the fashion cycle consists of three phases:

- Planning, design, and development
- Selling
- Production and delivery

For a wholesale product, selling comes before the production, while generally for a direct-to-consumer product, the production comes first. Either way, for each product or collection, you need a master production schedule that includes the steps of each phase. From ordering materials, developing patterns and samples, to cutting, sewing, and shipping, the schedule will help you track each material and process and keep you on time.

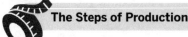

The Steps of Production

1. Research materials and concepts.
2. Design and develop silhouettes.
3. Select materials, fabric, and trims.
4. Create technical drawings.
5. Estimate cost and target pricing.
6. Create first patterns and prototypes.
7. Make adjustments and perfect fit.
8. Order sample cuts of materials.
9. Cut and sew samples.
10. Finalize collection of samples.
11. Photograph samples for lookbook and direct selling.
12. Create line sheets for wholesale.
13. Sell collection to stores and take pre-orders.
14. Finalize orders and production quantities.
15. Order production fabric and materials.
16. Sign off on production prototypes.
17. Digitize and grade pattern for sizes.
18. Create marker for cutting fabric and materials.
19. Cut, sew, and trim.
20. Pack and ship.

Start with the date when you need the product delivered to you or to the stores, and work backward through all the steps. Schedule plenty of time for unexpected delays and manage your time well. Industry experts are quite serious when they recommend that a designer designs her first two or three collections before even starting her business because she will never again have the luxury of that much time to design.

The production process takes months and as you create new product, the production schedules will overlap. The wholesale world lives on a set calendar with hard deadlines, and you must work within them if you plan to sell to stores. Designers who sell seasonal collections are shipping Fall orders at the same time as they are sampling for Spring and may be producing Resort. As you see from the sample production calendar, production for Spring is more crunched than production for Fall, and the seasons overlap significantly.

Sample Seasonal/Wholesale Production Calendar		
	Fall 2022	**Spring 2023**
September '21	Research fabrics. Start design.	
October '21	Select fabrics. Order fabrics.	
November '21	Create patterns. Begin samples.	
December '21	Develop collection. Review production strategy.	
January '22	Finalize collections. Begin sales.	
February '22	Show collection. Continue sales.	
March '22	Close sales.	Research Fabrics. Start design.
April '22	Order production materials. Create production samples.	Select fabrics. Order fabrics.
May '22	Begin production.	Create patterns. Begin samples.
June '22	Monitor production.	Develop collection.
July '22	Monitor production.	Review production strategy. Finalize collections.
August '22	Begin deliveries and collect COD.	Begin sales.
September '22	Continue deliveries. Collect payments.	Show collection. Continue sales.
October '22		Close sales.
November '22		Order production materials. Begin production.
December '22		Monitor production.
January '23		Monitor production.
February '23		Begin deliveries and collect COD.
March '23		Continue deliveries. Collect payments.

Fabric selection often starts earlier, and selling may extend longer depending on the market. Timing will vary depending on whether you create new fabrics or prints and whether they are coming from overseas or from the jobber down the street. Regardless, it's up to you to stay on schedule. The process of pattern-muslin-fitting-adjustments-sampling should take four to six weeks, assuming you make your approvals quickly. Jené from StitchLuxe says most delays during this process are caused by the designer making last-minute changes or being late getting fabric and materials to the patternmaker or sample maker.[1]

There is much debate in the fashion industry over the wholesale sales and production calendar. Designers are striving to minimize production time to deliver product to the store sooner to avoid markdowns, while also lobbying retailers to push delivery dates later to better coincide with the actual seasons and consumer shopping patterns. Currently, the primary market weeks for womenswear take place in February and September, and there are different dates for swimwear, childrenswear, and accessories. Menswear sells primarily in early July and January and ships in early January and August. Pre-collection and Resort have their own sales and delivery dates. But all of this is in flux as the industry grapples with the challenge of offering consumers fresh product while cutting back on waste and avoiding discounts.

Your production calendar will look different based on your business model and type of production. But whether you are direct selling, following a pre-order model, or dropping limited edition product each month, you still need a solid schedule based on your inventory and delivery needs.

Production Options

Production sources need to be lined up before you begin to take orders. In fact, many designers recommend that you research your production options before you even start your company. Although there are alternatives, the majority of designers choose to give their production to a factory or contractor.

Like the fabric suppliers, some factory owners feel that new designers are not worth the extra work. New designers have smaller orders and less experience and tend to make more mistakes, which take time to organize and fix. To a factory, time is money. Factories often require references or recommendations from someone in the industry. They are concerned about your credibility and whether you can pay. They will ask about your business history and, most important, the projected production run. If you are brand new and don't have any orders yet, you don't need to tell them.

Minimums

Factories require MOQ (minimum order quantities) because small production runs are time consuming and less profitable. When reviewing a factory, first find out its production minimum and try not to waste time with factories that are not an option for you. Many factories specialize in small lots or are at least open to negotiation, especially in New York and Los Angeles and increasingly in Europe, where competition with Asia forces them to be more flexible.

Designers utilize several tricks to try to get around minimums, but it's best to be straightforward and try to negotiate. If you don't meet the minimum, offer to pay more. For example, if the factory requires a 500-piece minimum at a price of $20 each, you can offer $22 each for 250 pieces. Realize if you negotiate this minimum up front and end up only needing 200 pieces, you must decide if you can take the loss on the extra 50 items and try to sell them elsewhere. Extra stock is wasteful, ties up your cash, and often results in some returns. Be very careful never to cut more than a 3 percent overage on your orders. If you can't sell enough to meet the production minimums, it's best not to produce the piece at all.

Make sure you understand the definition of minimum. Some factories may have a minimum of 200 of each style, but that may include all sizes and several color options. Try to convince the factory owner that working with you now will lead to a large production run in the future. Ask about the production capacity of the factory to imply that you are planning to have big volume soon.

Design Tricks

Cutting the same silhouettes in different colors and fabric combinations, and incorporating different trims, will save time and money on patterns and production and help meet minimums. Even though the garments look like different styles, the cutting and sewing steps are the same for the factory, and you will be charged a lower price as if it is all the same garment. Observe collections in the stores to see the smart ways that designers save money on fabric and production. At Rebecca Taylor, for instance, a tuxedo pant is offered in several different colors of wool, and the same silhouette is available in satin and with varying trims. Many brands use block patterns of the same basic silhouette and just tweak them from season to season.

Types of Factories

Every day, young designers in New York are seen schlepping from place to place just to complete one style. They carry fabric from the cutter to another place for marking, to another for sewing, and then wait in line elsewhere to have the buttons put on. Transportation from one place to another can be tedious and expensive, and the designer has to manage the flow between vendors and contractors.

Production can be simplified by choosing a factory that offers multiple services in one place. Having fewer organizations involved means less opportunity for things to go wrong and processes to run late. When one factory handles many steps of the process, it is more likely to provide accurate cost and timing estimates up front and take responsibility when things in the supply chain go wrong.

Consolidation can also result in efficiencies and savings. Factories that order fabric and trim place orders for multiple brands resulting in bulk discounts, particularly with standard fabrics such as denim and performance fabrics for swimwear or activewear. Designers don't have to run to the factory every time they are short a button because the factory sourced the button and can order more.

FPP (full package production). These factories offer "packages" that include everything from sourcing and sampling to producing, finishing, and shipping the goods. The process starts with an initial consultation in which you provide sketches or product examples, and then they make the patterns, source the materials and trims, create samples, grade, mark, cut, sew, and finish the items. During the process, they may make suggestions about the design, types of materials to use, placement of hardware, and order quantities. FPP is much more expensive than "cut and sew," and many designers feel the packages limit the choice of materials and processes too much. FPP limits your involvement in each process, leaving less room for maintaining quality standards and control over lead time.

CMT (cut, make, and trim). Also called "cut and sew" factories, these factories offer fewer services. They cut the fabric, sew (make) each item, and trim by pressing, tagging, hanging, and packing for shipment. The other steps of the process, such as marking and grading, need to be outsourced. A CMT factory will expect you to provide the patterns, tech packs, fabrics and trims, and a "sew by" sample before they begin. Many of the best factories only offer CMT because they specialize in these processes. With CMT, you have more control over fabric selection, special techniques, and lead times. You can work closely with your own patternmaker to develop and perfect the pieces before you even approach the factory. You can also manage your costs more carefully knowing the factory isn't marking up each button and label they procure. But as mentioned earlier, managing each process, and the sourcing and delivery of each item, takes a significant amount of time.

On-demand. The growth of on-demand manufacturing is a very exciting development for fashion production. Factories are incorporating technology and adapting their flow to turn around production in as little as 72 hours. This option eliminates inventory, minimums, and waste, allowing designers to order only exactly what has been sold and still deliver in just a few days. The product can be sold closer to the season and it enables customization at an affordable price. However, the convenience of on-demand production comes at a premium price, and it works best with simple designs and silhouettes. A designer must also be very organized to produce on demand. Development must be complete and the materials and trims ready and waiting at the factory before they can accept any orders. On Point Manufacturing in Florence, Alabama, is one manufacturer providing on-demand to independent designers.

Specialized services. In some cases, the best sewers for a fabrication might be in a sewing room that doesn't offer any other services, or the designs may require a cutter or sewer with special equipment. Sometimes it's simply less expensive to cut certain quantities in a cutting room or to hire an independent grading service.

ADIFF—Survivor Made

While still a student at the Parsons New School for Design, designer Angela Luna was impacted by the images and stories of the Syrian Refugee Crisis and used her senior thesis to develop utilitarian items that would support displaced people. Her signature item was an award-winning waterproof jacket, which could also configure into a tent. Since then she launched her brand ADIFF with outerwear and accessories made from upcycled life vests and UNHCR tents, among other materials. ADIFF aims to use no virgin materials and now makes everything in their manufacturing facility that ethically employs resettled refugees in Athens, Greece. Angela notes that some of the refugees are "the most amazing tailors I've ever encountered who used to have their own shops in Afghanistan." With her model of rapid development production, the design, pattern, and sample are made in New York and they can start selling within two weeks of the first design. Her mission of empowering people through job creation and making the right choices in sourcing and production attracts collaborations with other brands that want to upcycle their excess inventory and support her manufacturing. She says, "Our goals are to build a scalable model for upcycling and empowerment-based manufacturing that we can prove works within our field of design, as well as with other brands."[2]

Where to Produce?
Domestic Production

When starting out, it's highly advisable to produce domestically or even locally, if possible. As designer Annie Lewis of Lewis Cho says, "I love the hands-on approach of producing locally. There is more of a dialogue, and it can be a much more collaborative process. It is easier to control the overall quality, and minimums are usually flexible. I also think it is so important to support our local manufacturers to keep the industry alive in the U.S."[3] There are multiple advantages of producing in your own country:

- Local allows you to oversee each process, to learn firsthand, and to make quick approvals to keep production on schedule.

- In-person oversight helps uphold quality standards.

- Delivery to market is faster when you avoid overseas shipping and customs delays.

- Building relationships and negotiating terms is easier face-to-face.

- Producing nearby supports your local economy.

- Designs are safer from piracy, which is a greater danger overseas.

- Using less fuel for transport minimizes the carbon footprint.

- Domestic factories usually have lower minimums.

Anna McCraney of Blank Canvas Development says, "If you produce overseas, your price per unit may be cheaper, but the time you spend corresponding, the trips you take to the factory, and the frustration of the experience might not be worth it. Domestic production can be as quick as 4 to 14 weeks, with no minimums, while overseas manufacturers will barely get out of bed for less than 1,000 pieces per style. Even then, don't expect to have your product in less than three months. Not to mention, American consumers love knowing that they are supporting American-made products. This adds to the value of your product, and your ease of production will make you appreciate it as well."[4]

The downsides are that domestic labor costs are high and you may not find a factory with the expertise you need. As designer Annie Lewis says, "In the U.S., we have lost some of our manufacturing capabilities, so we need to rely on other markets around the world. Options can be limited at times, especially when searching for lower minimum suppliers, so it is helpful to explore other countries." In addition, many domestic factories that work with smaller companies are CMT and require the designer to source and deliver all materials.

In the United States, many small design companies produce in New York, but there are production opportunities everywhere. According to Makers Row, California is actually the largest producer of apparel in the United States, and driving your production around Los Angeles is easier than dragging it from block to block in New York. The California Fashion Association and the LA Fashion District can assist in finding factories and fabric sources. The Evans Group (TEG) is one of several vertical companies that will work with smaller brands and has on-site patternmakers and sample makers in both LA and San Francisco.

There are designers in Dallas, Denver, St. Louis, Chicago, Nashville, and Portland who manufacture locally and cite the advantages of being able to create specialized pieces, quick reorders, and small runs. Numerous cities also support their local fashion industry with fashion weeks and incubators to support emerging designers.

Offshore Production

Designers generally choose to produce overseas for either cost or quality reasons. Italian factories are credited with producing the highest quality of designer goods, from men's suits to shoes. They have highly trained craftspeople and artisans who have learned from generations of experts. Many leather goods brands want to launch with the cachet and quality implied by

"Made in Italy." Manufacturing overseas can give you access to specialized machinery or skills that are not available at home. Designers may go to Peru for knits, India for beading, or Mexico for embroidery.

After producing locally for a few years, many designers move some of their production overseas to lower their cost or increase their margin. China's dominance in apparel production is a combination of low labor costs and high productivity from automation and digitization. In recent years, Vietnam, India, Turkey, and other countries have significantly increased their share of global production. The myths that overseas factories are not interested in small designers and that their quality isn't as good are no longer true. There is a wide selection of factories in terms of size, quality, and expertise. There are artisanal factory owners everywhere who care about quality and the vision for the product. Most of these factories are FPP and will cover all aspects of your sourcing and production with the convenience of just one contact person for it all.

There are some challenges to consider before producing abroad.

Communication

Language. Even if your contacts speak English, small misunderstandings can cause big production problems. Communicate in clear, simple language, and take extra care to confirm that you understand each other. You may need to hire your own production manager or an agent who is fluent in the local language or at least find an intern with the necessary language skills.

Point of view. It's important to provide the overseas factory with very precise specifications and examples so they fully understand how you expect the product to look and fit. Don't take anything for granted. You can't assume the person looking at your job will notice the tailoring details or the importance of the grain lines.

Time zone. When you sit down at your desk in Minneapolis at 9 A.M. ready to work, it's already 8:30 P.M. at the factory in Mumbai. You can lose many days in your production schedule if you don't plan accordingly.

Cost

Shipping and duty. Even with inexpensive labor, producing overseas can cost as much as producing domestically because of international shipping expense and taxes. Sending materials to the factory, as well as samples back and forth to monitor quality, is costly. Tariffs must be paid when the product enters the country and the amount depends on the product category and the country where it was made. Trade wars between countries can cause spikes in tariffs large enough to force designers to find alternative sourcing and production.

Exchange rates. Designers who produce large quantities overseas follow the exchange rates daily because of how greatly they affect their costs. Always confirm in which currency you are dealing. A high valuation of the euro or the yuan versus the U.S. dollar can be challenging for American designers who produce in Italy or China.

Terms. Minimums (MOQ) are high at overseas factories. Many of them require a letter of credit from a bank, and most expect a 50 percent down payment with the remaining 50 percent due on delivery.

Timing

Holiday schedules. Different countries have different national holidays. European factories are generally closed for three weeks in August when designers may be finishing Fall production and Spring samples. China, Vietnam, and India have different festivals throughout the year during which businesses close for at least one week. Designers must allow for this time in their production schedules.

Weather and infrastructure. Many countries where apparel is produced have weather patterns such as monsoon season, during which flooding closes factories, power outages occur, and production and shipping can be delayed.

Lead times. Overseas production can take twice the time of domestic production. Designers should pad their schedules and ship materials and patterns early to try to prevent late deliveries. Customs paperwork can cause delays, and duty needs to be paid promptly. Many designers warn that samples from Europe can arrive too late to make critical trade show dates, and a menswear designer who was participating in his first New York runway show received only part of his collection when several boxes were delayed at customs. He sent models onto the runway wearing his well-styled shirts and jackets with only underwear.

Culture. The working practices and customs in each country are different, and people in some countries don't work the long hours or at the same fast pace as workers in the United States or Asia. In some cultures, it is considered rude to say "no," so when they say "yes," it really means "I wish I could." Designers often cite the challenge of getting work done quickly in Italy, where it always seems to be time to break for lunch.

Quality Control

It is more difficult to control the quality of production when you are thousands of miles away. Large brands have full-time employees who travel to or live in the production country and oversee the factory every day. New designers generally can't afford to do this and, therefore, must work with an agent or have the factory send samples at several stages of the production process for approval. This takes time and if there are problems with the final product when it arrives, you may need a local factory to fix it quickly.

Environmental and Human Rights Issues

Unrealistic expectations for low prices have led some factories to exploit and enslave their workers; use high levels of toxins, such as formaldehyde; or participate in unsafe practices, such as dumping dyes and finishing chemicals into rivers. While these things also happen domestically, it can be harder to monitor from thousands of miles away. See Chapter 5: Sustainability for important questions to ask regarding environmental and ethical practices.

Ultimately, you need to produce in the place that makes sense for your product, otherwise you may not get the right price or quality. If you design organic cotton block-printed dresses, you should make them in India where they have the expertise. Swimwear, activewear, denim, and T-shirts are more commonly produced in LA versus NY.

Fashion Revolution's transparency campaign
encourages you to ask "Who Made My Clothes?"
Courtesy of Fashion Revolution

How to Find and Choose a Factory

Finding and reviewing factories is time consuming, but critically important to your business. The best source is word of mouth. Ask for recommendations from designers, patternmakers, fabric sources, and others in the supply chain. The graders and markers know where their clients are sending their production. If you are making leggings, ask the supplier of the stretch fabric which factory they recommend to sew them.

Events such as Sourcing At Magic and FIT's CitySource let you meet factory representatives in person. Makers Row, the CFDA Production Directory, and WeConnectFashion are just a few excellent resources online. Adila Cokar of Source My Garment says, "Many sustainably focused brands are transparent about their factories and suppliers, and this can help you find proven sources." She suggests joining sourcing groups on LinkedIn and reaching out for contacts. She also recommends, "If you know where you want to produce, you can reach out to apparel associations in that country or to export development to help make introductions."[5] The Chambers of Commerce of China, Hong Kong, and India can help you find factories in those countries, and the Italian Trade Commission has been helpful for many shoe and accessory designers. These sources provide long lists of potential options, so you will still need to research, call, and vet several to find one that is right for you.

Take the time to meet with several factories and choose one that gives you confidence. A factory owner compared it to choosing a babysitter and said, "You don't just hand your baby over to anyone." Adila Cokar recommends, "'Date the factory.' Go out for dinner and get to know them before you commit. Listen to how they talk about the product and the work. See how communicative they are and if they are interested in your story."[6] This is a critical partnership. You will work closely with these people and need to trust them.

In reality, some factory owners care about the quality of their work and the success of the line, while others only care about getting the job done and getting paid. When you meet the owner or manager of each factory, try to get a sense of the person, their priorities, and whether they take pride in their work. Communicate your brand values up front to make sure you are aligned. There are several types of questions to ask, and if there are things you don't understand, ask for clarification. Don't be intimidated.

Expertise

What's their specialty? Each factory has areas of expertise with the corresponding equipment and knowledgeable workers. Factories usually specialize in a category such as knits, wovens, or leather goods. Factories that work with cotton or wool may not be competent with delicate silks. If a collection includes leather jackets, knit dresses, and woven pants, you may need to work with three different contractors.

Production services. Find out which production services the factory provides and whether they subcontract work out to others or do it all in-house. Many factories offer multiple services to attract more business and may use subcontractors for various processes. But subcontracted work is difficult to oversee and can add time to the production schedule.

Quality. Ask to see some of the factory's finished work. Do they make product similar to yours? Do they have product that meets your quality standard?

Factory size. How big is the factory and how many employees do they have? If there are more than 50 to 100 employees, you may get lost in the shuffle.

Delivery

Timing. Ask if the factory regularly meets deadlines and establish the lead time for each job. Show your contact a sample or ask her to have one made to help estimate timing as accurately as possible.

Reorders. Inquire about the turnaround time for reorders. Reorders should be finished faster than the initial run.

What does "delivery" mean? Confirm what the factory means by delivery. To some, it may mean the product is just leaving the plant or is on a boat, but you need to know when it will be in your possession.

Late delivery. What recourse will you have if the factory is late in delivering the goods?

Customer Service

Who is your main contact? Find out whom you will deal with every day. Try to meet them in person or at least on FaceTime or WhatsApp.

Responsiveness. When you email or call, how quickly do they respond?

Quality control. How does the factory ensure quality at each stage of production?

Cost control. Ask the factory owner for insight on how to lower your costs and improve the production process.

Insurance. What happens if your goods are damaged at the factory or during transport? What kind of insurance does the factory have?

Credibility

Experience and reputation. How long has the factory been in business? Which other brands are clients, and for how long? Ask for references and CALL them. They can provide valuable insight and advice.

Work conditions. Ask for a tour and as Adila Cokar advises, "Look for cleanliness, check out the bathroom, observe how people are talking and interacting with each other. How is the energy? How does it make you feel? Say 'hello' to several people and talk to managers, the production team, and the quality control staff."[7]

Standards and practices. Ask about certifications or standards that ensure ethical and fair trade practices. If you doubt if the factory is legal, ask to see their business license.

Confidentiality. Get a sense of how trustworthy the factory is regarding copyrights and private information. Probe the factory owner about other clients to see if the owner tells you things he shouldn't. If proprietary details about another customer are shared, the owner would likely share the same information about you.

Website. Don't judge a factory by their online presence. Maintaining a website is not a factory's business priority so they are often poorly designed or out of date.

Price and Payment Terms

Cost should not be your determining factor in choosing a factory. As a small company, you cannot compete on price and must focus on quality, value, and getting the job done on time. Know what you can spend before you approach the factories. Your target sales price and costing determines the budget you have. If the factory cannot keep costs to where you need them to hit the target price, they may be able to suggest changes to materials, finishing, or design to help you reach that number.

The factory will give you an initial cost estimate based on the sample and the specs or tech pack you provide. The more information you give, the more accurate the quote will be. Fabric swatches, technical drawings with details of stitching and placement of trims and embellishments, packaging and labeling instructions, estimated order quantities of all styles (with size and color breakdowns), and delivery dates help them better understand the job. You can also ask the factory to make a sample. This will help you judge the quality of the work and give you a sense of what it is like to work with them. Some factories will create a sample for free to try and secure your business, but others will charge you three times the production price to cover the extra work of sample making.

The greater the quantity of items produced, the less each item will cost. Remember that everything is negotiable, but if the price seems too good to be true, revisit any concerns about quality, delivery, or unethical practices.

Generally, a factory will require a deposit of at least 30 to 50 percent with the balance due on delivery (COD). Some factories require a line of credit from a bank while others may ask for progress payments as the job passes through different stages of production. Try to negotiate to get the best terms. Jené from StitchLuxe recommends, "Pay your deposits and balances on time or even ahead of time and your work will often get moved to the front of the line and completed more quickly. Future jobs will also get priority when the factory and suppliers know that you pay promptly."[8]

Pricing terms specify which party covers which parts of shipping. FOB includes the transportation to the shipping port but not the shipping, duty, or other costs from that point on. CIF includes shipping but not duty. LDP is landed cost in which the shipping and duty is included in the quoted price. Taxes and duty depend on the product category and the country where it was manufactured. Realize it is difficult to get an accurate quote for shipping and insurance until the product is packaged and you know the final weight, size, and number of boxes.

The Agreement

The purchase order agreement (PO) should include pricing; the number and description of items being produced; delivery dates for samples and production; the repercussions of late delivery; detailed finishing, packing, and labeling instructions according to your or the store's requirements; the shipping method (local messenger, trucking, sea, or air); payment dates; and the method of payment.

Before you begin, confirm the number of each SKU to be produced; which stages of production are being handled by which contractors; and that all samples, materials, and patterns will be returned to you. Be very clear about the delivery dates and make sure they are realistic. Delays happen and larger jobs take priority despite the agreement. If you pressure a factory to rush, you may get less quality and accuracy and potentially exploit workers. It's smart to pad your deadlines to be safe.

Factory Alternatives
In-house

Some designers produce all, or at least part, of their line in-house with a small team that generally includes a patternmaker and a few sewers. Obviously, this method can be expensive and requires a significant outlay of funds for cutting, sewing, and pressing equipment, as well as the permits, insurance, and licenses legally required to run a production facility. A designer I know with a very small in-house sewing room spends $20,000 a month to keep it running. She says it's worth the expense because of the control it gives her. With in-house production, the designer can oversee the entire process every day and manage the timing and quality of each garment as it's produced. There is no competition from other designers, and it's easy to react quickly for reorders, work around missing materials, respond to new opportunities, and create customized or one-of-a-kind product.

When designer Gustavo Cadile couldn't meet the minimums at the beading factories for his intricate eveningwear gowns, he pulled together an in-house team of talented and experienced couture sewers who handle all his beading, sample production, and special orders.

Producing in-house results in a tight team of people who learn to work together efficiently, and the designer has the opportunity to train and teach the team to become experts in signature fits and finishes. Some designers take their team on research trips to high-end stores, such as Saks Fifth Avenue, to analyze the technique and finishing of garments and set expectations. An in-house sewing room can help protect proprietary information about design and fit. A designer told me she sends out her jackets, blouses, and dresses to a factory but will never contract out her pants. She has worked tirelessly to develop a signature fit, and with many other jobs moving through the factories, she doesn't want to risk someone stealing her pattern.

Keep in mind that even with your own in-house team, you won't have all the special skills required for each collection and will still have to contract out specialty work, such as beading, pleating, or knitwear.

In-house production requires you or a production manager to be there every day with the sewers, giving direction and reviewing the work. Some designers who have an intense focus on quality are happy to spend all day measuring seams and checking finishes to ensure that each item is consistent. But not every designer wants the time consuming responsibility of managing manufacturing processes and people.

A full-time production staff brings additional pressure. The sewers are employees and bring a serious financial obligation in terms of their salaries and benefits. You need to have the work to keep them busy, and you know that if the business fails, you won't be the only one left without a job.

Freelance Sewers

If your orders are small or require special skills, individual sewers (or craftspeople) can be hired on a freelance basis. Freelance sewers are expensive and may take longer to produce, but they can be the best option when filling a one-time order for a store or creating specialty items that require detail or handwork. Several labels that are upcycling garments into new one-of-a-kind items work with tailors who have the skills to adjust the individual fit according to the fabric and shape of the previous item. But this skill is reflected in the high-end price of the new design.

If you anticipate a large reorder of an item, you may need to involve a factory to keep the production quality consistent on all runs and to take advantage of quantity discounts and cost-effective measures. Patch NYC started its business with a collection of crochet hats made by the mother of one of the designers and then embellished by designers John Ross and Don Carney. John says, "After one especially crazy crochet season, we realized Mom just couldn't keep up. We brought in two of Don's aunts and one of Mom's friends to help that season. Suddenly, there were all these variations in the hats since each person crochets slightly differently. We stopped wholesaling the hats and only added knits back into our collection seasons later when we found a factory that would produce quality hats and scarves."[9]

Natalie Chanin, the designer of Alabama Chanin, produced her signature hand-appliquéd organic cotton garments by engaging quilting circles in her hometown of Florence, Alabama. She supported the hometown economy by subcontracting to more than 100 women to do the stitching. Since then her hand-manufacturing operation has grown to include a machine-manufacturing business, an educational arm called The School of Making, a not-for-profit called Project Threadways, and a partnership with the nonprofit artisan-based organization Nest.[10]

Working with Artisans

Collaborating with artisans results in a unique product with a compelling story, and it can provide income and preserve ancient craft. Increasingly, appreciation for artisanal handwork and traditional techniques is a driving force in fashion purchasing. As *International Vogue* editor Suzy Menkes says, "I have long thought that today's greatest fashion luxury is found in things touched by human hands."[11] Unlike typical production, there are many special considerations when working with artisans.

Honor the craft and tradition. The beauty of artisanal product is its unique, small-batch, hand-touched attributes. It's important to learn about the craft technique, the individual artisan skills, as well as the historical, cultural, and social context of the work. Collaboration with artisans requires you to listen to their expertise and suggestions for design elements. As Aurora James of Brother Vellies says, she would never dictate to the Maasai what beading patterns to use—she isn't Maasai.[12]

Establish trust. It is important to create honest communication and understanding between yourself and the artisan community. Visit the workshop and the community. Be clear about what you want to create, why, and how you will present the work to your customers. Set the tone for transparency so the artisans feel open to communicate any delays or issues that arise.

Define quality. There is more variance in product that is individually made versus on an assembly line in a factory. Look at a range of samples to set your expectations for how much items vary in size, color, shape, and stitching, and be ready to communicate that to your customer.

Communication. Apps such as FaceTime or WhatsApp enable designers to communicate directly with artisans to answer questions, approve product, and even handle payments. However, using a local agent as a liaison can help navigate communication barriers. Explain your expectations clearly using tech packs, photos, samples, and common color standards such as Pantone chips or even Sherwin Williams paint. Request a sample to ensure an understanding of your design concept. Check in regularly during production and ask for photos, or hop on FaceTime to see the progress.

Sourcing. A designer needs to find trusted artisan partners who offer ethically produced product that aligns with their brand. The best approach is to ask people who are already working with artisan groups and can tell you about their experience. Trade shows NY Now, Maison & Objet in Paris, and Ambiente in Germany have artisan resource sections. For a fee, agents and consultants such as ByHand Consulting can source by product type and help manage production.

Capacity. While artisan workshops offer small minimums, there are limits to the amount they can produce. Ask how much product is realistic to create in a specified time frame. Ask about availability for local materials. If you are using rattan for bags or hats, in many places it is only harvested four months of the year.

Cost. Because of the small-batch, handmade attributes of the product and the expense of remote and/or international shipping, costs are higher than at a factory. Design, story, and mission come first when marketing artisan-made product; it is not about competing on price.

Timing. While being "on time, all the time" is a designer's goal, when working with a small handmade workshop, it rarely happens. Technology, infrastructure issues, and weather cause delays. Cultural norms and lifestyle differ from our fast-paced, work-focused society. Try to plan ahead and pad the schedule. Communicate delays to your customers with a reminder of why this product is so special.

Payment. WireTransfer is the most common method of payment. It requires trust on both sides because there is no one guaranteeing the transaction. Credit cards, Venmo, and PayPal are also common. Be sure to negotiate all financials before you place the final order. Check they have insurance and storage and packaging that considers conditions such as dirt floors or exposure to rain.

Audits and certifications. Many products are "artisan-made," but the artisans are exploited and paid unfair wages. It's incredibly important to follow fair trade standards to ensure the artisans you work with receive a living wage and that their culture is respected and preserved. NEST's Ethical Handcraft Program conducts audits to ensure home workers and artisans in small workshops have fair compensation, benefits, and safe working conditions. Certifications are also given by the Artisan Alliance, the World Fair Trade Organization (WFTO), and the Fair Trade Federation (FTF), which offers a verified membership. There are many small ethical workshops and artisan-based groups that don't have the funds to apply for certifications. Try to get recommendations, ask how artisans are paid, and share in the profits. Travel to meet with your suppliers face-to-face to support the relationship and verify the conditions.

Tell the story. Buyers, salespeople, and your customers need to hear the story of your artisan-made product to fully appreciate it. Explain that each item is handcrafted and available in limited quantities (you should even consider numbering very limited items). Educate customers on why a luxury product, made by hand, may not be perfectly standard or straight or takes longer to make. Explain how each purchase pays fair wages and supports a community and a heritage. Find ways for the artisans to tell their own story. Share experiences from your travels and learnings from the artisan communities.

Mireia Lopez and Vishrami Devi, weaver at Barefoot College, Tilonia, Jaipur, India
Mireia Lopez / Blinded By Color Project / www.milotricot.com

111

Ethical Storytelling
by Manpreet Kaur Kalra, Founder, Art of Citizenry

When crafting and sharing the story of your brand, it is important to be thoughtful of how you frame your narrative. When highlighting artisans, consider the words you use and what you share. Stay away from using language that is disempowering and sharing intimate details about the artisans' lives. Instead, focus on highlighting their skills and talents. Showcase the craft, handmade process, and talents of the artisans you work with. For all the greatness that has come out of the "Who made my clothes?" campaign, so has the need to share uncomfortably intimate details about the lives of the people making each piece. Transparency should not come at the cost of privacy.

When it comes to storytelling, **consent is important and non-negotiable.** If you are sharing photos of artisans or any information about their lives, ask for permission in a non-coercive way. Clearly inform the artisan of what you plan to share, where you plan to share it, and the degree to which people will be able to access the information. Make sure to do this *before* printing their name and picture on hundreds to thousands of swing tags. Also, it is important that artisans you work with know their work contracts are not in jeopardy if they prefer not to have their name and photo used for marketing purposes.

Production Management

Once you have taken the collection through the sales or pre-order process, tested product, made estimates, and confirmed wholesale orders, you will know which items to produce, in what quantities, and the required delivery dates. Now it's time to start production.

When asked "If you could hire just one employee, who would it be?" many designers answer "a production manager." The production process is extremely critical and time consuming. It requires daily management of each stage of the process, dealing with unexpected problems, communicating clearly, and avoiding delays. Whether you are fortunate enough to have a production manager or, like most start-up designers, you are attentively filling the role yourself, careful production management is critical to ensure quality construction, consistent fit, on-time delivery, and repeat customers.

Quality Control

The buck stops with you. You cannot accept bad work or compromise on quality. Quality control is critical at all stages of production right through to labeling and shipping. The buyers and the end customers have rules and expectations and if you don't meet their standards, they will return the product and will not give you another chance. The customer doesn't care if the factory messed up. It's your responsibility. Designer Nicole Miller tells of her experience when all the beads popped off an entire shipment of sweaters for Saks Fifth Avenue. She had to eat the loss for the shipment because the store could not accept it and the factory was already paid with a letter of credit and could not be held liable.[13]

Stay on Schedule

Once you hire your factory, request a copy of the production calendar for your job. Make sure it works with your delivery dates and includes time for approvals and transit. Use this calendar to follow along and stay on schedule. On-time delivery is key, and if you are late, orders can be canceled and returned to you and stores and customers may not order from you again. If you know that a shipment will be late, call the retailer immediately to ask for an extension and permission to ship. Find out if the store will accept a partial order on time and the rest later. Be honest with your online customers, inform them of the delay, and let them know when they can expect to receive their items.

Estimating and Ordering Materials

Wholesale orders make production easier because you know exactly how many of each style, size, and color to make and when they are needed. If you wholesale, you should "cut to order," only producing exactly what is necessary to ship. The mills do not accept returns, and if fabric is ordered in advance for a style that doesn't sell, the designer will be left with the excess. However, if some of your fabric is from overseas and has a long lead time, you may need to order the production yardage long before sales are finalized to stay on schedule. In this case, wait as long as you can and work closely with the salespeople to get accurate quantity projections. Know how much yardage it takes to produce each piece. A very small amount of excess can cover damaged or unusable goods, but too much will go unused and eat up your profit margin.

When you sell direct to consumer, deciding out how much product to make is a process of trial and error. Overly optimistic sales projections can result in money tied up in excess materials and product. A conservative estimate can result in missed sales and revenue. Some designers offer pre-order and made-to-order on some items to cut back the risk, but unless the product is really special, or limited edition, it is rare that customers are willing to wait. When starting out, your inventory may simply be determined by the factory minimums. As Adam Humphreys from La Bucq says, "At first it was how much can we possibly bear to make it work for our factory. Now we are growing, it's about how much we can sell. There's no formula."[14]

Don't forget hangtags, packaging materials, and anything else required by the factory for the packing or shipping services they provide. Confirm the delivery lead time, cost, and shipping information for each item.

Track the Production Materials

Create a system or chart to keep track of every material needed for production and where it is in the ordering process. The chart should include every item required for every style from fabric or leathers, lining, thread, and interfacing to buttons and zippers. Do everything you can to ensure all materials arrive at the factory on time and in the right quantities. Most factories won't start a job until all the components are there. They don't want to risk setting all their machines with your green thread just to find out that the zippers aren't arriving for three more days. If any materials will be late, tell the factory manager immediately so he can make arrangements to fit your job in later.

Production Pattern and Samples

Once you are ready for production, the factory will create the production sample or prototype for each style, in the actual fabric, to the exact specifications you provide. Check each one carefully. Confirm the measurements, stitching details, and fit. Wash it according to the care label and check for shrinkage. Take photos of any issues so you can easily point them out. The production samples that you approve set the standard for the rest of the production.

Shipping samples back and forth takes time. If possible, go to the factory to inspect the samples and discuss changes or quality concerns. Factory managers are busy, but you want to utilize their time and expertise. Ask them for their concerns about the samples and the overall job. They could suggest a slight change in seam allowance that could save significant cost. Each change adds to the time and cost of production so try and approve the samples quickly and within a couple of rounds. If you aren't happy after several rounds, maybe it's the wrong factory or the item just shouldn't be produced.

The Tech Pack

A tech pack contains all the information the factory needs to make your product exactly to your specifications. It generally includes:

- A list of materials

- Product descriptions

- Spec sheets with measurements and sewing instructions

- Technical drawings with details for seams, embellishments, and placement of hardware or closures such as zippers and buttons

- Fabric or materials swatches and color references

- A line sheet with every item in the collection, with style numbers

- Artwork and photo references

- Guidelines for size grading and marking for grainlines and cutting

- Labeling instructions including placement

- Required product testing

- Final packing and branding details

The more details you include, the less likely there will be errors. This level of information usually isn't required for local development and production when a sample and spec sheet will suffice. But if you are producing overseas or making swimwear, eveningwear, or other product with complicated construction, the tech pack is essential to getting the product you envision.

Cut Tickets

Cut tickets are actual orders for production that specify how many units of each piece need to be cut. These are used to check the order and as a basis for any disputes, so keep proof of the communication. The cut ticket should include the style number and the quantity to be cut in each size, color, and fabric. It should include the delivery date, a technical drawing, a fabric swatch, a list of all materials and trims per style, and sewing, finishing, and labeling instructions. Be specific regarding measurements and where to sew, details on how to lay the fabric, and whether it should be cut in a specific direction.

Grading for Size

For garments to sell, the sizing must be correct and consistent from season to season. While there are no standard measurements for size and it differs from brand to brand, it does need to relate to general consumer expectations. Grading is the process of adjusting the production pattern up and down to create a size range for a garment. Grading is often offered by the factory or contractor, and there are grading services that specialize in this work. Grading is charged per pattern piece and affected by the complexity of the pattern. Although it is usually too costly for new designers, some recommend testing the grading and fit by ordering a full size run of samples before continuing production to avoid problems on delivery.

Marking

The marker determines the best layout for cutting pattern pieces from the fabric or material. A good marker will save time, eliminate fabric waste, and help you determine exactly how much fabric you need. Depending on the number of garments produced, a quarter inch saved by a good marker can eventually save yards of production material. The marker ensures that the pattern pieces are properly laid out with the grain of the fabric and accommodate any patterns, such as lining up stripes. A new marker is created for each size in the range.

Cut and Sew

Once the marker is set and the fabric has been carefully checked, it can be cut. Usually the fabric is spread on tables and cut in large stacks. Pieces from the same dye lots must be cut together, or else the pieces within one garment may not match. Once cut, the pieces are bundled together with the thread, trims, and other items ready to be sewn.

Don't Forget Labels

Brand labels, size labels, fiber content, and care labels all have to be sewn into your product. Labels must state the country where the item was made. Additional information and even placement of the label differs by country where the item will be sold. For example, Canada requires bilingual content and "made in" labels. In the United States, information about labeling is regulated by the Federal Trade Commission. Make sure your factory has the required information and it is included in the tech pack and on the production sample.

Overseeing the Factory

It takes time and experience to learn all that you need to know to manage production. Factory owners and industry experts often advise designers to spend a few months in an internship or job at a factory. While students prefer to intern in the design room or even the production area of a big company, a few months in a factory will provide a wealth of useful experience and knowledge. Ask people at the factory to take you around and explain processes to you. It is so helpful during production if you understand how things are made. Adila Cokar of Source My Garment suggests, "When getting started, I recommend managing production yourself to better understand the factory's manufacturing process and to build a solid relationship."[15]

Communicate clearly. When you work with a factory, be specific and communicate clearly and often. Know what you need before you call or show up. Don't be afraid to ask questions, but don't be difficult or annoying. You need the factory's patience in case materials are late or cut tickets change during production.

Most factories assign a production manager or merchandiser to each job. Have their mobile phone or WhatsApp number, and use the production calendar to follow along with the processes and check in often to see that things are on schedule.

Do as much as you can to communicate your quality expectations. Provide reference samples, and point out stitching details. It may be necessary to train the sewers on some aspects of the garment. Show them illustrations of the garment being styled and worn to provide greater understanding.

Relationships are everything. Designers often cite factory owners who have become important mentors. Some receive financial investment from their factory, and occasionally, a factory will produce a designer's sample collection at cost. Relationships grow and become easier over time as you get to know how each other works, and eventually they will offer better terms, discounts, and flexibility on minimums. The more work you give them, the happier and more supportive they will be in terms of price and service.

Say thank you and treat them as a partner who genuinely wants your business to grow. Share your "wins," such as new accounts, press coverage, or customer feedback. Some designers send a monthly email to all of their supply chain partners to keep them up to date on their brand and recognize the suppliers' contributions. If you have a dispute or misunderstanding, take a breath and react calmly.

Be there. If at all possible, you need to be there. Call and visit the factory often during all steps of the production process. Big companies pay big bucks to have their production finished quickly, and the young designers get pushed aside. If you show up regularly at the factory, it can ensure that your job isn't continually bumped.

A designer should catch mistakes as they are happening, before the product is complete. Workers are often paid by the piece. Their incentive is not to be careful but to be fast. As they speed up, they may take shortcuts, and the quality could suffer. If you show up regularly or check in daily via video calls, they will take more care with your product. At a very minimum, check on the work during the beginning, middle, and end of the production run.

Respond immediately. The factory should call you when things go wrong or if something doesn't look right. If your factory calls you for each concern, consider yourself lucky, because others will only call once for every ten mistakes. Respond immediately, and if the factory needs you to come in, get there as soon as possible. Sometimes NY designers will go to the factory four times a day to deal with problems. Factory owners say that 95 percent of small designers don't call back right away, and because time is money to the factory, they won't sit around waiting. The factory will move on to something else and won't bother to call next time.

Designer Mandy Kordal says even though her production is far away, everyone is very communicative. She was making handwoven indigo-dyed dresses in Peru, but the dye was washing out and needed to be overdyed, which caused a shipping delay. She says, "They let us know there was a delay and then we let our buyers know. We understand that things change—everyone is human and our buyers understand that too."[16]

Check quality carefully. Once production begins, ask for a "top of production" sample to be pulled from the production run for quick approval. Compare everything against the standard set by your preproduction sample. Measure the seams, test that the buttons and labels are secure, and check that the stitching is straight. Look for color consistency and for stains from the machine oil or glue. Inspect the pressing and packaging. Inspect a number of items again before you pay at the end of production, and refuse to pay if they're not up to standard. If the factory can't get the quality right, change factories.

Overseas. If you choose to produce overseas, ideally you will have a production manager or agent whom you trust to babysit production for you. As consultant Adila Cokar says, "If you work with a buying agent to source your production, they will also manage quality control and make sure the factory follows the production calendar to stay on schedule. However, these arrangements are expensive and can leave you somewhat removed from the process. An alternative is to work with a quality control company such as Intertek and pay a day rate for an agent to go into the factory and inspect the job for you. Just be sure to communicate your standards and expectations clearly to the agent."[17]

Even if you have an agent or manager there, you may need to go as well. Designers have moved from Los Angeles to New York specifically to lessen the flight time to Europe where they do their production. Without proper oversight, you can't ensure quality. In fact, you may not even know if the factory is outsourcing the production to somewhere else. One designer sent a production manager to check on their factory in China just to discover the factory was using their pattern to make cheaper garments in different materials to sell as their own. Producing in Italy has its own challenges. Flying in for 24 hours to check on everything is not enough. Both clothing and accessories designers cite their biggest frustration producing in Italy as being constantly pushed back by bigger brands, resulting in late deliveries.

Shoe production is complex and challenging, which is why many of the big brands license their shoe lines rather than produce them themselves. Shoe designers are experts on Italy because they spend significant time there. Most visit several times a year, even if they have a local production agent. Also, attending the Linea Pelle leather show is key for meeting with tanners, heel makers, and fit specialists. Shoes have many components and when coordinating with tanneries, sole makers, last makers, heel suppliers, component suppliers, and dye houses, just one delay can cause the whole chain to go off schedule. Even if production takes place in Brazil or Portugal, designers still often have to source their leather and hardware from Italy or Spain.

When designer Alicia Bell first manufactured some pieces overseas, she received her shipment, and along with the beautiful beaded pieces, there were endless problems—stains and dirt on the garments, pen marks where the buttons were sewn on . . . even a size 6 shirt with a size 12 sleeve on it! She had to spend many days fixing the garments herself at her U.S. factory. Fortunately, she had an iron-clad contract and didn't have to pay for the faulty production. Since then she has worked out the kinks in production and says, "Your relationship with your factory is KEY to this business. It is one of the most important components in succeeding in the fashion world."[18]

If you don't have someone to monitor production at the factory, have them send samples from multiple stages of the production run for your approval. Shipping will become a significant expense because of the constant back and forth, but it's critical to guarantee good quality. Many Asian factories have very efficient and quick sample approval systems in place, and some visit New York each season to meet with their U.S. clients, review fabric and materials options, and even test first samples.

Packing and Shipping

At most small companies, the designers and their staff personally pack and ship the goods. On the bright side, it's an ideal time to be in touch with each product and check that quality standards have been met. The designer can control the packing process, include personalized notes, and make sure that directions from the stores are carefully followed.

Retailers, and in particular department stores, have specific packing and shipping instructions that must be followed or the store will refuse the goods or issue charge-back fees. Read the routing guide from the store thoroughly and follow the directions. Packing details cover whether the garments should be on hangers or packed flat in bags, wrapped in plastic, or tagged in a specific place with specific information. Shipping instructions indicate the shipping method that should be used, the documentation and packing slips required, and the format for labeling the boxes. Don't forget to order packing materials in advance. While some of these requirements seem overly demanding, realize that the stores receive thousands of items each day. To get your goods onto the selling floor quickly, the box labels, packing slips, packing bags, and hangtags must provide all the information to help the stores quickly process the boxes and items. They should be able to tell the style name and number, the size, the color, and even the neckline or sleeve length without unpacking or unfolding each item.

Take your time and pull each order, one at a time. Confirm whether the shipment is insured by the shipper or the retailer. Once shipped, track the deliveries. When shipping small amounts overseas, FedEx, DHL, or UPS can act as a customs broker, and if you work with one carrier regularly you can request a bulk discount. Software such as ShipStation can help manage e-commerce orders or streamline your shipping process. Once you start shipping in volume, it's preferable to use a freight forwarder or fulfillment service, which can help with paperwork and international shipping regulations, book the shipping, arrange for insurance, and save money through consolidation.

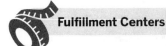

Fulfillment Centers

At some point, you may want to work with a fulfillment center rather than handle all the tagging, shipping, and packaging of product in your own studio. As volume grows, shipping becomes too time consuming and complicated and takes up too much space. When selling to department or online stores, a fulfillment center can help you drop ship and meet the vendor compliance requirements correctly to avoid charge backs and returns. A label that produces shoes in Italy, bags in Korea, and apparel in New York may need to coordinate items coming from all over the world to be packaged together in mixed orders for multiple accounts in a short time frame.

Fulfillment centers offer a range of services and capabilities, and you can negotiate a package based on your needs. They may offer warehousing and inventory management, garment on hanger (GOH) shipping, pick order or batch order processing (assembling those mixed orders of items from different manufacturers), processing returns, customs clearance, hangtag and price ticket application, credit checks, invoicing, and a range of barcode and EDI-compliant services.

Most department stores require vendors to use electronic data interchange (EDI) barcode technology on their boxes and hangtags. They receive thousands of items each week and need to track and process them quickly to get the goods onto the selling floor. It is expensive for a new designer to invest in this technology, so you should definitely ask the store for an exemption for the first few seasons. If your fulfillment center has the EDI and barcode software, you will be able to comply earlier without making the investment yourself. As a result, the stores will get your goods onto the floor more quickly, allowing them more time to sell at full price, and you will avoid the expensive charge backs that result from packing and shipping errors.

Many fulfillment companies have a minimum, so make sure you have the orders to meet the requirements. Make sure your fulfillment company has insurance, and ask what discounts it has with the major shipping companies, how fast it can turn around orders, and if it offers same-day shipping.

8 MARKETING AND BRANDING

The fashion business is as much about branding, marketing, and storytelling as it is about design. There is already so much fashion product in the world. But the brand you create, through the story you tell and the way that you tell it, can break through the clutter and provide meaning and value to your customer.

Build the Brand Story

Branding is how you shape and present every aspect of your company and product to form a clear identity and consistent impression. It differentiates your label, communicates your values, and establishes an emotional connection to the customer. Versace consistently embodies an ornate and glamorous lifestyle, while Stella McCartney stands for easy, cool luxury with a commitment to sustainability. Successful designers market their identity and story as much as their product. It extends to all areas of life, enabling Ralph Lauren to sell paint and Dolce & Gabbana to sell toasters.

Spend time researching the brands you admire and observe how every communication and image reflects the same message and aesthetic. A strong brand identity will be clear and consistent in the visuals, social media content, collaborations, models, packaging, and even where the product is available.

Brand Mission

The foundation of your brand goes back to the *mission* that drove you to start a business and design the product. Why are you creating this product? What is your vision for the company? What promise are you making to your customer? Use the answers to these questions to hone in on no more than three specific messages you want your brand to communicate at all times.

Brand Values

Consumers expect brands to stand for something more meaningful than just their product design. They want to understand what makes you authentic and whether you share the same mindset and values. As Laura Moffat of Kirrin Finch says, "There is too much product and noise, and the only way to filter it out is to make connections with brands that make us feel good and share our values—the brand has to be much bigger than just a product."[1] The brands that stand out have a strong point of view and a compelling story of the inspiration and beliefs behind their product and company culture. Create a list of words to describe your values. Words such as *ethical, honest, luxury, inclusive, easy, glamourous, functional, minimal,* and *affordable* all reflect different values. Work to narrow the list down to three to five words that succinctly describe what you offer the marketplace.

Brand Image

The brand image is conveyed through every visual aspect of your brand—starting with your logo and encompassing the color palette on your website and packaging, the sets and models in your images and video, the lighting and filters on your social media, and the fonts you use in your copy. Create a mood board of visuals and then brainstorm descriptive words, such as *bright, soft, pale, vibrant, vintage, elaborate, minimal, modern,* and *contrasting,* to help you focus your aesthetic to a look that can stay consistent across all channels.

Brand Voice

The language and tone you use to communicate make up your brand voice. Create another list of descriptive words to describe the "attitude" of your brand. Adjectives such as *fun, calm, humorous, intelligent, spiritual, thoughtful, silly,* and *reverent* set the tone for the words and phrases you use in product descriptions, captions, newsletters, and customer service interactions. Music is also a powerful component of brand voice. Think about what appeals to your customer and feels authentic to your story.

Put It All Together

The combination of the mission, values, image, and voice you craft for your brand make up the *brand story* that lives in the mind of your audience and gives context to your product. Use all of the elements above to create *brand guidelines* to reference in all of your communications, design, and marketing decisions. If this overall story is distinctive, memorable, and cohesive, it will be the driving force for your label to expand and grow.

Paige Novick—A Brand Journey

Designer Paige Novick launched her fine jewelry collection with an emphasis on 18k gold, gemstones, and traceable diamonds. This led her on a journey of learning more about the stones and their link to crystal healing. She created her line Powerful Pretty Things to complement her signature collection and to focus on stones with healing properties. The success of PPT evolved into other lifestyle and well-being focused products, such as a line of balancing essential oils used in combination with crystals to help channel, focus, and harness energy. Paige is now certified in crystal healing, angel healing, and meditation and leads workshops in the field and offers private client services.[2]

Focus and elevate

ASHYA's Passport Bolo bag @ASHYA.co

Canava sustainable, high quality leisure and intimates @canava.co

Paul Marlow Studio

Made-to-measure and custom menswear by Paul Marlow @paulmarlowstudio

Grammar's focus on perfecting the white shirt @grammarnyc

Showcase the product

Perspective shows personality at Duckie Brown @officialduckiebrown

Photo: Chloe Horseman

Image: Courtesy of Adam Humphreys + Labucq LLC

Focus on product in a 'slice of life' shot by Labucq @labucq

Diego\ Credit: AW'20 Love Binetti Collection at 080 Barcelona, Spain

Classic full look shot from the LOVE binetti runway @lovebinetti

Copyright 2016 Good Omen NYC Photographer: Anthony Rigo

Good Omen flat lay shot shows detail and texture @good_omen_nyc

Enhance with backdrop

A coordinated backdrop at Autumn Adeigbo reflects the color and energy of the line. @autumn_adeigbo

Christine Alcalay complements a romantic dress with a romantic setting @christinealcalay

Photo: Olivia Malone

Breathtaking landscape reflects the Lindsey Thornburg jacket and lifestyle @lindseythornburg

Focus on inspiration

The Bliss Lau suspension line inspired by the Brooklyn Bridge @blisslau

Image courtesy of Bliss Lau

Courtesy of Helena Fredriksson

Courtesy of Helena Fredriksson

Nature and form inspire at H. Fredriksson @hfredrikssonny

Photo: Carolina Palmgren

Focus on process and materials

The signature Alabama Chanin hand-sewn reverse applique technique @ alabamachanin

Photo: Robert Rausch for Alabama Chanin

Photo: Gary Graham Model: Sophia Hall

Gary Graham 19th century reproduction print over muslin Lillian dress @garygraham422

©FloraObscura

Natural fibers at Flora Obscura are dyed and printed with botanicals @floraobscuranyc

Photo: Chloe Horseman

The Kordal quilted jacket is made with Upcycled Cotton by The New Denim Project in Guatemala @kordalstudio

Focus on lifestyle

Kirrin Finch creates conscientious menswear-inspired apparel @kirrinfinch

The beach lifestyle of Bell Collection and Little Bell @bellcollection

The Thea Grant vintage inspired lifestyle infuses all aspects of the brand @theagrantdesign

Expand with purpose

Photo: Jess Richmond

Inspired by the refugee crisis, the Adiff trench coat which also functions as a tent, evolved into a mission driven brand which empowers resettled refugee tailors who produce the collections @adiffnyc

Courtesy of Paige Novick

The gemstone-based jewelry collection of Paige Novick evolved into well-being focused products that harness the power of gemstones and crystal healing.

Photo: Jess Richmond

Courtesy of Paige Novick

Paige Novick Gem Story Essential Oils

Inspired by culture

Ruthie Davis
2020 Pride
Love Pump
@ruthie_davis

Gustavo Cadile's
gown inspired
by the flag of his
native Argentina
@gustavocadile

Lulu Frost
necklaces made
with original
bronze numerals
from NYCs
Plaza Hotel
launched an
iconic collection
@lulufrost

Keanan Duffty Bearbrick collaboration with Jon Savage - noted UK
rock journalist and author of 'England's Dreaming' @keananduffty

The Customer

While great product is the driver, and branding sets the scene, strong customer relationships are the key to success. Very few shoppers NEED anything. But customers are seeking to "join" brands for community, meaning, and entertainment. As designer and educator Keanan Duffty says, "There's an emotional connection in fashion and people want that connectivity."[3]

Who Are They?

To serve your customers, you need to understand them. While demographic information such as age, income, and where your customers live and work is useful, it's vital to understand them at a deeper level. Knowledge of what they care about, what fulfills them, and what problems they want you to solve is the basis for a real relationship with a brand. When it comes to serving customers, successful brands sell benefits, not features.

How to Get to Know Your Customer
by Laura Moffat, Cofounder and Director of Marketing, Kirrin Finch

One of the key factors in branding and marketing is identifying and deeply understanding your customer. When I ask designers to tell me about their customer, I often hear back something like "women aged 25-45." It feels better to say your customer is all the women in an age group, but your product is not going to truly resonate with all those people. If you try to market to everyone, your message will be diluted and not break through the noise of all the other thousands of marketing messages people see every day.

The goal is to first identify a specific group or groups of people with shared characteristics who are most likely to be interested in your products or services. Then dig deep and get to know everything about them, down to where they shop, who they associate with, and what they believe in. In order to gather this information, you need to ask four key questions:

1. **Demographics: Who are they?** This is often the easiest place to start. It's the factual information about your customer. Find out their age, gender, race and ethnicity, sexual orientation, occupation, income, social status, religion, and family status.

2. **Psychographics: What is important to them?** This relates to their lifestyle and personality and goes beyond the surface to get inside their hearts and heads. You want to understand their motivations, attitudes, values, opinions, interests, and hobbies. Who influences them? What do they care about?

3. **Behaviors: How do they behave?** This data gives you a view as to how they are interacting with your product or competition. When do they purchase? How are they buying, and how often? What other brands are they considering in the path to purchase? What channels (i.e., mobile, desktop, online store, in-store, catalog, etc.) do they use for purchase?

4. **Needs and frustrations: What is your product going to do for them?** People don't want what you make. They want what it will do for them and how it will make them feel. Identify what they want out of your product by understanding their desires and pain points. What problem is your product going to solve for them? What need can your product satisfy?

You are probably wondering where and how to find this information. In one word: research. There are lots of different types of research, but the simplest place to start is online. This is called secondary research and allows you to find information from existing sources. For example, say you are creating a performance suit for men who are always on the go and need their suit to remain crisp throughout the day. You likely already have a general idea of who might wear your product—let's say, men who travel internationally for work. The first step is to use Google to find out as much information as you can about these types of people (how many fly internationally, what types of men are they, where do they go, what occupations do they have, what brands are they wearing today, etc.). You are going to stumble upon a lot of different information, and the goal is to synthesize this to get a rough idea of what your customer might look like.

The next phase is to fill the gaps using primary research. This is research that you design and conduct yourself. This often takes the form of an online survey, one-on-one interviews, or a focus group with multiple people. The key is to ask questions that will give you the answers you cannot find elsewhere and to validate findings from your secondary research.

A simple but very effective technique is to use the "five whys." If an interviewee says they like your product because it is stylish, probe further and ask why. They might say, "Because style is important to me." Ask why again. They may elaborate further and say, "Because my friends value style." Keeping asking why until you get to the root of the issue. You might find out that their choice in clothes has little to do with style and more to do with their fear of being rejected by their peers. We all like to think that we make decisions based on facts and figures, but 90 percent of decisions are driven by emotions. With a deeper understanding of your customers' emotional needs, your marketing message can be that much more relevant.

At the end of all this research, you should develop a detailed customer persona. This persona is a semi-fictional representation of your ideal customer based on market research and real data about your existing customers. Every time you are writing content for your website or designing a new product, you should review the persona and do it all with that exact person in mind. If you can embody how the customer thinks, feels, and acts, then your marketing efforts will be that much more successful.

Example of a customer persona:

Working Mom Miranda

Age: 45

Lives: Westchester Country, NY

Income: $120,000

Family: Married with 2 kids

Education: B.S. in Psychology

"I rarely have time to myself, so anytime I am buying something I don't waste much time and just get it done"

Background
Miranda works as a SVP at a branding agency in New York City. She is a working mom who is balancing her aspirations to have a successful career with raising her two teenage boys in Westchester. She commutes daily to the city and has to leave early in the morning to be back in time for the kids dinner and bedtime. Her husband also works full-time so they trade off who picks the kids up from school during the week.

Characteristics
- Socially and environmentally conscious
- Technology savvy
- Prefers to shop online vs in store
- Cares what people think of her
- Values brands that represent her values
- Health and fitness conscious

Goals
- Wants to look professional at work so her peers and clients recognize her talent

Frustrations
- Feels like her career has been halted because she has had to make sacrifices to raise her kids
- Does not have enough time for herself and often feels overwhelmed by all her responsibilities

Relationships Are a Two-Way Street
Engage

Awareness of your brand can happen on social media; through search results, referrals, press exposure; or at an event or in a store. But once someone is paying attention, you must connect with them through content they authentically enjoy. You cannot just show product. But you can share educational, entertaining, humorous, or inspirational content that fits the personality of your brand. So much goes into making your designs—the people, the music, the places. Take your audience on that journey with you and cultivate the feeling of belonging to something special.

The best way to build a loyal following is to spark conversation and encourage feedback and community. Respond, comment, and thank the people who are paying attention. Start discussions, retweet, ask and answer questions, and be honest and real. Explain your pricing and be willing to change or create things based on customer comments to let them know you are listening.

Reward

Your current customers are your most important customers. They are already showing up and supporting you. Most designers agree, the best marketing comes from customers who are satisfied and spread the word, so find ways to make these customers feel special. Recognize them individually with thank-you notes. Reward their loyalty with sneak peaks of new product and upcoming sales or a code for free shipping. Offer pre-order, limited-edition items or customizations, and invite them to be in your campaigns and to visit you in the studio. Definitely encourage them to write reviews and post selfies with your product, and offer them good rewards for referrals.

Find Ways to Meet Them

There is nothing more powerful for a designer than meeting customers face-to-face. Real-life interaction allows you to exchange ideas, hear informal and genuine feedback, and learn more about their perceptions of your product and brand. Trunk shows, pop-ups, workshops, happy hours, studio tours, and sample sales are all ways to get off-line and in person.

What single thing is most important to the relationship you have with your customer?

"Trust. My customer must trust that they are receiving a product of value, that it was produced under the most ethical of conditions, and that they are receiving a design conceived of an original idea." —Paige Novick[4]

"Respect. Don't insult their intelligence by skimping on quality, charging an inflated price, or having a shady supply chain. Respect them and they will respect you back." —Autumn Adeigbo[5]

"Trust and consistency—and they go hand in hand. Our customer trusts and knows we are always consistent with our products. They know they are getting something good every time, which is why we have been able to build a brand over 20 years." —Alicia Bell, BELL[6]

Content Strategy and Creation

Content is how you show your product, tell your story, and relate to your customers. People are exposed to thousands of messages and visuals every day. To capture and keep their attention, you must offer a diverse and relevant mix. Good content takes time to create and you will need a lot of it. In all of your content, *always* keep top of mind the brand guidelines you created for image, voice, and personality. Imagine if you were to hang every piece of content you create together on a wall; despite the variety, it should all connect and feel uniquely you.

Set the Goals

Each time you create and shoot content, be focused on its objective. The detailed product shots you need for retail buyers are different from glossy editorial photos designed to attract new Instagram followers. Whether you are providing product news or playlists, all content should be tied to a specific goal. Brands use content for many different purposes: to create awareness, capture email addresses, drive people into the stores, build loyalty, spark referrals, announce new products, and trigger quick online sales. Be clear on the specific message you want to send to the audience with each communication. As you grow, you can create even more unique and targeted content for specific markets, locations, and customer types.

Curate the Themes

While there is pressure to create a lot of content, it must all keep your specific customer in mind and stay consistent in telling the brand story. To avoid having a menagerie of disjointed topics, curate a tight set of content themes within those guidelines. There are many ideas to consider:

- **Behind the scenes.** A glimpse into the photo shoots, factory visits, fit sessions, or fabric weaving.

- **Inspiration.** Share the art, nature, travel, culture, social issues, mood boards, or people that inspire your brand.

- **Education.** Teach about fabric and materials, explain the beading or natural dye process, and share knowledge about the refugee makers or environmental issues that inspire your product.

- **Tutorials.** Product-related instruction can demonstrate how to hand wash the cashmere, customize your denim, or clean the brass. Tutorials can also reflect the brand's lifestyle, showing how to frost pastel cupcakes or mix essential oils.

- **Entertainment.** Short film, runway footage, drawing challenges, interviews, quizzes, fitness classes, games, and playlists entertain and affirm shared mindset.

- **News and moments.** New product launches, spontaneous product drops, guest curation, media coverage, promotions, holidays, and events.

- **Guides.** "How to get the look" styling and trend advice, gift guides, and self-care.

- **Lifestyle.** The destinations, careers, hobbies, and habits that inspire the brand.

Make It Personal

One thing that makes buying from small brands so special is the ability to have a personal connection to the designer and their process. All of the above themes offer opportunities to show YOU. Share how you think and show what you love. Invite customers into your personal world to see how you pack for travel or make your favorite foods. Once you do, your white shirt takes on much more meaning than every other white shirt.

Create the Content

Fashion is very visual and you need a lot of visual content to tell your story, show your product, and keep customers engaged so they come back for more. Content needs to be presented in a variety of ways to work across different channels. Visual formats range from a variety of still photography to graphics and illustration, long- and short-form video, and live formats. Before social media, jewelry designer Bliss Lau did photography once a season for her lookbook. Now she has learned how to shoot her own product and invested in a full lighting setup. She schedules a five-hour photography session every week.[7]

Plan ahead to determine what content you need to fill each of your marketing channels. A content calendar can be drafted far in advance to establish a consistent schedule for website, social, and email content. Most web and email platforms include tools for content management, and many designers employ software applications such as Planoly, Sproutsocial, and Hootsuite Plus. Be prepared to create for multiple formats each time you shoot, and develop content that is not tied to the moment so you can divide it up for later use. In addition to visual content, it may suit your brand to have written editorials for newsletters, op-eds or a digital magazine, or audio content for podcasts.

Photographs

Your photographs will work harder for you than anything else. They are your most important sales and marketing tool and often the sole reason for landing a new client, attracting new followers, or hearing from a celebrity stylist. Designer Christine Alcalay says, "The one thing I never skimp on is the photography. You work so hard trying to tell the story every season, if the photos are not produced in the best way, what is the point?"[8]

Be purposeful and edit carefully. Take many photos often and be focused on how they will be used. People are inundated with thousands of images every day. The photos need to be beautifully shot, show the product, and be consistently styled to reflect the culture of your brand. You will need photographs for social media, e-commerce, and a digital lookbook for buyers and press. You will need a combination of straightforward product shots, close-ups that show texture and detail, and carefully styled photos to grab attention and express story and inspiration. Formal shots may be best for some platforms with casual shots needed for

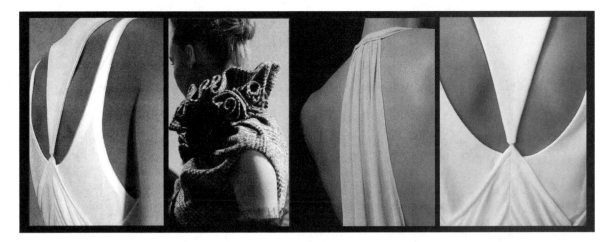

Four exquisite close-ups show details of the Doo.Ri collection.
Printed courtesy of Doo.Ri
Photo by Lee Clower

others. Plan to also have photos of your atelier and creative process.

Good photos are not cheap to create, and you need to watch your costs carefully.

There are photographers, stylists, and hair and makeup artists who are new to the business and have lower rates or may even work in exchange for prints and a photo credit. Look for interns who have these skills and can help you on a regular basis. Be honest with yourself about your own abilities, and choose your team with care. A good photograph requires the photographer, models, styling, and set all to work together holistically.

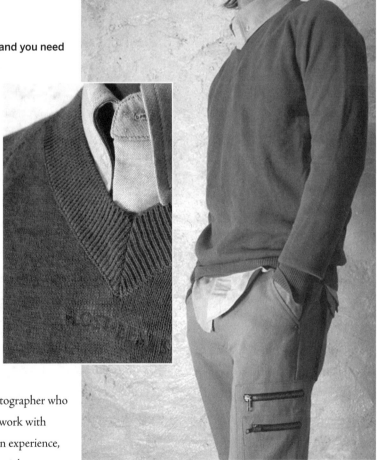

Photographer. Photographing fashion product is a specialized skill. Ideally, you will have an experienced photographer who can shoot clear, impactful images. If you work with an amateur or someone who lacks fashion experience, several things can go wrong. The photos might come back blurred, or they may be shot from the wrong angle. The cost for a photographer varies greatly and can be extremely high. Shop around, meet with several, and review their portfolio

These photos give two perspectives on an outfit. One gives a sense of the overall look and the other focuses on texture and detail.
Printed courtesy of Obedient Sons

and social media feed to get a sense of the quality and style of their work. Word of mouth is the best way to find a good photographer. Modeling agencies can also recommend photographers and stylists who want to test.

This outdoor backdrop reflects the inspiration for the collection.
H Fredriksson F15 collection Printed courtesy of Helena Fredriksson
Photographer: Redrick deLeon

Models. Clothing should be photographed on a live model to give dimension to each piece and emphasize detail and fit. Casting the right model, who fits the personality of the brand, will communicate the right mood and energy without distracting from the clothes. If you don't have personal connections to an appropriate model, you will need to call an agency. Know in advance the type of model you want for your shoot. Be up front with the booker about your budget. Reassure them that you are a professional with a serious business and you are working with a decent photographer. Be sure and meet the model in person before the photo shoot to make sure they are a good fit. While you don't have to have a live model to shoot accessories, jewelry does look better when photographed on a three-dimensional form.

Lighting. The lighting is critical to the quality and mood of any photograph. Natural light will affect the timing of your photo shoot as well as where it will take place. Lighting equipment is more consistent and easy to control, but requires investment and the knowledge of your photographer.

Set and background. The background for your photographs should not overwhelm or distract from the clothes. A good choice is a simple white wall, but of course, you can create a background that lends mood and ambience. A romantic Victorian-inspired collection could be photographed in front of antique wallpaper with the model on an antique settee. Just be careful to not overwhelm the product with the set. Shadows from props and furniture or a model's pose can bury the product. The key is for the viewer to be enticed by the story, but still able to see the product clearly.

The background in this photo compliments the shoe fabric and style.
Courtesy of Tashkent, Photo: Greg Morris/Insight Visual www.iy-photo.com

Styling. You want to style each look appealingly, using shoes, accessories, hair, and makeup to reflect your inspiration and brand. Be careful: Too much creativity can overshadow the purpose of the shoot or be confusing to your customer. While the designer drives the overall vision for the shoot, it can be beneficial to work with a stylist who can give creative input as well as help find your location, accessories, and other needs. Accessories and shoes can be your own, borrowed from a showroom, or, in the manner of many stylists, purchased and then returned to the store. Hair and makeup should be carefully conceived to complement the story. An additional concern is that some buyers and consumers are better than others at separating the clothing from the styling. If you have cotton prairie skirts rocked out with heavy leather jackets and biker boots, the online customer who really loves prairie skirts may not relate to the rocker image.

A well-styled product shot that positions the bag in the life of a chic customer
Photo from Rafe, Photo by Micaela Rossato

Some designers add their logo to a lower corner of all of their product shots online so they are credited if copied onto Pinterest or other social media.

The models' pose and styling in these photos project dignity
and strength while clearly showing the clothes.
Photos from Maria Marta Facchinelli, Photographer: Cecilia Glik, Stylist: Clarisa Furtado

Video

Video tells a broader story of your brand and lends movement and context to your product. You need plenty of video content to keep your social media and website fresh and engaging. Because video is expensive to produce, make a lot all at once and slice it up to use at different times and on different channels. A five-minute film or documentary may be best for your website or YouTube channel, but short clips are needed for stories and messaging apps. It doesn't always have to be perfect. Sometimes casual, spontaneous video created on an iPhone gets the best response. Just make sure its relevant to your brand and customer, and it should make sense with both sound on and off.

Fashion film offers a particularly rich and imaginative platform for storytelling and entertaining. A film can present a compelling narrative not just to show product, but to draw the viewer into the world of the designer's inspiration and vision. The flexibility of film allows for distribution online or a real-life screening during fashion week, or it can even be taken on tour. Film can tease a future collection or be shown in coordination with the arrival of the collection in stores, or timed with various product drops.

With their narrative films, designers Ashley Cimmone and Moya Annece, of luxury travel accessories label ASHYA, seek to encourage thoughtful post-tourist exploration and cultural awareness through design and storytelling and to pay homage to the largely unseen and underrepresented Black and indigenous communities that nurture and inspire their work. As they say, "We seek to push conversations beyond planning your next best trip, but instead sparking dialogue around moving thoughtfully throughout the world, being a contributing visitor while touring. The fashion industry is notorious for 'borrowing' from culture without proper representation. We seek to do quite the opposite."

They also create their "how to wear the bags" films to showcase how their bags and accessories function, as well as the many ways of styling them. As Ashley and Moya explain, "Some of our design details are quite unconventional so we want to use these instructional films as an educational tool, all while keeping the messaging, look, and feel playful and beautiful."[9]

Other Marketing Materials

Printing is expensive and digital images save designers thousands of dollars that used to be spent on glossy lookbooks and elaborate press kits. However, for in-person meetings, trade shows, and sales events, you still need a takeaway reminder of your label. A postcard with a great product shot, a short brand summary that mentions key retail accounts or celebrity clients, a business card with a discount for online purchases—you don't need much. Just make sure the materials are professional, fit your brand guidelines, and always include your website and contact information.

In a world of digital communication, mailing a low-cost postcard, a fold-over mailer, or a printed invitation to customers, press, or buyers can break through the clutter of a crowded inbox or social media feed. A single eye-catching photograph or sketch that is representative of your brand can serve as a reminder and an incentive to visit you online.

A postcard with a bold statement to create intrigue for the line
Printed courtesy of Lost Art,
Photographer: Marco Guerra www.marcoguerraphoto.com.

Line Sheets

Line sheets show each item in the collection with the information needed by wholesale buyers and press. They include a flat technical drawing or a clear, simple photograph that shows the shape and details of each item. The line sheet is arranged with several items on one page and includes the style number, name, description, wholesale and suggested retail price, colors and sizes available, and fabric and materials. They may also come with fabric swatches. Your company name and contact information should be on every single page. Don't just hand these out to anyone. Line sheets show the specific details of your items and are a good guide for knockoffs if they fall into the wrong hands.

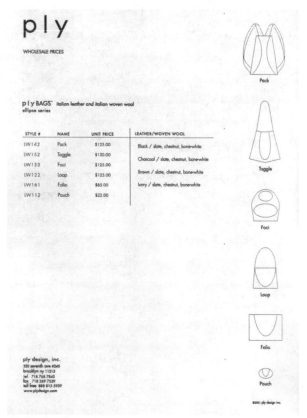

This line sheet focuses on product pricing and descriptions with simple flat drawings.

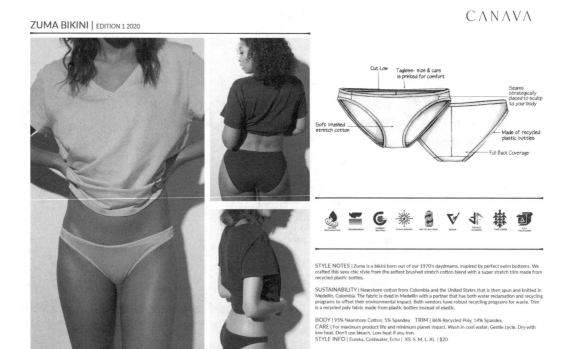

This line sheet includes detailed information about raw materials, production, and social and environmental impact.

A lookbook spread of full looks with highlighted details

Printed courtesy of Lewis Cho, Elizabeth Young (photographer), Denise See (layout)

Biography and Brand Summary

Buyers and editors want a brief paragraph or two about the designer, the product, and the brand. Keep it short and to the point and don't forget to spell-check. The bio should include the designer's origin, education, and relevant work experience, along with anything special and intriguing. Designers use childhood experiences, such as visiting their father's chemistry lab, playing dress-up in their mother's closet, or spending years in teenage rebellion, to tell the story behind the clothes. Describe your brand and mission, and as always, explain why you are different. Provide some framework for the current collection. Include where it sells, celebrities who have worn the product, and any industry awards or recognition you have received.

Packaging and Tags

Boxes, envelopes, and hangtags are important offline communications of your brand. As designer Autumn Adeigbo says, "Presentation is everything. You want to present the product in a way that aligns with what the customer should feel when they get it. For a luxury brand, it should be a premium experience that makes them want to come back."[10] The iconic Tiffany blue box with its white ribbon emulates affluence, while a compostable tag embedded with flower seeds reinforces a brand's commitment to the earth. Design these materials with your brand values in mind, and use the tag to remind your customer of special processes, inspirations, or materials. Try to keep your costs down—simple and elegant says a lot. Consider what you include when you ship from the tissue paper to the return instructions or even a handwritten thank-you note.

Press Coverage

Copies of press coverage and photos of celebrities with your product make for good content on your website and social media and should be included with your sales materials. Don't include every press item you have ever received, and take out anything that is not relevant to your current work. If your item is included on a page with many other products, circle or highlight it to make it easy to find. Customer testimonials and positive comments can also be influential.

Samples

Proper, well-made samples are critical for photos as well as for sales and press appointments. The buyer assumes that these items are an exact example of what she will receive if an order is placed. The quality of stitching, fabrication, and construction will set expectations. Buyers stress the importance of first impressions when previewing a new collection. A store will never take a chance on a new collection that doesn't look professional.

Before each appointment, check that your samples are clean and undamaged. Clothing should be pressed and carried in a sturdy garment bag on good hangers. Accessories and jewelry should be packed in neat bags, boxes, or trays. Hangtags should include your company information, style number, size range, color options, fiber content, wholesale price, and where the item was made.

Samples are expensive and I usually advise being conservative, but if you can afford it, cut the sample in a few of the available colors. Although you can show the items in one color with swatches of color options, several designers tell me that the buyers have trouble envisioning the choices and are more likely to buy if they see the actual item in each color.

Marketing Channels

Once you identify your customers, you must determine where you can reach them—and you will want to reach them in several places. You don't have to be everywhere, but the right mix of email, search, web, and social media platforms will solidify your brand in the mind of your customer.

The beginning is hard and you have to be realistic. Unless you already have a huge social following, or Beyoncé or Ellen wear your product, you won't grow your audience from 0 to 100,000 overnight. You will have to diligently work on your keywords and hashtags, build your email list, and eventually try to get some press.

Search Engines Deconstructed

by Manpreet Kaur Kalra, Founder, Art of Citizenry

As online shopping continues to grow, your website is as much about showcasing your brand to the world as it is an essential sales channel. Ever wonder how to make your products show up in Google's search results? It all starts with understanding how search engines work. The goal of any search engine, including Google, is to provide users with the most relevant answer to their search query. Search engines do this by crawling your website and "indexing" it based on factors ranging from quality of content to user experience. While search engines continue to become smarter, you can help your website rank higher on search engine results pages (SERP) by investing in your website's search engine optimization (SEO). After all, more quality traffic means more sales.

Quality is queen. SEO is not just about increasing the *quantity* of traffic to your website, but also the *quality* of your website's traffic. This means optimizing your site to get in front of the customers who care most about what you have to offer. When optimizing your website, think less about making search engines happy and more about making your customers happy. SEO success is about understanding what your customers are searching for online, what words they use to describe the products you sell (culotte vs. wide-leg crop pant), and the type of content they are looking for.

Think about keywords when naming and describing products. When working in the fashion space, it is incredibly important to be thoughtful about how you name the products you sell. Many designers like to give each piece a unique name, which can make your product harder to find in search results if someone is not already familiar with the piece or with your brand. If you want to maintain a unique name for each piece in your collection, couple the name with the product type.

For example, if you design an organic cotton maxi skirt with a floral print and name it "Manpreet," list it on your website as "Manpreet Floral Maxi Skirt" instead of "Manpreet Skirt." The phrase "floral maxi skirt" is something a potential customer might be searching for, so include that string of keywords into the name of your product to make sure they see it.

What about organic cotton? Depending on your target customer and what they care about, you may decide to include organic cotton in the name of the product or in the product description. Remember, the key is to include words or phrases that your customer cares about and is searching for.

Pro Tip: Broad keywords like "maxi skirt" have high search volumes, but often have a lower purchase intent. Although their search volume may be lower, targeted long-tail keyword phrases like "floral organic cotton maxi skirt" have a higher purchase intent.

Define your *title tag* and *meta description*. Each page of your website has a unique *title tag* that lets customers know what to expect when they visit the corresponding page of your site. The title tag displays as a clickable headline in search results. Your *meta description* is the short paragraph of text that appears below the clickable headline. While meta descriptions are not used to index your website by search engines, they are used by customers to get a preview of what to expect and impact the likelihood that someone will click on your link. Meta descriptions are the perfect opportunity to pique the interest of your customer. Your title tag and meta descriptions should include the keyword or phrase you are targeting (i.e., floral organic cotton maxi skirt). For product pages, your title tag should be the name of your product and your meta description should be a variation of your product description.

Pro Tip: Your title tag should be 70 characters or less, and your meta description should be between 150 to 160 characters. Well-crafted meta descriptions include a call to action (CTA), extra points for adding an incentive like "Free shipping over $50."

Don't forget about photography and user experience. Without a website that holds the interest of your customers, you will struggle to rank highly in search results even if you spend hours optimizing your product names and metadata. Make it as easy as possible for customers to find what they are looking for, add it to their cart, and make the purchase. The more successful your customers are at engaging with your website and navigating the purchasing process, the better it is for your SEO.

For design-driven brands, photography is key. However, photos can really slow down your website, negatively affecting your user experience and, in turn, your SEO. Do not let your photos hurt your online presence. Instead, reduce the file size while maintaining image quality using an image-editing software or an online image-compression tool.

Pro Tip: Define the *alt text*, or image tag, of all website images. This helps your images rank higher in an image search. It also gives you another opportunity to optimize your website for keywords you care about. A well-written alt text describes the associated image and includes keywords.

From SEO to SEM. While SEO is about generating organic (unpaid) traffic to your website, SEM (search engine marketing) is about paying to get in front of high-intent customers. Ever notice how the first few entries on the search engine results page are always ads? That's because search engines reserve the first few spots for those who pay to rank. While SEO takes time, SEM starts generating results right away. You can set up paid search ads using Google AdWords, but be sure to invest in your website's SEO before you begin. After all, a well-optimized website is more likely to generate sales irrespective of whether your traffic is from paid or organic sources.

Think big picture. Optimizing your website is an important component of your digital footprint. However, like any other marketing tactic, SEO alone only goes so far. Think about your marketing as an engine. Instead of approaching your strategy from purely a sales-driven mindset, focus on brand loyalty and relationships. The more people enjoy what you have to offer, the more likely they will share it—leading to more visits and more love from search engines. Remember: Each marketing channel builds on another and serves a critical purpose in helping customers discover, shop, and love your brand.

Manpreet Kalra is a digital marketing expert, activist, and social impact educator. She currently serves on the board of NYC Fair Trade Coalition, a grassroots fair trade advocacy organization. She is an advocate for fostering cultural humility in impact through inclusive brand narratives. She has dedicated her career to exploring the intersection of digital media, social impact, and diversity in the sustainable fashion movement. Manpreet is a thought leader in impact communication. She launched Art of Citizenry to coach conscious businesses on how to maximize their impact through business development, branding, and strategic marketing. With a background in venture and start-ups, Manpreet uses her knowledge to help purpose-driven organizations and brands think of creative ways to grow and address inclusion in every aspect of the business.

Website

If you have an e-commerce business, your website is where you want your customer to be. Whether they land there from social media, an email link, or a Google search, once they are on your site you can control their experience and lead them to purchase.

Even if your entire business is wholesale, your site is a critical marketing channel to provide content and information to build your brand and drive sales for your retail partners. When consumers visit your site, they should get a compelling brand story, fresh product imagery, understanding of your inspiration and materials, exciting news, and of course, links to your retail stockists. A password-protected area on the site for buyers can include lookbooks and line sheets for upcoming collections, as well as high-resolution photos with descriptions for media use. The majority of fashion brands do design their website to drive direct-to-consumer sales, therefore websites are discussed in-depth in Chapter 9: Sales.

Social Media

Social media blurs the lines between marketing, sales, and public relations. Designers can send images to stylists, answer customer questions, and process sales all on a single platform. Most important, with social media you can share your story and product directly with millions of potential customers across the globe—building personal relationships and receiving real feedback.

Social media is affordable, but it can also be ineffective. It takes the right content on the right platform to break through the clutter and resonate with the people most likely to buy your product. The number of your followers, likes, or views is not what is important. It's the quality of the interactions and how they will build the community and relationships that lead to sales. As designer and educator Keanan Duffty says, "I wring my hands when designers say they want to build their brand on social media. The best marketing is when someone buys your product and their friends like it and then it goes viral. Too many customers on social media experience a brand and become a fan of a brand, but never actually buy the product."[11]

You Don't Have to Be Everywhere

To some designers, Facebook is a waste of time, while others say it drives the majority of their sales. Success on any platform depends on whether your audience is there and if you can connect with them in a meaningful way. Almost every fashion brand is on Instagram in some form, but there are designers who have the best engagement on LinkedIn and others who connect best on TikTok. There will always be new platforms and opportunities emerging in social channels, gaming platforms, private chat and messaging apps. The important thing is to do the research to find where and how your customers engage in each place. Be sure to check your competitors to see where and how they interact with their audience. With social media, it's easy to test and explore, but if your audience doesn't respond, don't waste time—move on.

The content you create must not only make sense for your brand and customer, it must also fit the individual platform. Instagram is more glossy and polished than Snapchat, which is more personal, and TikTok, which is silly and unfiltered. People tend to read longer posts on Facebook, but Twitter is quick and snappy. Even within a platform, content types can range. An Instagram post may live on your grid and represent your brand over time, but Stories can be spontaneous and less "official," and Live can be both scripted and off the cuff. New features such as stickers, augmented reality, and selling tools are launched frequently, and you will want to tweak and freshen your approach for each platform while still maintaining consistency.

Be Social on Social

To maximize your brand on any platform, it is critical to be an active member of the communities of your customers. It's not enough to just be responsive, you need to join the conversations and spark dialogue between your followers by commenting, asking questions, and soliciting opinions. Create challenges or fun interactions based on your customer values and engage with communities and causes that align with your brand's mission. Always acknowledge the people who are interacting regularly with your brand, thank them, and encourage them to create content for you to share.

Research the hashtags and keywords your audience follows, and that your competitors use, to learn more about your customers and to connect with them in more places. Brands can create their own hashtags, such as #LMFgirlsonholiday, which celebrates Lisa Marie Fernandez swimwear, to be used by friends, influencers, and fans to both create community and attract new followers. Hashtag challenges and contests encourage users to create their own content, and location tags can help you grow specific local followings.

Join the interest-related communities where your customers engage. Because there is so much content on social media channels, it is worth exploring smaller groups and micro-communities, which have more curated forums and feeds. The closer you can get to your customers' interests, the more attentive they will be. Don't forget to also comment and share the posts of the buyers, influencers, and editors who would be a good fit for your product.

The community of social media provides a great opportunity to create cross-promotions and social "events" with other like-minded brands and organizations to reach new audiences. Ask your retail partners to host a meet-the-designer event for you on their social media.

Negative Feedback

Everyone online gets negative feedback or is called out at some time, and it can even be valuable if there is truth in it. If you make a mistake, apologize quickly and sincerely. If it's not truthful or useful, it's best to just let it go. Attorney Nicholas Rozansky warns that attempting to delete or suing over a negative comment or conversation puts you at risk of creating a "Streisand effect" situation—a phenomenon where an attempt to hide or remove a piece of information brings even more attention to it.[12] Instead you can ask friends to post positive comments to drown out the noise and try to move on quickly. Others also recommend messaging the person to try and diffuse the situation without a public audience.

Test, Test, Test

The beauty of online platforms is how easy it is to experiment with different images, messages, timing, and captions to see what resonates with customers. When you are starting out, this is an important way to hone your style and approach to find the combination of elements that have the maximum impact. Some brands rely on high-production glossy video and images, but others discover that more personal content, shot on their iPhone, works best.

There is no true formula for how often you should post on social media. Quality is more important than quantity. If you post something irrelevant just to post, you will confuse people and lose them. If your content is fast paced or news breaking, such as announcing limited product drops and flash sales, you will post more than a company narrating a story around two small collections per year. Some brands purposely post high-quality content with limited frequency to create desire, but this can result in overall lower traffic numbers.

Brands tend to post as much as three times a day on Twitter, but only a few times per week on Facebook or LinkedIn. Short-lived content such as Instagram Stories can be posted more frequently. It's up to you to test small variances in time and frequency on each channel to discover what works best. Whatever your strategy, it's important to be consistent so your followers know what to expect.

 Caution!

If you see a photo of Selena Gomez wearing your outfit and the photo is owned by someone like Getty Images, you need their permission to post it. Attorney Nicholas Rozansky recommends you review the FTC guidelines for social media. He says, "Rules for false advertising claims apply to social media and so do the laws for product endorsements. If you have someone else managing your social media, or you have influencers endorsing your product, it's your job to make sure they are following protocol."

Pay to Amplify

While it's tempting to just throw money at social media advertising and hope it will deliver, the costs add up quickly and it doesn't always work. First, do what you can for free to determine what type of messages, platforms, and images work best for your customer. Then, unless you already have a huge following or fan base, you will probably need to invest.

When you identify your best performing posts, consider putting some budget behind them to reach more potential customers. As Adam Humphreys of the shoe label Labucq states, "There is a lot of competition on Instagram, but for us it performs. We have to pay a little bit for everyone who might be interested in our product to be able to see it. That makes me feel in control—it's something you can do that doesn't just rely on your existing social media following."[13]

With online advertising, you can choose who to target based on their location, their interests, and their activity online. The platforms create "look-alike" audiences based on the characteristics and behaviors of your existing following, website visitors, and customer list. You can target different groups by when and where they are online and experiment with different messages, images, and strategies to get the best response.

Different ads are designed for different purposes, and you should be conscious of your goal each time you spend. *Brand awareness* ads and boosting your posts ensures greater exposure. *Lead generation* ads incentivize people to provide their email. *Conversion* ads drive consumers to interact or make a purchase. *Dynamic* ads are customized to retarget individual customers based on their past actions, such as reminding them of product they looked at before.

Budget. Online advertising is most often sold on either a cost per mille (CPM) basis, which focuses on *impressions* or how many times the ad is seen, or a cost per click (CPC) basis, which tracks consumers who actually interact with the ad by clicking, signing up, or linking to a website. Generally, the closer you get to the purchase point, the more expensive the ad. Designers often allocate a percentage of their sales for advertising. Your sales cover the cost, and as sales increase, so does your advertising budget.

Return on ad spend is your most important advertising measurement. It tracks how much money you make in sales for each dollar you spend on advertising. For example, if you are only making one dollar in sales for every three dollars you spend, it is not a good investment. You may need to experiment with the image or video, the caption, and the channel to try and increase the response. Try posts versus stories as well as different times and days. Success takes time and as you experiment and learn, you will build momentum. After a few months of learning, your investment will yield better results.

Frequency. Ads can be annoying. They are not as authentic as other content, and some designers say that as soon as a price appears next to their product, the engagement goes down. Pay attention to how often your ad is showing up. You should pull it before it's seen too many times by the same people, but you do need them to see it enough to remember you. It's a fine balance between too much and too little, and it's different for every brand.

Email Marketing

Email is often the most valuable channel for brands. It is a direct line of communication to the customers who have shown interest in your label and are the most likely to buy. Email builds on the awareness of your brand to communicate your story and values in a more personal way to generate loyalty.

Build the List

Emails must be individually collected and carefully maintained. Most brands grow their email list by offering a discount or special promotion. Others are successful with granting access to exclusive content such as a playlist, first access to a limited-edition product, or collaboration with another brand. The key is to entice the person to be curious enough, or value what you offer enough, to give up their email address.

Have email sign-up incentives and opportunities on every page of your website, on all marketing collateral, and at events. Post a link to your site on your social media profiles and include it on your hangtags. Many designers start with a list of friends and family who are supportive of their line. Eventually, you may invest in social media advertising to lead more people to your brand and entice them to click and sign up.

What to Send

When people first sign up for your email, have an automatic response to thank them for signing up and deliver the discount, newsletter, or other promised content. Then every email going forward should focus on getting the viewer to your website to explore and buy.

It's okay if people unsubscribe from your list because they simply aren't interested in your product. But you don't want them to unsubscribe because you are boring, annoying, and just cluttering up their in-box. Don't send continuous product shots and discount offers. To build genuine interest in your brand, you need to mix product and offers with interesting content and news.

Promotional emails announce a new product, a sale, or a discount to entice the viewer to the website. They should capture attention and have a clear and specific offer. Be creative with reasons for new offers such as answering a quick question or taking a fun survey. Offer birthday discounts, holiday-related promotions, and discounts for referrals. Focus on just one offer at a time, and all offers should have an expiration date.

Content emails reflect brand values, process, and community. The content themes you employ such as "behind the scenes" or "entertainment," can offer profiles of artisans, interviews with customers, mood boards, or playlists to share the culture of your brand.

News emails announce events, a new retail partner, a sighting of a celebrity in your product, or exciting media coverage.

Behavioral emails respond to consumer action—or inaction. If they left something unpurchased in the shopping cart, you can send a reminder or offer a second look at a product they viewed several times. A "we miss you" email can provide a discount or special message to a past customer.

When a customer purchases something, they should automatically receive confirmation and information on shipping, payment, and expected delivery.

As you grow, you can become more targeted, offering loyal customers previews or friends and family discounts. Influencers, editors, and wholesale buyers can get news of the next season or an upcoming celebrity placement. Local customers can be invited to a sample sale or a party at your store. Many designers also send monthly updates to their suppliers and manufacturers to share positive news about the brand.

Design

Regardless of the specific message, emails must always look like your brand and be consistent in tone. It is definitely worth hiring a designer up front to create an email template to keep things consistent. Pay attention to the "above the fold," or preview area, which the viewer sees first in their inbox. This should grab their attention and encourage them to click or scroll to see more.

Don't Oversend

The frequency of email depends on your brand, product, and what your customer wants. If you offer daily flash sales, you need daily emails. If you release one new product every quarter, or the customer signed up for a monthly newsletter, you aren't adding value by emailing them every day. On the bottom of every email, you must include the option to unsubscribe.

Use the Information

Email platforms monitor the response to every email you send and can provide a lot of useful insight. Pay attention to the following:

- **Open rate.** The viewer opened the email showing they are either interested in you or your subject line. If your open rate drops, you are probably sending too many emails or your content lacks value.

- **Click-through rate.** The content of the email was interesting enough to click through to your website.

- **Conversion rate.** The viewer not only clicked through, but they also did what you asked, such as signing up for your email list, completing a survey, or purchasing.

- **Forwarding/sharing rate.** How often the email was interesting enough to share.

- **Unsubscribe rate.** The number of recipients who are no longer interested in either your product or your email. If this is increasing, consider how you might need to adjust your overall strategy.

As with social media, you should test different types of content and subject lines and also experiment with the day and time of delivery to see how that affects the open and click-through rates. Be sure to only test one variable at a time.

Text

Text message marketing is offered by most email platforms, and you have to decide how this fits with your brand values and whether your customer will see texts as helpful or just interrupting their day. The key is to use text for more personalized communication based on specific interests and behaviors. Customers may not want a text for every discount you offer, but they will want a text when the shoes in their cart go on sale.

Understanding What Works

Ultimately, designers say the only number that really matters is how much money you make, but it's important to use the data and information available to figure out what marketing efforts are working best for you. Once you see the actual facts of who is responding to your content and in what way, it may surprise you.

Before you dig into the official data, you can make your own initial observations on whether your number of followers, comments, and shares are growing, and if your email list is expanding. This alone can help you develop a sense of which type of content has the best response for its goal.

Try to understand why something did well so you can replicate it. Content goes viral when something in it causes an emotional reaction, which might just be related to timing or current events, and it is not something you can always predict or control. Designer Angela Luna from ADIFF woke one morning to find her website buzzing with 8,000 users from Japan. Unexpectedly, the brand went viral because of a retweet about their Kickstarter project three years prior.[14]

There are a few specific measurements that online platforms provide to monitor the success of your marketing efforts.

- **Reach** defines the number of unique accounts who saw your content.
- **Impressions** are the number of times your posts have been seen, possibly multiple times by the same person.
- **Engagement** measures the number of people who actually interacted with your content.
- **Conversions** are when someone is actually led to buy.

With this data, you can evaluate your content by comparing how many people see it versus how many actually engage. Try to find parallels between the content that is most viewed and most shared and brings visitors to your profile and website. The products with the most clicks, and the videos that were most watched, are worth emulating in future posts and emails. As with email, note the days and times *when* consumers are most likely to engage, and plan your content schedule accordingly.

The consumer analytics from each platform provides more detailed information on exactly *who* is engaging with your content. Google Analytics connects to your web platform and tells you *where* your visitors come from and exactly what keywords they used.

Web analytics reveal *what* visitors do once they are on your site. In addition to seeing the products they looked at, where they clicked for more information, and what they put in the cart, you can see how long they stay on your site and whether they look at one product or browse many pages and products. Tracking how much time customers spend looking at return policies or sizing charts can give you insight into their concerns and *why* they may be leaving things unpurchased in the cart.

Ultimately, the data itself is not what's important and you don't need to monitor it all. It's understanding which metrics are meaningful to you and how you should respond. If you see a lot of sales in a specific city, you can use that data to entice stores in that area to buy the collection or you could stage a pop-up there on your own. At Kirrin Finch, the data revealed that many customers were searching their website for "vests," so they designed a vest for the next collection.[15] The knowledge you acquire over time, along with a deeper understanding of your customer, should inform how you continually evolve your communications, sales strategies, and even design.

Beware of relying too much on data in decision making. While data drives many of the big brands, what often makes a small label interesting or special cannot be quantified. Even if certain design-driven product doesn't sell well, it may be critical to attracting the customer to your core items. Don't forget the importance of your intuition, unique vision, and personal understanding of your customer when making decisions.

9 SALES

Regardless of design talent, the designers who focus on selling are the ones who stay in business. As designer and educator Keanan Duffty says, "The only way to prove yourself is your sales."[1] Without sales, the effort put into designing the collection and developing the samples is irrelevant. Today there are so many ways to reach customers and sell your product. You can build an e-commerce business on your own website; a wholesale business to department stores, boutiques, and online retailers; or open your own independent stores.

Start with One, Then Add

With so many options for sales, it's best to initially focus your resources on one channel and have it running smoothly before you add. It takes years to develop each sales channel, and where you start depends on your product and type of business. Some brands may launch with wholesale and eventually add a small direct e-commerce business. Others will build a large e-commerce base and then support it with pop-ups and one or two wholesale accounts.

If you start with a direct-to-consumer business, eventually adding wholesale can be a smart marketing strategy. A high-end store can lend credibility to a brand and provide a place where people can touch and try the product, and where the designer can hold trunk shows and meet customers in person. The best stores are more likely to partner with a brand that has a solid online customer base, and that base gives the designer more negotiating power.

If you first build a wholesale business, later expanding to direct to consumer delivers better margins and an opportunity to control the full customer experience and brand message. It will also offset the risks that come with wholesale relationships—when Barneys NY closed in bankruptcy, the designers who had their own stores had somewhere to sell the inventory from cancelled orders. During the COVID-19 quarantines, designers relied on e-commerce to reach consumers who were only shopping online.

For most designers, the ultimate formula will be an "omni-channel" approach, which reaches the customer with a seamless combination of online direct-to-consumer sales, some wholesale accounts, and an in-person, real-life component. The channels also work together to financially support the business as direct to consumer keeps cash flowing throughout the wholesale calendar, and wholesale orders add consistency and volume to manage inventory and increase financing options.

Direct to Consumer (D2C)

Direct-to-consumer selling accounts for a significant portion of all fashion business. It cuts out the middleman between the designer and customer, and allows brands to start small and test a few products on a basic website, or in a small pop-up, with very little risk. As shoe designer Ruthie Davis says, "By selling direct to consumer, I don't need to have big collections to satisfy the buyers. I can listen directly to what my customers want, and sometimes they simply want a similar style with slight tweaks. I can deliver collections when I want and put things on sale when I want. In general, I have more control of my business and its ultimate success."[2] There are several avenues to sell directly to the consumer in-person or online.

Direct to Consumer: Online

Your Own Website

Most designers who sell directly to their customers start by launching their own e-commerce website.

There Are Several Advantages

- **Easy.** With existing platforms, such as Shopify, it's easy to set up and launch your website.

- **Access.** You can reach millions of potential customers around the world.

- **Higher margins.** You aren't sharing revenue with a wholesale partner.

- **Competitive pricing.** The low overhead and higher margins will enable you to price your products more competitively.

- **Customer connection.** Your website will provide more direct and personal contact with customers and access to data about them.

- **Flexibility.** You can release styles at your own pace rather than following an industry calendar.

- **Control.** Managing your own site gives you control over your brand storytelling and the customer experience.

- **Responsiveness.** You have the ability to respond quickly to cultural moments, media coverage, or a spike in interest.

- **Direct payment.** Payments can channel directly to you from customers throughout the year versus waiting for the stores to pay.

- **Creative freedom.** Without the pressure or filter of a buyer, you are free to design, adjust, and test new product as you wish.

There Are Several Challenges

Despite all the upside, designers often underestimate the challenge of building a business online. As Adam Humphreys of Labucq says, "The first mistake is to set up a website and think people will just come."[3]

- **Competition.** There are so many brands online, it can be very difficult to break through the clutter and attract enough of the right customers to build a business.

- **Marketing expense.** The costs to create fresh content and invest in search and other paid advertising can quickly eat up what you gain in wholesale margin.

- **Inventory risk.** It is difficult to predict how much of each product will sell, but you need inventory ready to deliver. The product ties up cash as it waits to be sold.

- **Responsibility.** In addition to design and production, without a wholesale partner you need to manage the marketing, customer service, planning, shipping, and returns on your own.

- **Technology.** Investment in e-commerce platforms isn't cheap, and growth requires more sophisticated payment systems, inventory management, web hosting, customer service, and distribution technology.

- **Credibility.** Without a wholesale order in hand as proof of sales, it is more difficult to obtain production financing, such as a line of credit or a factor, or to convince suppliers and factories to work with you.

Design and Function

As mentioned, it's easy to set up a website on a platform such as Square Space or Shopify, and it's much less expensive than hiring a web developer. These platforms have a variety of design templates and e-commerce abilities with payment solutions. Eventually, as you grow, you may want a developer to create a site that can better integrate with your email marketing, analytics, accounting, shipping, and other systems.

Whether minimal or elaborate, every element of your website must reflect your brand guidelines. The colors, fonts, graphic layouts, and copy will work together with your content to bring your brand to life. Images and video must have strong impact and draw the viewer in. The copy and product descriptions, which communicate features and origin, should also add personality, value, and more reasons to buy.

Spend time researching other fashion e-commerce websites to see how they lead the customer through the site to the different products and eventually to the shopping cart. It should be fun and easy to choose favorites, make a wish list, share with friends, and find suggestions for complementary products and accessories. Make sure the pages load quickly, the search works well, and that it all looks just as good on a mobile device. Ask friends and family to test the browsing and purchasing experience on your website and offer suggestions to make it better.

The site should be updated regularly with fresh product and new photos, videos, and layouts. Highlight limited editions or one-of-a-kind pieces to bring more interest to the mix. Post media coverage or exciting company news such as collaborations, and find fresh ways to repeat both your unique story and the best attributes of your products. Don't forget to have an email sign-up opportunity and social media links on every page.

Inventory Issues

Online businesses need to have inventory to fulfill orders. Consumers want to purchase a product and have it shipped the same day. But as designer and educator Keanan Duffy says, "Inventory can be a killer."[4] It ties up cash, and you need to sell it at full price or risk training customers to expect discounts. It's very difficult to predict which colors or sizes will sell and to decide how much of each style to produce. Unsold inventory is wasteful and can be difficult to unload. Until you have a few years of experience and build some data, it's just trial and error. On-demand manufacturing is definitely an option worth exploring for online brands.

Pre-order

Pre-order can balance some of the risk and reduce some of the waste from estimating production quantities. Many designers offer a selection of new or special product by pre-order even as they create inventory for the rest. Some customers are eager to be first to a new item or style especially if there's a limited quantity. Pre-order generally doesn't work for items that are too similar to what is already available elsewhere—it should be something special. Most pre-orders require a deposit, which helps with cash flow for production. Be sure to set accurate delivery date expectations to avoid disappointing clients who could get tired of waiting and cancel their orders.

Limited Edition

Offering new styles or capsule collections, in small quantities, lets you test product and gauge response with less risk. If the limited-edition product sells out, you can increase quantities in the next production run and use the opportunity to incorporate any customer feedback, such as the heel being too high or the hem too short. Dropping limited-edition product throughout the year also keeps customers engaged so you can lead them back to your core product. The challenge here is to find production partners who will be flexible with their minimums. It may be helpful to increase the production quantities for your best sellers to encourage the factory to be patient with your test styles.

Customer Service

A designer, who ships all her own orders, came down with the flu after offering a big discount for "cyber Monday." She immediately sent out an email to all of her customers explaining that she was ill, and because she personally ships everything, the shipments would be delayed. Instead of angry responses, she received notes of condolences and understanding because she was honest and up front. Some local customers even offered to come and help her with the packing.

Communication Is Everything

Being open, honest, and responsive can build loyalty for life. Find ways to thank your customers and make them feel special. Ask them for feedback and respond quickly to their questions and comments. Include personal notes in your shipments, and offer repair services when it makes sense.

Mistakes will happen. Packages get lost and arrive late and orders end up wrong. When you make a mistake, own up to it immediately and fix it. Express your commitment to doing better and use the opportunity to make an extra effort to increase the loyalty of this customer. In addition to a sincere apology, offer a credit or free shipping for a future purchase.

Before you launch, go through the entire order and purchasing process yourself to see if there are parts that are confusing. Try to predict the questions that could arise, and make the answers easy to find. A FAQ section can answer common questions, especially around the shipping and delivery details and time frame. Make it easy via text, email, or messaging for customers to ask questions, and consider adding Live Chat to your site during times when someone is available to service it.

Products need clear and detailed descriptions of the materials, care instructions, and dimensions, and you definitely need an accurate sizing chart. After purchase, encourage your customers to write product reviews and customer comments, or conduct a survey to better understand ways to improve the product and service. A customer review section on your site can foster trust with new visitors and result in more sales.

Be sure to have secure and reliable payment systems to process credit cards, and include alternatives such as PayPal, Stripe, ApplePay, and payment plans such as Affirm and Afterpay. Be very clear on all of your policies, especially for returns. Don't forget to include terms of service and privacy policies that comply with the laws of where you do business.

Set Expectations for Shipping

Most customers expect free shipping, but it is very expensive for a small business and hard to accurately budget. Shipping costs vary by weight and distance, so a package to a nearby state may cost $10, but shipping the same item to California may cost $25, eating up the designer's margin. The best way to approach free shipping as a small business is to set a minimum order amount, such as $100 (depending on the price range of your products), to qualify. Or only offer free shipping on specific products. Free shipping offers are a good reward for first-time customers and as holiday promotions.

Set clear expectations for your customers regarding when their items will arrive. Specify whether the time includes days for processing and how the shipping time is affected by weekends and holidays. Be clear about taxes and shipping charges and explain how the policy is different for international orders.

Avoid Returns

Easy returns are the new normal and are a key reason consumers are willing to shop online. Many consumers and personal shoppers purposely buy multiple items with the intention of trying them all and returning at least some.

For the designer, returns are costly and time consuming. Avoiding returns should be your first priority. As shoe designer Ruthie Davis advises, "For a brand to be successful online, you cannot have a lot of returns. It is critical that your sizing is really consistent across every style. And we put a lot of energy into taking care of the customer and having personal shoppers available via email or Instagram to answer every question."[5] Again, take great care to make the product images and descriptions on your website clear and accurate. Include views on a model from multiple angles, along with high resolutions of fabric texture and close-ups of prints and details. Include product measurements and an accurate sizing chart for clothing and shoes. Descriptions should include details about the materials used and mention what size the model is wearing and whether the item runs small or large. Definitely ask for detailed reasons for all returns. If multiple customers are saying the same thing, you may want to make changes to the design or production.

Be extremely clear in your return and exchange policy. Include any restocking and shipping fees and requirements for timing, condition, and packaging of the item. For example:

"We gladly accept returns of full-priced merchandise for refund, exchange, or store credit. Items must be unworn, unwashed, undamaged, with the original tags attached. All items marked FINAL SALE are final. To qualify for a full refund, return authorizations must be requested within ten days of receiving your order. Items approved for return must be received by us within ten days of approval. Refunds will be processed after the return is received, minus the cost of shipping."

When drafting policies, spend some time online researching how other small brands handle their shipping and returns. While most start-up labels handle their own, as you build volume it's worth it to work with a fulfillment house or a shipping platform such as ShipStation to get the best shipping rates (see more about packing, shipping, and fulfillment centers in Chapter 7: Production).

Use the Sales Data

The analytics from actual online purchases is the most valuable data you own. You might have a vision of your perfect customer, but transactional data gives you truthful insight into exactly *who* is purchasing your product. This data will help you *refine* your content, communications, and customer service. Information on *when* customers are buying certain products, and which products are bought together or in multiples, can help you refine the merchandising and seasonal offerings on your site. The products that are regularly abandoned in the cart, and the merchandise that is never considered, should inform your policies, your pricing, and your product development.

Cybersecurity

Unfortunately, small businesses are often the targets of phishing schemes, ransomware attacks, fraud, and stolen data. Be vigilant with messages you receive about financial accounts, and make sure you confirm the validity of an email and the contact before you respond. Follow the PCI security standards for credit cards, and use verification systems and strong password management systems. Keep your website and software up to date, make use of anti-virus programs, and look into outsourcing security to a managed service provider.

Selling on Social Media

While social media is a critical marketing tool to drive sales on your website, it's also an important sales channel on its own. "Shoppable" posts, storefronts, pins, and tags all link customers to the designers' websites for purchase. But social media channels also offer ways for consumers to buy product without leaving their platform so they can buy from multiple brands in a single transaction. These opportunities can expose your product to new customers who are shopping other brands and make it more convenient for the customer to buy. The platforms charge a transaction fee for each purchase and sometimes charge an additional payment processing fee. Unfortunately, the platform owns the full customer data and, other than shipping, the designer loses control over the customer's purchasing experience. As with any opportunity, you need to weigh the benefits against the costs and maintenance to decide if it makes sense to try it for your brand.

Livestream

These shopping events feature influencers and hosts who present product online for immediate purchase on mobile apps. They host shopping tours of stores and showrooms to show, describe, and try on product while answering real-time questions from viewers. Initially popular in China, it is catching on throughout the world, with a lot of exciting potential for creative entertainment and interaction with your customers. ShopShops is one app that sells in China and also has an English-language version of its service.

Online Marketplaces

Brands can still make their first start on Etsy or on marketplaces specifically created for emerging fashion labels, such as NJAL and Nineteenth Amendment. These platforms facilitate the discovery of new brands and allow designers to test and sell product without the expense of building their own site and the pressure to lure all of their own traffic. Some also offer the advantages of on-demand production and fulfillment for all orders, eliminating the need to hold inventory. The downside is the lack of control over brand image and management of customer experience. Various platforms can add a "crafty" or "amateur" stigma to a brand, and some are curated better than others. While this approach can offer a designer a good first taste of running a business, it is challenging to build traction as a brand or achieve enough volume to sustain it.

Direct to Consumer: In Real Life

While e-commerce does drive sales, it simply cannot replace the human interaction and in-person experience of a brand.

Your Own Store

Having a store offers a valuable opportunity to control the image and the storytelling of your brand, as well as provide a steady revenue, higher margins, and in-person engagement with the customer. Designer Tory Burch launched her line with her own store in New York rather than launching through the traditional wholesale route. She felt that this would ensure consistency in the image and brand of the company and she could control more details regarding the store environment and the shoppers' experience.[6]

With their own store, a designer can get direct customer feedback, test product, and immediately see which sizes, colors, and styles sell best and to whom. A designer can still operate an online or wholesale business from the store, and use it as a showroom and as a place to sell overstock and merchandise returned from wholesale accounts.

But a store is an expensive and risky investment. Rent, equipment, fixtures, and staff add up, and you have to hold inventory and bring in new items on a regular basis to keep it fresh. Always test the market before opening a store. Host a pop-up or a trunk show, or participate in a local street fair or market. Choose your location carefully and try to negotiate the cost and duration of the lease with the landlord. A store can easily take up to a year to earn back the cash required to open it.

Running a store is a full-time job. Someone must be there to keep it open during regular retail hours and on weekends and holidays. If you are busy servicing customers, it is hard to find time to get to the factory to oversee production or to meet with fabric suppliers. As you hire help for your store, look for people who really believe in your product and mission and who will be passionate and informed when interacting with customers.

One advantage of having a store is the ability to host in-store events, such as collection previews, cocktail parties, and workshops, to keep it busy and attract new people. Be creative and align with artists, restaurants, and other neighborhood businesses to build community and generate buzz. Bring in other brands to flesh out the product offerings and appeal to more customers. Be sure to collect contact information from people who visit so you can keep them informed of sales, events, and the arrival of new merchandise.

Thea Grant: A Journey from Wholesale to Direct Retail

Thea Grant, launched by designers Thea Grant and Nico Bazzani, was a 95 percent wholesale company selling to stores globally, at trade shows, and through private appointments, but always with the middleman. Occasionally, they would participate in retail events and sample sales, and realized it was a great way to try new things and hear directly from the customer.

They set up a booth with friends at Brooklyn Flea, and Thea says, "After that it was like following bread crumbs. We could not sell the same product we were selling to Barneys NY and Anthropologie, so we started bringing many different items to the market and eventually started creating product based on what the customer liked." They added fine jewelry, signet rings, engagement rings, and wedding bands to meet demand while staying true to their antique aesthetic. They enjoyed the direct feedback and the ability to explore and test product and pricing.

When people started requesting custom items, Nico began creating pieces and stamping brass on the spot at the market. People were fascinated watching him work, and Thea and Nico realized that seeing something being made was as important as the final product. At this point, with their vintage antiques and tools, every aspect of the space and decor, the process, their personal style, and the product had come together fully, conveying the Thea Grant story to the customer. After two years at Brooklyn Flea, they slowly tapered off their wholesale accounts and opened their own Brooklyn store.

Thea says, "The amount of money we would make in a weekend or two at the Flea was the same as we were making at wholesale for a lot more product." At the market, they could control the story of the brand, interact with the customer, and add fresh product all the time—making it the week before instead of with the long lead times of wholesale.

She says if you compare the business to running, "Brooklyn Flea is like a sprint. There are thousands of people each day commenting, experiencing, and purchasing, and you have to be there when it's happening. Our store is the marathon. There is less foot traffic, and you need steady hours, certain comforts, and problem solving such as repairs, gift items, and custom work to slowly build community and ensure repeat customers. With wholesale, we were completely removed from the race—only allowed to be at the start and finish lines."[7]

Pop-Ups

Temporary pop-up stores are an opportunity for customers to experience your brand in a way they can't online. The designer gains access to in-person feedback and the chance to observe as customers touch and try on the product—without the risk and commitment of a permanent store. Pop-ups can reach a new audience, test a market, unload excess inventory, and drive traffic to your online community. Pop-ups can also be costly, so be clear on your goals and have a concrete plan to achieve them.

Location is key to the positioning of the brand and to attracting the right traffic. Rents vary based on location and ideally you should look for a space that includes electricity, insurance, and Wi-Fi. To sell product, you will need displays, inventory, and a reliable system to capture customer information and process payments. Agencies such as Parasol Projects in New York or Appear Here, which operates in several large cities around the world, can help you find the right space. It's good to get recommendations from others who have booked with the agency and who have had pop-ups in the area.

Once you have a space, bring in the right decor to express your brands personality and to attract people into the space. Partner with nearby restaurants, candy shops, art galleries, and flower shops to cross promote and fill the space. Maximize online promotion of the shop with daily offers, flash sales, guest curators, and in-store event announcements. Create a hashtag to encourage your visitors to spread the word. Be sure to capture email addresses, and give visitors an incentive to check out your website after the event.

Designers can save expenses by using their own studio spaces to occasionally invite VIP customers and key social media followers to "shop the showroom." This allows for a more intimate approach for customers who want to meet the designer and get a glimpse into the design process.

Markets and Events

Markets and events take place in cities and towns across the globe, offering designers, craftspeople, and artisans a chance to sell directly to the public in a fun atmosphere with food and entertainment. Designers can test product, make a little cash, unload samples, and connect with buyers and creators outside of their usual circle. Various events may highlight home and gift items, furniture, or artwork. Future and Fauna focuses on female makers, Field and Supply targets the interior design world, and others are tied to holidays or charitable causes. Music festivals and conferences such as the Women in the World Summit are a great fit for certain brands. Usually designers pay a fee to participate, but some organizers also charge transaction fees or take a commission on sales.

If you decide to participate in a shopping event, find the one with the right mix of designers and appropriate target market for your image and product. Some product categories do better at these events than others, and you should ask the organizers which vendors have the most success. Ask how and where they promote the event to ensure enough traffic, and do what you can to spread word of your participation.

Concession Models

Rather than buy or consign the collection, some stores or independent spaces offer designers an opportunity to sell product for a monthly fee and/or a percentage of their sales. The space curates a mix of brands and hosts events and programs to draw traffic. If a designer isn't selling in a physical space elsewhere, it can be a great opportunity to test product, spread the word, and meet your social media followers.

The spaces usually have their own staff, but you may want to hire your own people or man the space yourself during busy times to get the personal interface with customers. Definitely find a way to capture email addresses for people who visit the space, and ask the organizer for weekly sales reports and the related customer data. There is always a risk that the space won't draw enough customers and that the mix of other designers and products won't be positive for your brand. Visit the space several times in advance to get a sense of the traffic and ask the participating designers about their experience. Examples of these stores are Showfields in New York, Re:store in San Francisco, and The Canvas in both New York and Antwerp, which focuses on brands that address the United Nations Sustainability Goals.

Private Sales and Trunk Shows

Private clientele can boost your sales, help with cash flow, and become loyal advocates (or even investors) for your brand. Many designers hold trunk shows in various cities where customers can try on and purchase or pre-order product in an intimate and private setting. In some cases, clients host friends in their homes where they can meet the designer and shop together. Designers also travel on multi-city tours hosting their trunk shows in high-end hotel suites.

A trunk show format can also involve partnering with a local retailer who invites its own customers to meet you and shop the line. This is a great way for the retailer to test a new brand and for designers in different product categories to cross promote and share customers. Brooklyn designer Christine Alcalay holds a regular trunk show at the store of a hat designer in LA who has a similar product price point. Her clothes complement the hats, and they both invite their customers to introduce them to each other's brands. She says, "You have to be smart about it. When I do trunk shows, I call the store before I go and ask what sells really well in the store, what is the weather, what is the customer like—so I know which product to bring."[8]

Co-working spaces, hair salons, and other businesses occasionally host trunk shows for jewelry and other product to offer something new to their clients. Be sure to promote the event in advance and invite wholesale buyers from local stores where you want to sell.

Made to Order

Made-to-order businesses focus on custom garments for individuals. The financial risk is low because there's no need to invest in materials or production until there is an order. The margins are high and the client pays a deposit. Menswear designer Paul Marlow was a finalist in the CFDA/Vogue Fashion Fund with his brand Loden Dager. He now runs an exclusive made-to-measure custom suit and shirt business. He says, "It's a different approach to satisfying customers. They end up with something that fits them like nothing has ever fit them before. The greatest compliment for me is when a client says I have ruined the rest of their suits."[9]

Individual customers are time consuming because you have to service each one. But this leads to loyal clients who will spread the word. Paul Marlow says his business growth relies entirely on word of mouth. "When my customers wear their suits and feel good in them, people notice. It's much more effective than an Instagram story."

It takes many individual customers to build enough volume to sustain a custom business. Ideally, you want to try to grow the amount that each client orders, rather than just the total number of customers. Social media and press can help spread the word, as does traveling to different cities to host trunk shows in a client's home or a luxury hotel suite. Ask clients to invite others who may be interested in bespoke clothing.

Wholesale

Many still believe that wholesaling to retail stores is the best sales route for new designers. The stores are known by consumers and they have the resources to quickly build a customer base for an unknown brand. The buyers have data to predict sales and place specific orders so you know how much to produce. As Tim Moore of Hilldun advises, "Start first with wholesale as that is very simple. You get orders, you figure out your financing, you know exactly how much to produce, you deliver, and you get paid."[10]

Keep in mind, the goal is not just to get the merchandise into the stores. When you sell to a store, you partner to achieve a common goal. You both believe the customers will want what you design and will pay the price to buy it. While it is exciting to have a store interested in buying your designs, smart selling requires a careful strategy for working with the right stores, negotiating the best terms, and helping the goods sell.

Types of Stores

Department stores. Designers want to be in department stores because of the prestige, exposure, and sales volume they can provide. One buyer from a department store such as Saks Fifth Avenue can land your merchandise in 20 locations across the country, dramatically growing the business and providing economies of scale for sourcing and production. The department stores have established customers and regular traffic and benefit from extensive promotional budgets and online sales reach. They can put new designers in the company of established, highly desirable brands. However, department stores also put significant stress on designers to contribute to their margins and to cover their costs. Many are owned by large public companies pressured to make money for their shareholders. Their decisions are based on daily sales and don't allow time for a new designer's business to develop.

There is a saying that at department stores "the clothes are on wheels." The store wants to wheel the clothes in completely prepped for the sales floor and, if they don't sell, wheel them back out without any loss or responsibility. Big brands, such as Ralph Lauren, essentially rent real estate from these stores. They spend thousands of their own dollars to build branded areas in the stores and hire the people who staff them. It can be difficult for a small brand to compete in this arena.

Boutique and specialty stores. New designers should start by selling to small boutiques, and many continue working primarily with small stores once they are well established. Small boutiques are more flexible regarding delivery, and they share in the risk. They expect to pay in full for their orders and don't demand markdown money or issue significant charge backs. If they return items that didn't sell, they are more likely to accept credit for next season rather than demand a refund. Working with small boutiques allows you to keep more control, to try out new things, and to make sure you have your production thoroughly in order before you enter the department store business.

A product that doesn't sell well in a big department store may do well in a small boutique. Department stores tend to overbuy, and your label must compete with hundreds of others on a crowded floor with bulging racks and too few salespeople. In a small store, the owner is generally the buyer, knows the customer well, and buys specifically for them. The sales staff in the store often includes the owner or is made up of people whom the owner personally hired and trained.

Working with smaller stores does have its challenges. Each store needs to be tracked and serviced separately, regardless of how big or small its order. Each believes it is your most important account, and because it places small orders, you may need several stores to buy an item to meet its production minimums. Most importantly, small stores are less known and can be financially unstable. They may go out of business or simply not pay. You have to be meticulous about checking their credit before accepting an order. As designer Andy Salzer of Hiro Clark states, "Servicing small boutiques and special 'cool' stores is often harder than servicing the big box retailers. Boutiques are great for brand recognition and testing new ideas, but on the flip side, they often order just three of something or don't pay for six months."[11] Some of the more influential and trendsetting boutiques want to buy on consignment or demand discounts because they know the designers really want to sell there. These key boutiques can be instrumental in building a new brand, but they won't necessarily contribute to your profitability.

Chain stores and boutiques. Some multi-label boutiques, such as Intermix, have numerous locations, which increases their influence and the size of their buy. As a result, many make the same demands as department stores. Other national chains, such as Anthropologie, buy new designer product and partner to sell the product either under the designer's own label or as private-label merchandise for the store. Any of these accounts can launch a new label in multiple markets, but they also increase the risk of doing too much business with a single customer. While it is efficient to grow the amount of product with each account, designers should not rely too heavily on one customer for the majority of their sales. If the store drops you or goes bankrupt like Barneys NY, it can put you out of business. You need to spread the risk over multiple accounts.

Global opportunities. Overseas stores open the door to entirely new markets. It's best to focus first on selling and delivering successfully one at a time and slowly expand to others. For many young designers, their first overseas accounts are in Japan, where there is interest in new labels and the stores are very reliable in paying on time. There are also lucrative markets in Europe, other parts of Asia, and South America.

In general, the rules are the same, but there are additional challenges. It is more difficult to collect late payment from a store on the other side of the world than from one across town. If you are far away, people may try to take advantage of you and offer consignment or difficult terms. Factoring, COD terms, and letters of credit will help protect you, but if you aren't working with a showroom, you may want to ask for payment up front and only sell to the stores that agree. Fortunately, markdown money and charge backs are less prevalent overseas, but there are differences in labeling requirements, sizing, payment terms, markups, sales commissions, and contracts. Shipping and insurance costs are high, plus there is duty and the expense of handling overseas returns and customer service. All of the costs can fluctuate with foreign exchange rates and trade disputes. A designer needs to adjust their pricing to cover the variance in costs and the shipping terms. Lead times are longer for shipping, customs paperwork can cause delays, and you can't deliver late in overseas markets, either! Delivery times may differ dramatically in a foreign market, putting additional strain on your production.

To land overseas accounts, you can contact specific stores directly. Some large department stores have buying offices in New York, London, and other large cities or make regular buying trips overseas. Other methods include participating in overseas trade shows or hiring a showroom in the market where you want to be.

Alternatively, a distributor can represent you in another country. Distributors buy goods directly from the designer at a significant discount. They handle credit checks, delivery, and collecting from each store. Many designers advise that to really grow in Japan and other markets, you must have a distributor agreement. Designer and educator Keanan Duffty says, "Distribution agreements are the only way to go overseas. It's too much hassle to collect payment, deal with customs, and negotiate who pays shipping and landing duty with dozens of small foreign stores."[12] A distribution deal can also provide pricing leverage with fabric suppliers and factories. But like everything else, with a distributor there are risks. You must thoroughly check their credit and have a lawyer review the agreement, because there can be big differences in law and business methods from country to country. Research the distributor's other clients and pay attention to how it promotes them. Distributors can hurt your brand by oversaturating the market, selling to the wrong stores, and discounting your product.

Online multi-brand stores. Net-a-Porter, Matchesfashion, and Shopbop are just a few of the online stores selling millions of dollars of designer fashion each year. They have the power to extend your market reach globally and bring thousands of new customers to your brand. Online stores capture extensive information the buyer can share with you about where your product sells best and who exactly is buying it. They have marketing and promotion budgets and email lists to bring more traffic to their site and more exposure to you.

There are a thousands of online stores and many appeal to specific customers and product. Some specialize in expensive, high-end labels; some in edgy new lines; and others in fun contemporary product. As with any store, you need to make sure the site is right for your product and will draw the appropriate customers. Find out what it will do to promote and support you and if your merchandise will be included in their emails, social media, and website editorial.

Do Your Research

Often, when asked where they want to wholesale, new designers predictably list the same high-end, high-profile stores, such as Bergdorf Goodman, Dover Street Market, or Net-a-Porter. I can't stress enough how important it is to research carefully and find the stores that are right for your specific line. Designers must target places that cater to their customers and have the appropriate product mix.

If you aspire to sell to a specific store, go there in real life or online and study it. Look at the layout of each floor and each section of the website. Review the merchandise, visual display, and price points. Observe the customers and how the store markets to them. Before you contact a buyer, you need to know exactly which floor your product should be on and what designers you should be next to in terms of aesthetic, price point, and customer target. Note whether the store has lines similar to yours or if you would fill a gap. Research where your competitors sell to discover new places.

Talk to the salespeople in the store and ask them what sells well, what doesn't, and which items fly off the floor as soon as they arrive. Ask them about your competition and the lines you admire—how many deliveries do they have and how do they support the product? Find out what items are on a wait list and notice the merchandise on sale because those things won't be reordered. Review the store's social media accounts to see how they present the merchandise to their customers and how they communicate. Read comments to see how customers engage with them.

This research will help you significantly at your sales appointments. The buyer will see that you have done your homework and are serious about working with them. As Susanne Rehnstrom, owner of W29 Showroom, says, "Invest money on going to the store and get to know the market and meet the buyers and sales people. That makes a big impression. There is so much fashion out there—it often comes down to 'who do you want to do business with?'"[13]

Be Selective

Wholesale is not about trying to sell to just anyone. You want to carefully select the stores where you sell and create strong retail partnerships that feel authentic to your brand. Choose stores with a strong point of view that promote and support the smaller brands. Build your accounts slowly to avoid excess inventory and to control quality and image. Be strategic about adding the right partners to reach new types of customers or to enter a new market.

The best store for your product is wherever your customer shops. As designer Lindsey Thornburg, who designs her signature cloaks from Pendleton wool blankets says, "You have to be creative. My cloaks do the best in western and mountain towns and with wealthy people and celebrities. I try to reach them when they are in a 'vacation' or 'away' mindset and can be a little more detached from the cycle of fashion. So where do they stay?" She currently sells at luxury properties including Paws Up, the Yellowstone Club, and the Ranch at Rock Creek.[14]

Know the Risks

Stores do not like risk, and they put pressure on designers in numerous ways to share costs and guarantee profit. A designer must understand the store policies and make her own retail terms and conditions known on sales agreements and forms. Realize that stores make exceptions all the time. *Negotiate everything.* In the end, you must weigh the pros and cons of each demand and decide if the account is worth it.

Charge backs. Fees charged to the designer for not meeting specific requirements of the store are called charge backs. Do what you can to keep these charges to a minimum. They add up quickly, can eliminate your margin, and can damage your relationships with buyers, factors, and your showroom. Most department and chain stores have strict policies for packaging, labeling, and shipping product. They may require clothing to arrive on specific hangers, while other items need to be poly-bagged. Product may need to be pre-ticketed for the sales floor, and both the packing slip and the shipping label must include specific information. Department stores provide a *routing guide*—an extensive document that outlines all of their requirements—and if you don't follow it precisely, you will be charged. The charges are expensive—$0.10 per item for not attaching price tags, $5 per carton for no packing slip, $60 for boxes that exceed the weight requirement, $250 for sending a box to the wrong address. Charge backs may also be issued if items arrive damaged or need to be repaired at the store. Many retailers keep copies of their routing guide on their websites under "vendor relations."

The best way to avoid charge backs is to read the routing guide carefully, and if there are requirements you can't meet, tell the store up front. When you receive a charge back form, inquire immediately if a charge is unjustified. Don't be intimidated; you *can* dispute it.

Markdown money and guaranteed sell-through. Guaranteed sell-through requires the designer to agree that a certain percentage of goods will sell at full price. If that percentage doesn't sell, the store can charge the designer *markdown money* or a *markdown allowance* to cover the loss when the goods are put on sale. For example, if you sign a sell-through agreement of 70 percent and 72 percent of the goods sell at full price, you won't have to pay markdown money.

But if only 60 percent of the goods sell at full price, the store can require you to pay money to cover the markdown for the 10 percent that was guaranteed, as well as for the remaining 30 percent.

The arrangement protects the stores by taking the risk out of the buy and allowing them to overbuy. Big manufacturers are able to support these policies because they have high volume and still make a profit with the markdowns. But for small companies, the allowances eat up profit quickly. Many designers and showrooms successfully refuse markdown allowances and guarantees by explaining that the company is too small to support the policy financially. Showroom owner Greg Mills advises designers to say no to markdown allowances or at least negotiate.[15] Tell them you will agree to the sell-through guarantee if they make a commitment to buy for the next two years or offer the markdown money as a credit toward their next season's order. Ultimately, the best approach is to try to sell only what you believe the store can sell at full price.

Discounts. Most department stores, chains, and online stores expect to receive a discount off the wholesale price. Their reasoning is that they buy in greater quantities and will sell more product in total. The discount can range from 3 percent to 15 percent and can dangerously eat up your profit. Decide how much you think the store can sell for you and whether being there will lead to bigger buys and other accounts. For example, a store like Bergdorf Goodman can be very important to new designers, even if they don't sell much. Being there grants prestige to a brand, and if buyers from other stores see your label there, it can result in new business. If you really want to be in a store, determine whether you can afford to give the discount and try to negotiate. The better your relationship with the buyer, and the better the goods sell at the store, the more bargaining power you have.

Cancellations and returns. Stores will return merchandise for a multitude of reasons, including overshipment, unauthorized substitutions, bad fit, early or late delivery, low sell-through, or defect. While some reasons for returns or cancellations are justified, stores may try to refuse shipments without cause or return them for absurd reasons. One designer received a large department store order for a blouse, but before delivery, the buyer saw a knockoff version of the blouse in a fast fashion store window and canceled the order.

If merchandise is returned, first try to fix or replace the unacceptable product and get it back to the store immediately. If you can't replace the items, ask the store to accept a credit for next season, rather than refunding any money. If the merchandise is old, don't accept it. When one department store tried to return styles to a designer that it had held for eight months, the designer rightly refused the return.

Another designer had a dress returned to the store by a customer who had worn it once, leaving yellow stains in the armpits. The store returned the entire shipment of dresses to the designer, even though only one dress was affected and the stains were probably caused by the customer's deodorant. If something like this happens, try to push the responsibility back on the store or take one garment back to do an inspection before accepting the entire return.

To avoid returns, always call the store before you ship. Many stores require designers to make a *delivery appointment* with the receiving department; failure to keep these appointments results in a charge back. Try to negotiate if a store wants to cancel. A designer had a store call mid-production to cancel an order, and the designer simply refused based on the fabric's being purchased, cut, and already on the machines. The negotiation resulted in a tedious shipment plan, sending small batches every few weeks, but at least the merchandise made it into the store.

Making the Sale
Whom to Contact

For small boutiques, you will often be dealing with the owner of the store. The bigger stores have fashion directors whose job is to find the next new thing, and they spend considerable time researching new sources. If the store has a fashion director, contact that person first. You can also call a store or ask a salesperson for the name of the buyer who covers the specific section or category in which you should sell. You can also identify the right people on LinkedIn and other social platforms. Once you have the contact, start by sending a message or an email with a strong image to entice them to visit your Instagram or website.

When to Contact

Get your collections ready early. Many buying decisions are made before market week, when the stores have their full budgets for the season. Womenswear designers should try to meet the buyers a few weeks before New York Fashion Week and the trade shows. The menswear market officially takes place in mid-July and mid-January, but buyers ideally want to start seeing samples in late June or December. If you sell early, you will be able to start production early and avoid being pushed to the back of the line at the factory.

Once market week comes, buyers are besieged by dozens of brands all vying for their attention. They have limited budgets for new sources, and if you wait, you may miss out. If you simply don't have anything ready to show early, you might be better off waiting until market is finished and the buyers are less busy and are spending any reserve money. Realize that in this case, you will have less time to produce and more challenge in meeting the required delivery dates.

In reality, buyers are interested in new items to keep the store fresh year-round. Some have bigger budgets for pre-collections, such as Resort and pre-Fall, which are delivered between the main collections.

Traditional Sales and Delivery Dates		
Collection	**Sales Dates**	**Delivery Dates**
Spring Womenswear	Mid-August through October	Late January and February
Spring Menswear	Late June and July	January
Fall Womenswear	Mid-January through March	August and September
Fall Menswear	January through February	August
Pre-Fall	November	May
Resort/Cruise	June/July	November

*Accessories and shoes are generally planned and purchased in sync with ready-to-wear.

As mentioned in Chapter 7: Production, there is much dissatisfaction among designers around the sales and delivery calendars. Many believe the early delivery of pre-collections leads to mid-season discounting rather than waiting until the end of the season to put things on sale. If deliveries were closer to the season, when the consumers actually need the goods, they would be more likely to sell at full price. Industry leaders, designers, and retailers are working together under the umbrella of Rewiring Fashion to develop a calendar that makes better sense for all. Regardless of where they net out, as a small brand, it's best to be early.

Landing an Appointment

First, contact a buyer by sending them a few strong images of product by email or message with a link to your online portfolio or digital lookbook. Include a brief sentence or two about you and the line. It should provide a quick and enticing taste of your product to encourage the buyer to see more and to give them a point of reference when you follow up.

Be professional and allow them a little time to respond. Don't contact a buyer more than once per week, but do follow up as they are busy and often need reminding. Send a new image or fresh news to get their attention. Buyers are busy so be brief. If you email, give them all the information in one concise email so when they go back to it, everything they need is right there. If you don't hear back, follow up with another message or a quick, concise phone call. Be professional as you introduce yourself, and remind the buyer of the email or message and ask for an appointment. Mention anything that makes you stand out, such as successful sell-through at another store, a large social media following, celebrity clients, or unique production. Don't ramble on or your good impression will fizzle quickly. Most of the time you will get their voice mail, so leave a brief, polite message with your name, contact number, and reference to what you have sent. For a designer, it can be nerve-racking to pick up the phone and place these calls, but it will get easier over time, and gradually you will develop relationships with the buyers.

Keep in mind that buyers are contacted by hundreds of people each week. If they are short on the phone or in their DMs or emails, it's not personal. If the buyer responds with a no, ask for feedback in hopes that you can learn from it.

If you send emails through an email platform such as MailChimp, you can see whether an email has been opened. If a buyer has opened the email several times, they are probably interested and you should make a bigger effort to sell to them by calling or contacting them on social media. When you just can't get a response, be creative and think about what you can do to help them see a link between your product and their store. Follow, comment, and share on their social media. Research to see if there is something they personally love that authentically relates to your collection. It won't go unnoticed if you make a sincere effort.

The Appointment

Once you get in the door, be concise and to the point; buyers have limited time. Present your collection in a professional, friendly manner. Share your successes, such as a strong e-commerce business, loyal followers, and media coverage. Let your store research pay off to make it easy for the buyer. Explain how the product fills a void in the market and how it will specifically fit into this store. Have your pricing, options, and delivery dates ready.

What Do They Look For?

There is already plenty of product in the marketplace so the stores are interested in "new," and buyers look to fill a gap and avoid repetition of the lines they already carry. Many stores carry the same large brands, and the buyers rely on the small designers for the "spice" that brings excitement and innovation to the store. A clear and authentic brand vision is critical, as well as a product that makes sense or fills a need for their customer.

There are buyers who are mostly interested in hype: the social following, the celebrities, and who else is buying it. One buyer says, "If you don't have at least 30,000 followers on your Instagram, you are not on our radar." However, others say that while buzz might make them reconsider a designer or item if they are on the fence, it won't sway them on something they don't like.

Your collection must have "hanger appeal" to look good as well as a good story to attract customers and help it sell. Buyers also look at the value and the quality of the production and how well the silhouettes, colors, and fabrics fit with current trends. Some stores are more trend-driven than others. P45 in Chicago focuses on promoting individual style; therefore, owner Tricia Tunstall does not go to market looking for trends. If sequins are hot, she may buy a few sequined items from her best designers, but in general, she feels that trends too often cause customers to burn out on a good thing.[16]

Consistency is key. Buyers want to look at the product and immediately understand your viewpoint, even if they don't like it. They look for a clear identity that stays consistent from season to season. The price point must also make sense for the store.

The buyer also must believe that you are ready as a business. The store's credibility is on the line, and buyers need to be confident in your production ability and quality control. Business stamina is important as well. Buyers don't want to pick up a line, promote it, and start building your customer base just to have you burn out financially, flake on your deliveries, and leave them hanging. You are a risk, and as we've already established, stores don't like risk.

Buyers Are a Great Resource

Buyer feedback is important whether or not they buy (and whether or not you agree with them). They know what sells and what succeeds. Listen to their comments as they review the line and note what they do or don't like. The meeting is a rare opportunity for free, qualified advice that can help enormously with development of the line and with the next sales appointment. However, keep in mind that retailers tend to look back too much at what worked well in the past. A designer needs to weigh the feedback against her own vision and make sure she stays true to the focus and direction of the line.

When a buyer sees a new designer, he may pick up the designer right away, but more often will wait a season or two. Accessories are easier to pick up quickly because they require less space, but generally before a buyer commits to any line, he will watch to see if the business is stable and the product is creatively consistent from season to season. Don't be afraid to ask the buyer directly, "What do I have to do to have a place at your store?"

After the appointment, promptly send a thank-you note and provide any requested information or materials and a confirmation if they placed an order. If the store doesn't order, remember that rejection is not personal. Send them periodic emails with product updates and brand news to keep you top of mind.

Technology for Sales

Even before the COVID-19 crisis canceled trade shows or moved them online, buyers struggled with the time and expense required to leave their stores and travel to the many shows and different markets to buy. Increasingly, technology is offering alternatives for selling that are efficient for designers and buyers alike. Wholesale ordering platforms, such as NuORDER, Joor, and Zedonk, make buying and reordering items much easier for the buyer. The designer pays a fee to link their inventory to the system so buyers can search by brand or browse specific product categories and place orders. Generally, the platforms work best for core product, basics, and items that are easy to understand. Some of the platforms create invoices, monitor inventory, and even link to accounting software such as Quickbooks. Brands and showrooms also host virtual markets on platforms, such as Zoom, complete with models to show the fit and movement of the garments. Three-dimensional fit technology, 360 views, avatars, and high-definition close-ups of materials and fibers will increasingly give buyers more confidence in placing orders online.

The Order

Only take orders you can produce and deliver on time. An enthusiastic buyer who loves your product and wants to place a large order may seem like a dream come true, but you need to be realistic and up front about what you can and can't do. Generally, first orders are small, and chain or department stores will test a new vendor in one or two locations. Designer Rebecca Taylor warned not to take on too many department store doors or locations too soon. She shipped more than 20 doors at Saks Fifth Avenue in her first season and says, "They came back with some charge backs and it practically put us out of business right then and there."[17] She recommends shipping only six doors at the most in the beginning.

Large orders require more up-front financing and create more risk of shipping and delivery problems, charge backs, and returns. Large orders leave you more vulnerable if the store cancels. It's better to keep the stores wanting more than to end up with a surplus of unsold or discounted inventory. If you let a store buy too much, you risk overexposure, bad sell-through, and discounts, which train customers to expect to buy your brand on sale.

Know your production schedule, and if the buyer requests a delivery date you can't guarantee, don't take the order. Try to negotiate the date. Be up front and tell the buyer you don't want to jeopardize her business and therefore need to wait until she can provide more lead time. While some designers have successfully taken on crazy deadlines just to land an important account, there is significant risk. If the store is important and you miss the delivery or have a quality issue because of the rush, it won't order from you again.

Delivery Dates

As your business grows, offering more deliveries can spread out the production payments and help with cash flow. The buyers like to keep fresh product flowing into the store, and additional deliveries each season provide more opportunity to sell and stay in contact with the buyers. However, you do not need to design new product for each delivery. Small designers should aim to create two collections a year and spread those out in multiple drops. You may start with one or two deliveries each season and eventually grow to have ten or more per year. Eventually, an annual schedule could include three Spring deliveries, three Fall deliveries, one for pre-Fall, and another for Resort.

Generally, designers break up their deliveries by category. For example, the first Fall delivery would be T-shirts, lightweight pants, and jackets. The second would be heavier fabrics and fall colors, and the third would be winter coats. Seasonless product can be delivered year-round.

Most often, the designer sets the delivery dates, but the store sets the terms, which affect the dates. For example, for Spring, the designer may set a date, such as January 30, or specify a window, such as January 15 to January 30 to allow some flexibility. The store may specify a start date, which is when it will begin to accept the goods, or it may ask that the goods be delivered "as ready." There is always a cancel or complete date, which is the final deadline for delivery. If product arrives after this date, the store can refuse it with no obligation. Stores with very fashion-forward customers may request early delivery to get fresh product on the floor before their competitors. For example, while most Spring menswear deliveries are in January, these stores may want delivery as soon as December 15.

As previously mentioned, designers should strive to deliver on the early side of the window to have the product in the store longer with more time to sell at full price. But only promise what you can truly achieve according to your production ability.

Is It Worthwhile?

Know the quantity of each item you need to sell to justify producing it. Consider your factory minimums, and if an order is too small, decide if it's worth it to pay the high sample cost to make it. Sometimes a special item is worth producing because it draws attention to the rest. In some cases, you may be able to make up the production numbers with direct sales on your own website. Once you have all of your orders for the season, you may need to call the buyers to drop a style. Communicate this as soon as possible. Although the buyer won't be happy, they understand minimums and expect this to happen occasionally. Try to get the buyer to replace the dropped item with another style in your line, rather than just canceling the order. Tell the buyer about other pieces that have been best sellers or point out similar styles. It's worth communicating the quantity you need to sell to produce the dropped style. If the buyer really wants it, he might adjust the order to meet the minimum.

Production limitations can be used to your advantage. Menswear label Duckie Brown often has only enough fabric to make a limited number of each jacket style, and its sales representative tells the buyer this up front. The limited quantity makes the jacket more exclusive and creates demand. It's okay to be sold out.[18]

The Selection

A great collection can look terrible on the store rack if the selection is wrong, and a buyer can make you look good or bad depending on what is chosen. Several designers caution against letting a store order too many of one style. A large rack with all the same style can look like a sale rack, and customers might assume no one wanted it.

It's important to keep some control. Make suggestions on the right styles, sizes, and color combinations for the market. While some buyers have a great sense for curating a collection and know what works for their store and customer, others need to be coached and pushed to take risks. Have options ready. For example, if a dress is at a high price point because it's made from expensive silk jersey, offer the dress in cotton as a lower-priced option. Avoid overexposure by mixing up the selection between different stores. Try to avoid having the same offerings everywhere. Once you assist the buyer with the selection, step back to avoid pressuring them when writing the order.

When buyers review a line, they look at both collections and items. Key items are often where they see themselves doing the most volume. Some designers are reluctant to sell items to a buyer who isn't interested in the whole collection, but showroom owner Denise Williamson says, "Designers should be flexible on that. The buyer knows what the store wants and if he sees the potential within the blouses, and that's what he really wants to promote in the store, I think it's great. It's a stepping stone. Perhaps next season he will come and say those blouses did so well, the pants look great too, let's add those on."[19]

Special Requests

Buyers often ask designers to alter product or even create a special item to round out a collection or fit a trend. They may want a skirt to be shortened or request special colors or fabrics. It's important to listen to wholesale customers and help them meet the shoppers' demands. However, when making special items for stores, there are no guarantees. If it doesn't sell, the designer is stuck with something they didn't intend to produce in the first place. Designers shouldn't agree to special requests unless it makes sense for their line. If a buyer requests crochet and crochet is not what you do, no one will win. Buyer influence can also push a designer too far into the mainstream, diluting what makes the brand special.

Exclusives

Stores compete to differentiate themselves and have unique offerings for their customers. They don't want to sell the same items as their competitors, especially if they are in close proximity to each other, and so they ask designers for the exclusive on their line. An *exclusive* means you can only sell the line to that store according to the terms of agreement.

Exclusive is loosely defined and changes according to each retailer. Some specify a geographic area. For example, in New York, an uptown exclusive may mean you can only sell to Bergdorf Goodman uptown, but you can still sell to The Webster downtown. A Los Angeles store may require the exclusive for a five-mile radius and a Midwestern boutique may require the exclusive for their state. Some exclusives specify a particular competitive store, and most require a period of time, such as a season or two, before the line can go elsewhere. Online stores such as Net-a-Porter and MatchesFashion often sign online exclusives with designers for a number of seasons.

Exclusivity is not always a bad thing for a new designer. You don't want to over-distribute your product and if you are new to wholesale, it gives you a chance to test your production and make sure you can deliver on time before you expand to more partners. Womenswear designer and *Project Runway* contestant Alison Kelly designed an exclusive collection for Shopbop and says, "It was a very good move for me, as it was my first wholesale order and I felt I could handle only one retailer that season."[20]

Loyalty is important to the buyer when they take a risk on a new name. When Tricia at P45 in Chicago picks up a new designer, she wants the exclusive in the city at least for one year in exchange for helping to launch the designer. When deciding between exclusives, be strategic and pick the store that supports you the most with marketing, placement, and good payment terms. Showroom owner Denise Williamson says that from her point of view, "You should never promise an exclusive until you see the actual order. If the order amounts to $3,000, it's probably not beneficial to your business to only be at that one store. If it's a $15,000 order and the store is willing to get behind you with promotions, an in-store event, or by putting merchandise in the windows, it probably is worth it."[21]

If a buyer really wants the exclusive, ask for promotional support, such as inclusion in their store catalog, email blasts, and online editorials, to be part of the deal. Be wary on multi-season exclusives, which could limit your expansion as sales increase. Try to keep the door open for renegotiation each season. Be *very clear* on the definition of exclusive. Most large online exclusives will still allow you to sell on your own website and in brick-and-mortar stores. If you really don't want to agree to a collection exclusive, you can offer exclusive items to be sold only at that store. Even if you have exclusives, stay in contact with other stores in the area. Designer Alicia Bell once had an exclusive with a store in Texas, and another nearby store wanted the goods. When the original store suddenly closed down, she was able to transfer the product to the other store, avoiding returns and ending up with an even larger order.[22]

Immediates

Retailers often want fresh product delivered quickly in response to a cultural moment, an issue with another brand, or new trend caused by a celebrity or influencer. The ability to fill *immediates* can help a designer land an elusive store or seize the opportunity when another brand cancels a delivery and the buyer needs a quick replacement. At trade shows, many designers offer immediate delivery on specific items. While it may be tempting to overcut best sellers to use for immediate delivery during the season, there is always a chance that the store won't reorder and you will be stuck with the overstock.

Immediate can mean tomorrow if you already have the items, but at others times, it depends on how quickly you can produce. Anywhere from two to five weeks is considered immediate. Despite the incremental sales and increased cash flow provided by these orders, a designer has to be honest about what can be managed. Immediates increase the pressure to produce and deliver quickly and can cause confusion in the simultaneous production and selling of other collections.

The Purchase Order

The purchase order should include the store's delivery address and billing address, the style number and description of each item ordered (including fabric option, size, and color), the quantity of each, the price of each, and the correct delivery due date. The order form should be numbered and include your company information and terms (see the following sample).

Sample Order Form

Designer Name	Customer P.O. _____
Designer Address	
Designer phone and fax	Department No. _____
BILL TO _____	SHIP TO _____
ADDRESS _____	ADDRESS _____
CITY _____	CITY _____
STATE _____ ZIP _____	STATE _____ ZIP _____
PHONE _____	PHONE _____
FAX _____	FAX _____
BUYER NAME _____	ORDER DATE _____
TERMS 6/30	START DATE As Ready
SHIP VIA UPS	COMPLETE DATE 6/30
SALESPERSON _____	IN STORE DATE _____

SPECIAL INSTRUCTION:

			A	29	30	31	32	33	34	35			
			B	2	4	6	8	10	12	14			
			C	XS		S		M		L			
Style	Color	Description	D								Total Units	Unit Price	Total
2417	Navy	Wrap Tee			1		2		2		6	20 00	120 00
2789	Beige	Pocket Skirt				2	2	2	2		8	39 00	312 00

THIS ORDER SUBJECT TO TERMS AND CONDITIONS AS NOTED ON OTHER SIDE OF THIS FORM	TOTAL	432 00

BUYERS SIGNATURE _____

TERMS AND CONDITIONS

1. This order is an offer upon the terms below that cannot be withdrawn by Buyer prior to cancellation date. It shall be a binding contract upon acceptance by Seller. Seller shall indicate acceptance by shipment of goods to Buyer. Buyer understands that certain styles and/or sizes and/or colors may be unavailable. Buyer will accept all available styles, sizes, and colors.

2. This order is not cancelable prior to completion date and shall be subject to the terms and conditions.

3. No returns accepted without Seller's written permission.

4. Seller will not issue credit for any allowances, deductions, or materials returned unless Buyer obtains the Seller's written consent of same within 14 days of receipt of goods.

5. Any merchandise returned to Seller which is not found to have been non-confirming in breach of the herein warranty shall be returned to Buyer.

6. Buyer shall be responsible for all shipping costs incurred in returning the allegedly non-conforming merchandise to Seller and the merchandise must be shipped pre-paid.

7. Deliveries against this order are subject to credit approval by the Seller's credit department and/or its factor at time of shipment. Seller or its factor may, at any time and from time to time, in its sole discretion, limit or cancel credit of the buyer as to time and amount, and as a consequence, may require anticipation or demand payment in cash for delivery of any untitled portion of this order.

8. Terms are F.O.B shipping point and title passes to Buyer upon delivery to buyer or the carrier.

9. Prices on this order are based on present contracts for finished garments, yarns, fabric, and supplies, and on present labor cost. Should prices for any items be increased, the prices on this order will be subject to increase.

10. All orders are taken subject to delays or non-delivery caused by any reason beyond our control.

11. All claims must be made within five days of receipt of goods.

12. Past due charges at the rate of 1½% times the prime rate will be accessed on invoices not paid when due.

13. No waiver, amendment, or modification of this agreement by Seller shall be effective unless in writing and signed by Seller. No failure or delay by Seller in exercising any right, power, or remedy shall operate as a waiver of the right, power, or remedy. No waiver of any term, condition, or default of this agreement by Seller shall be construed as a waiver of any other term/condition or default.

14. To be Shipped By means Day By which goods are shipped from our warehouse.

15. C.O.D POLICY
    a. A 25% to 50% deposit is required at the time each purchase order is written.
    b. All shipments must be paid by cash or certified check.
    c. All or any part of the order that is not accepted is subject to a non-refund or your deposit. If a shipment is refused there will $50.00 handling fee deducted from your deposit.
    d. Your deposit amount will be applied towards your outstanding balance once the last shipment of the corresponding purchase order.
    e. Due to processing, The Shipper will be allowed to ship 15 days after completion date.
    f. Your store will be contracted before any shipment is made. If you do not respond to our initial call (with an approval) within 7 days, your order will be considered cancelled and your deposit will not be refunded.

All the pertinent information should be in writing. Review the terms and make sure they work for you. Confirm who is paying the cost of shipping and insurance. FOB (free on board) is preferable because it means you cover transportation to the shipping point and, from that point on, the costs are covered by the store. Many stores require the designer to cover the cost of shipping to the store's warehouse, and then the store will cover shipping to each individual location. Double-check the packing requirements to make sure that you understand them and tell the store up front if you can't comply. Don't process the order until you are satisfied with all the terms.

Discuss the store's policy for discounting goods. Ask for exclusions from discounts on key items and core product. Negotiate a sale break date that is later in the season to give more time for the goods to sell at full price. Provide a suggested retail price to discourage some accounts from offering better pricing than others.

Set a date to stop taking orders for the season. Once you close the selling season, confirm all the orders and organize them on a master schedule for production and delivery.

Other Arrangements
Consignment

Sometimes, rather than place an order, a buyer will offer consignment at the store. The buyer doesn't buy the product, but will place it in the store and pay you, minus a commission, for anything that sells. Consignment has pros and cons that largely depend on how much you value the store. It can get you in the door at a place you really want to be, and it's a great way for you and the store to test your product. Michelle Smith from Milly agreed to sell her first season at Bergdorf Goodman on consignment to get in the door. The collection sold well, and the next season the store bought.[23]

Consignment in one store can entice other potential accounts and position your brand in an exclusive setting where you could also meet customers and test product. However, some designers resent the lack of commitment from the store. Consignment definitely works to the retailer's advantage as the designer is taking all the risk by producing stock, which will be returned if it doesn't sell.

Dropship

With dropship, the store doesn't buy or stock the product they sell. They operate like a showroom in which the customer sees the product at the store (or online), but when they buy it, the store processes the sale and informs the designer who ships it directly to the customer. The store never handles the actual product—just the payment—which they send to the designer, minus their commission.

Dropship gives a designer an opportunity to be in a store that doesn't have budget or space for a new line or a full selection of colors and sizes. It introduces you to a new audience and can lend credibility to your line if it's a well-known store. The brand is able to package and communicate directly to the customer when they ship, and they don't have to worry about store cancellations or charge backs.

However, these agreements put all of the risk and most of the work on the designer. The store doesn't buy anything or commit to any inventory. They don't have to deal with shipping and returns. Many online stores even require the designer to upload all the images and descriptions for each item onto the website. One showroom owner considers dropship agreements "really rude," and she would never accept those terms for her designers. In addition, because the store processes the payments, the designer may still have issues getting paid.

As with everything, you have to weigh the pros and cons of each opportunity. It's more appealing to dropship with stores that share the workload and have the capability to integrate their systems with yours to make orders, shipping, and payment easier. The store should pay the shipping fee and share the customer data. You may agree to dropship in an effort to get into a specific store. If so, work with them and promote the relationship to help the products sell so they will be more likely to actually buy from you next time.

Trunk Shows

If a buyer isn't ready to make a commitment, but really likes the product, she might offer to host a trunk show. This allows the designer to bring product into the store to sell or take pre-orders for a day or two. It's a great opportunity, but realize it's a test and you must do everything you can to get the good results that will get the buyer to place an order with you. Try to schedule the date during a busy weekend, and promote the event on social media and via email to encourage as many people as possible to come. Moda Operandi is one online store operating a trunk show model to allow customers to pre-order from designers' upcoming collections.

Getting Paid

Designers John Ross and Don Carney of Patch NYC said, "There are so many challenges working with stores and, unfortunately, the biggest challenge is getting paid."[24] While large brands are usually paid pro forma before the goods are shipped, the small brands, which bring the most flavor to the mix, are often the last ones paid. After several calls to a well-known, reputable store, one designer who has been in business for ten years had to show up personally with an intimidating friend to collect $20,000 in late payments. Another designer lost $45,000 to a well-known chain store that kept the goods and never paid. The story is too common, and while there are few guarantees, you can take measures to help get your money.

Check Credit

It is critical to check the credit of stores before you work with them. Set up an account with a credit service such as Dun and Bradstreet to get credit ratings on each new store. Have the store fill out a credit application and provide references. Call other designers who sell at the store to ask if it pays on time. Alternatively, you can rely on a factor. Designer Wenlan Chia says, "Factoring is like buying insurance on the store orders."[25] She deals with numerous unknown stores, and her factor handles credit checks and guarantees payment on the stores it approves. She knows that she will get paid whether the store pays or not. (See Chapter 3: The Money for more on factoring.)

Payment Terms

Some stores won't pass a credit check or be approved by your factor, but this doesn't mean you shouldn't sell to them. You simply eliminate the risk with the appropriate payment terms. The terms greatly affect your cash flow, and the goal is to get your money as soon as possible. Everything is negotiable, and stores make exceptions all the time. A store may pay a 50 percent deposit if a combination of hype and consumer demand has them eager to stock your product.

Credit card. Accepting credit card payment from small stores is a great arrangement for both parties. The designer is paid immediately, and the store can pay off the balance over time. Ideally, you want full payment on the card up front, but the store may only agree to half up front and half on delivery, or full payment on delivery. To accept credit cards, a designer needs to set up an account with Visa, Mastercard, and/or American Express, which will charge between 1 and 4 percent of the credit card sales. This expense needs to be built into your pricing.

COD (cash on delivery). When a store pays COD, it pays (usually via a bank transfer or an electronic payment system) immediately upon delivery of the product. Some designers have had a bad experience letting a store pay COD with a business check that then bounced. If this happens, it is a hassle to call and chase after the store owner to get your money or, in the case of one designer, go there and personally escort the owner to the bank. As you build trust, you can adjust your COD terms in good faith for the store. For example, COD 30 gives them 30 days after delivery to pay.

Deposit. While not always easy to obtain, a deposit provides much-needed cash to use for production. For new stores, you can ask for a deposit with the balance due COD until their credit is proven. Alternatively, if they pay a deposit, you might allow them 30 days from delivery to pay off the balance or even give them a discount on the total cost of the order. Many small stores justifiably refuse to pay a deposit because of being burned by paying up front for product that is delivered late or does not meet quality expectations.

Letter of credit. A store can also pay with a letter of credit from a bank. It essentially vouches for the store's creditworthiness and guarantees the bank will pay you. With a letter of credit, you can be confident you'll receive payment, but many stores refuse to provide them because they are expensive to obtain.

Net terms. Generally, you should offer the big well-known stores, and your best customers, terms such as net 30. Net 30 gives the store 30 days from the date of the invoice to pay you for the goods. Some stores even ask for net 60 or net 90 terms, and the delayed payment can severely strain your cash flow. With any terms, be sure to invoice immediately when you ship to avoid further delays. It is common to offer stores a discount if they pay sooner. For example, 8/10 terms offer the store an 8 percent discount if it pays within ten days of the invoice date. The terms on your sales forms should include a penalty fee of at least 5 percent for all past due payments.

Tips on Terms

"While designers are often proud of only selling to stores that pay deposits or pre-pay, ultimately you want to build your wholesale business with 80 percent of your accounts being the highest quality stores that carry the best brands and will consistently increase their orders. These are the stores that expect terms. Stores that pre-pay are often small, lower quality stores, and because they use their limited cash to pre-pay, they order less. Generally speaking, for any store that is approved with good credit, you should automatically give them 30-day terms. For stores that are declined for credit, you can require pre-payment by credit card before shipping for smaller orders and a 30 percent deposit up front for bigger orders." —TIM MOORE, EVP/DIRECTOR OF GLOBAL BUSINESS DEVELOPMENT, HILLDUN

Past Due Accounts

Collection is tedious, frustrating work and takes up valuable time. However, as attorney Nicholas A. Rozansky says, "If it's a store that is important to you, giving them some leeway can be a good business decision."[26] Your showroom may help you follow up, but while a designer desperately wants to collect $5,000, a $500 commission is not as motivating for them. Most often the amount owed does not justify the cost of retaining a lawyer.

The problem is in your hands. Legal-looking letters can be helpful and there are collection letter templates available online. In the worst case, you could turn it over to a collection agency to see if they can get anything.

They key is to try to prevent the problem by being firm with your terms when the buyer places the order. Again, ask for COD or credit card payment or offer a discount conditional on receiving payment on time. Designers sometimes bully or even threaten stores, but the simple reality is that often the money just isn't there.

Supporting Sales

The relationship with the store really kicks in once you have the confirmed order. Then you need to service each account and partner with them to sell the product.

Delivery Is First and Foremost

"Nothing will kill a collection quicker for a retailer than for it to come in late," says Robert Burke, consultant and former senior vice president of the Fashion Office of Bergdorf Goodman.[27] A collection is expected to sell best during the first few weeks on the floor. The buyer needs to have the merchandise there, proving the right choice has been made. If the merchandise arrives late, the store can cancel the order, send it all back, and issue significant charge backs.

Avoid late deliveries at all costs. If for some reason the product is going to be late, let the store know as soon as possible to give it a chance to make allowances, or if it cancels, to give you enough time to try to resell the goods elsewhere. Many stores will try to work with you, but others won't. A store may put a late shipment on the floor, but if the merchandise doesn't sell, the store won't take responsibility and the situation will make it very hard to justify doing business with you again. If the buyer wants to cancel, offer a discount as an enticement to take the goods. If you can't sell them anywhere else, you may even want to offer them on consignment.

You Are As Good As Your Sell-Through

Retailers measure your success by sell-through—the percentage of items they buy that sell at full retail price. For example, if they buy 100 pairs of pants and sell 5 pairs in the first week, the sell-through for that store thus far is 5 percent. Department and large chain stores issue sell-through reports each week and judge the product, and whether or not they will order it again, based on these reports. Each store is different, but as a guideline, 75 to 80 percent sell-through is fantastic, 60 to 65 percent in the designer area will probably give you a reorder, and 30 percent is really bad—buyers will definitely not reorder. Sell-through expectation changes by classification. Up to 90 percent may be expected in a highly competitive category such as denim, T-shirts, jewelry, and accessories.

Good sell-through gives you power. Designers testify that buyers will negotiate discounts and be lenient with charge backs and allowances if the sell-through is good. A designer told me about a store that claimed it would never buy from him again because of delivery problems, but ultimately because of his strong sell-through, he is selling there still. Good sell-through can entice new accounts, larger buys, and better terms for next season.

Your Job Is Only Half Done

Monitor the sell-through reports from the bigger stores, and call the small boutiques regularly to check on sales. You can't rely on the store to move the goods. Stores provide an opportunity, but designers need to take things into their own hands to make sure the product sells. There are several things you should do.

Confirm delivery. Always confirm with the buyer that the merchandise was received and verify when it hits the floor. A designer once shipped her goods to a famous flagship store in New York and called the buyer a few times to check on sales. After a couple of weeks, the designer was shocked to hear not a single item had sold. She went to the store herself to check on the goods and couldn't find them on the floor. After an intense search, the store located her collection still in its box in a storage room. It had never been put on the floor.

Go to the store. The above example is one reason to visit the store once your merchandise arrives. Of course, you may be limited to visiting only the stores in your area, but many designers and sales reps travel to their accounts to check on the merchandise and find out what is selling.

It's important to see where the merchandise is placed at the store and how it is displayed. Check to see that your product is positioned with other appropriate lines. Nothing will sell if it's mashed together on an overcrowded rack or hidden in a corner. If the display or location is bad, tell the staff on the floor and inform the buyer. When designer Shoshanna Gruss launched her line Shoshanna, I saw her multiple times at Bloomingdale's, checking to see what was selling and making sure her product was neat and displayed properly. I'm sure her dedication and ownership affected her sell-through and was instrumental in the success of her line.

Help the salespeople sell. The sales staff on the selling floor can be your greatest ally. They interact with the customer every day and can greatly affect your sell-through. Ask for an opportunity to meet with the salespeople and personal shoppers at the store to teach them about your collection. Sales seminars are a common practice at both big and small stores and the buyer can arrange a time for you. If you don't have a formal opportunity to train, stop by the store on your own and introduce yourself to the staff in your section.

Salespeople love to meet the designer, it creates a personal connection and gives meaning to the line. Share your story and inspiration and educate them on the product, the materials, and where and how it is made. Show them ways the items can be combined and worn. If the sales staff has met you and understands the product, the next time a customer wants a black skirt, the salesperson will be more likely to suggest yours. This is even more important as shopping apps such as Hero connect online customers to store associates via livestream. The store associate is more likely to feature and promote product when they have a lot of knowledge to share.

Designers can also work with the buyer to arrange incentives and rewards for the salespeople. A free handbag could be given to the person that sells the most that month. A pair of earrings could be the prize for the first person to sell one of the new necklaces in the line.

Learn from the sales floor. Salespeople have valuable information. They are on the front line dealing with the customer every day. Ask them to describe the customer who buys your product. Inquire whether there are loyal repeat customers and if shoppers tend to pick up one item or several. Find out which items get the best reaction, which get the worst, and why. Salespeople are the link to real feedback—they hear the customers' comments as they see your line and try things on. They can tell you about fit problems, issues with the fabric, or complaints about the price.

If you can, get behind the counter for a day or two at a store and sell your own product. There is no better way to have firsthand contact with your customers and to understand what the salespeople need. Menswear designer Thom Browne worked weekends at Bergdorf Goodman selling his own line. No one knew the product better than he, and I'm sure he received valuable feedback from all the customers shopping for suits.

In-store appearances. Many designers complain that the stores are not loyal and are more focused on building their own brand than yours. Too often, a customer who buys merchandise from a new label can tell you where the item was purchased, but cannot name the brand. The best way to make the store more loyal is to connect to their customers and create demand and satisfaction there.

Customers love to meet the designer. It provides a special experience to enhance their purchases. Customers can show their friends a new handbag and tell them they met the designer and learned firsthand about the inspiration and materials used. Personal connection results in loyalty. If you make the customer feel special, they will come back for more. Personal appearances also result in sales. Oscar de la Renta once sold $2.4 million in clothes at a single trunk show at Bergdorf Goodman.[28] Anytime you travel, try to arrange a trunk show or an appointment at a local store. The buyers appreciate the support and a reason to invite their best customers into the store.

Store advertising and promotion. When a designer's merchandise is featured in a store catalog, email, or online magazine, nine out of ten times, the designer paid for it. The designer shares the cost of the promotion with the retailer to support the goods in the store. This advertising is expensive, and for a new designer, it is often cost-prohibitive. Your best bet is to try to negotiate inclusion in promotions and online edits at the time of order.

Stores hold special discount days, holiday events, and "friends and family" type promotions that you can choose to support. Participation may require you to cover the discount or the cost of customer incentives, such as a free gift with purchase. As always, weigh the cost for each opportunity to decide if it really results in more sales and enhances the relationship or just eats up your margin.

Spread the word. From the moment your product hits the shelves or the e-commerce page, share the news of your retail partnerships on social media, in your emails, and through other channels. Post images of the product in store and share news of the latest deliveries and in-store events to help drive traffic to the store.

Reacting to Sell-Through

Stay in touch with the buyers throughout the selling cycle, and answer all emails from the store promptly. If your merchandise is selling out, you need to know to offer a reorder or additional sizes and inventory you may have. If merchandise isn't selling, you need to take action to help it. Schedule an in-store appearance, create an incentive for the sales staff, or swap out some of the merchandise.

Swap outs. If specific items are not selling at a store, offer to send other items that do sell well to replace them. You want the store to have product it can move to increase your overall sell-through. For your own image, you want to keep your goods off the markdown rack. If swap outs don't work and nothing is selling, consider having the store return the merchandise before it is marked down so you can sell it elsewhere. Less merchandise in the store will make your sell-through look less bad.

Realize that each market is different. One store may tell you the clothes are running big, and another will tell you the same clothes are running small. Different markets respond to different product, and designers can often swap items between stores. If a particular store is really struggling with your line, send them a few bestsellers to see if those get a response. If it doesn't help, the store is probably not right for your product.

Don't get beaten up. As much as you need to take sales responsibility into your own hands, sometimes it's appropriate to be firm in dealing with the stores and push responsibility back onto them. For example, if your line is selling great at some stores, ask the buyer why it isn't performing well at his. Tell him about your success elsewhere and discuss what he could be doing to improve sales.

How Buyers Decide to Buy Again

The efficient way to grow your business and brand is to not to just grow the number of accounts, but to deepen your existing relationships and grow the amount of product and sales in the best stores. For a designer collection that is selling well, a 10 percent increase in sales is typical for the next season.

The key to getting a store to return is having good sell-though and keeping your goods off the markdown rack. However, other factors are influential as well. It's important for the product to mix well into the store and to provoke good customer response. The stores also consider whether the designer did a good job in promoting and supporting the line. Designer Mandy Kordal says she received email reorders when buyers saw a lot of social media engagement around her quilted jackets.[29]

Overall customer service and professionalism is another important factor. If a designer isn't willing to build the relationship and provide customer service, a buyer may choose not to work with her. There are plenty of designers out there without having to deal with ones who aren't pleasant. As Susanne Rehnstrom of W29 Showroom says, "What really matters is the personal connection to the buyer—that is the number one."[30] If the stores tell you they manage reorders on a wholesale platform such as NuORDER or Joor, it can be worth the expense to join.

Leftover Merchandise or Overstock

You should try to sell off leftover or returned product before it becomes dated and results in a financial loss. Ideally, you can sell it on your own website, at a sample sale, or a group shopping event. Some designers also create additional stock from leftover fabric and materials for these sales. You can also work your creative mind and upcycle items into new designs for the next season. If the product is brand new and not dated, perhaps the result of a canceled retail order, you may be able to offer it again next year.

What is the single thing that most affects your sales?

"Talking to my customers. I always love hearing what my customers have to say, what they love, and what they can do without. Listening to them helps me understand their desires and what inspires them." —Christine Alcalay

"Email marketing—100 percent. We expand reach on social and get new followers, but every time we send an email we get sales." —Angela Luna, ADIFF

"It's having the two-point system where a person can see us at the shop or the flea market and then cross-reference with what they see online or on Instagram. That creates trust." —Thea Grant

"In our annual survey, people wrote time and time again that the reason they buy from us is because our values are shared with their values, and they see themselves in our brand." —Laura Moffat, Kirrin Finch

"Celebrity—100 percent." —Lindsey Thornburg

"Building a story around the process of creating the garments. And whether it's digital or in person, customer service is very important and something that doesn't get talked about often enough." —Gary Graham

"Our relationships with our wholesalers, our customers, and our community. Each one builds off of the other." —Mandy Kordal, Kordal

"In terms of branding and customer acquisition, Instagram is where people find me the most. Then email drives conversion and reorders." —Althea Simons, GRAMMAR

"This is always changing. One season I'll do great with boutique wholesale clients, another season I'll do amazing at direct to consumer pop-up markets. I still don't know the perfect way, and now it seems that since we have less direct contact, the best opportunity is online sales." —Karelle Levy, Krelwear

"Currently, the single most effective thing I do to affect my sales is having a relationship with my followers on social media (mostly on Instagram) and generating consistent, inspirational content that speaks to what the brand represents. In addition, I need to be a brand that stands for something and is authentic in the messaging." —Ruthie Davis

"I currently utilize a unique process called botanical contact printing, where I use actual flowers and plant-based dyes to make patterns and colorations on natural fibers. I believe the organic concept of this process, and good photography to illustrate it, is what drives people to buy. They are buying into the story and the sustainability of the line." —Alison Kelly, Flora Obscura

"Building a relationship is critical. Having flexibility and trust between all parties, including our production team. Long-term interest for all is what makes it work." —Diego Binetti

"Getting people's attention. We love our brand, and to keep growing, we will always need other people to love it as much as we do. Hiro Clark is still small, mostly digital, and still relatively unknown. We are super dependent on new customer acquisition and new people discovering the brand. Social media drives most of the sales—influencers and digital ads." —Andy Salzer, Hiro Clark

Trade Shows

Trade shows create a group-selling environment by bringing hundreds of designers into a single location to meet hundreds of buyers. There are dozens of shows in the United States, Europe, and Asia that attract buyers from all over the world, allowing designers to show their line to numerous buyers they wouldn't otherwise meet because of time and travel constraints. In addition, editors attend the shows, and there are opportunities to make contacts with showrooms and distribution companies from other countries that could represent your line.

The biggest downside of trade shows is the expense. The smallest booths generally start at $4,000 and can be as much as $10,000, depending on the show. It costs money to build your display, ship it, create promotional materials, and hire staff. Buyers are generally reluctant to place an order with a new line and may put you on their mental list for next season. Returning for a second season adds up to a $20,000 expense for the year. This can equal a significant percentage of your annual sales.

Choosing a Show

There are shows for womenswear, menswear, and accessories throughout the world, and many host shows in multiple cities. Designers and Agents, Coterie, Liberty Fairs, Woman, and Reassembled are just a few of the shows in New York for womenswear. Tranoi is in Paris, and Pitti Uomo in Florence, Italy, is the biggest show in menswear. Cabana is a swimwear show, Sole Commerce is for shoes, and shows such as Shoppe Object and NY Now feature a variety of jewelry, clothing, home, and lifestyle products. Each show is different, and while the large shows bring in thousands of buyers, new brands often do best at a smaller shows where they are with like-minded designers and can target more specific buyers.

Review the show's website and the list of past attendees to see whether the show attracts the buyers from the stores where you want to sell. Also look at the list of exhibitors to see if the brands you most align with in terms of style, target customer, and price point are there. Talk to other designers, past exhibitors, and even buyers about their experiences at the shows and ask for their recommendations. Try to visit the show before you sign up. Walk around and see the booths to get a sense of the quality of the traffic and whether the exhibitors are actually writing orders. One person's experience will differ from another's. A bad show for one designer could be a great show for you, based on who walks in the door.

Before you pay for the trade show, discuss your location at the show. Small, lesser known companies aren't always given the best spots on the floor. Make sure you aren't stuck in a bad location at the back of the show or in a corner that won't get much traffic. Also ask about who you will be next to and if they have a similar price point. You don't want to be next to a dress label that is similar to yours and much less expensive.

Going to Market: Getting the Most Value from Trade Shows
by Alexandra d'Archangelo, Brand Director, COTERIE

Trade shows and market centers don't sell booths; they sell brand alignment and exposure to retailers. Consistency is as important here as it is in other parts of your sales and marketing strategy, such as when and what you post to social media. Once you've identified the show that is the right fit for you, you should commit to showing with them for at least three successive seasons. There really isn't such a thing as testing a market by participating in a show once as a new brand. New brands need the most support, and it's confusing for the buyers when these brands bounce around from show to show or disappear altogether. Unfortunately, you may not recuperate your costs the first season. But over the course of three seasons, you should be able to build a business—if you are selling the right product at the right price for that retail audience.

Keeping Your Costs Down

Understand what's included: Before you sign a contract, clarify what is included with your "booth package." This refers to display fixtures, furniture, signage, etc. As an emerging brand, it's advisable to look for a show or area of the show that offers a standard "turnkey" display package. This means that everything is included in the booth price and that you walk in with only your collection, hangers, and sales collateral. Exactly what is included varies from show to show. You will likely hand carry your collection into the venue. However, if you are having anything shipped direct to the show site at a convention center, be sure to clarify pricing and/or what exactly is included re: drayage. Drayage is the cost of the labor used to transport your delivery from the loading dock to your booth and can result in an unanticipated expense.

Deadlines: Make note of all deadlines as late requests can result in extra fees and missed opportunities.

International freight: If you are showing internationally, use the official freight forwarder of the trade show. Though it may cost more, it also is the most likely to result in your collection being at your booth upon arrival. If there does happen to be any type of customs issue, the show organizer will be able to help expedite resolving it. Though services such as UPS, DHL, and FedEx may be cheaper, the show organizer will have less ability to help with any issues. If you must use these services, have your collection delivered to you at your hotel or where you are staying, and drop it off at the actual shipping center after the show. Booths are not real addresses, and delivery people have no real way of knowing how to deliver to your booth. They may also not be admitted on the show floor, due to loss prevention issues.

The trade show is not only three or four days. It's more like three months because your preparation and outreach before, during, and after is as important as anything that happens on the actual show floor.

BEFORE THE SHOW

What if you don't know any buyers? Whether you've been building your brand direct to consumer, or you only know the stores in your immediate vicinity, you can and must do buyer outreach before the show. Make a list of brands that you want to be aligned with and check out their stockist lists online. See which stores follow them on Instagram, and look up their contact info on their website and on LinkedIn. Direct message them on Instagram with an image to get their attention. See who the showrooms are following on Instagram. Some buyers have public profiles on Instagram. Follow them and engage with their posts. Once you have connected with a buyer, request an appointment at the show. They may decline, indicating that they'd rather drop by. Try to narrow down which day they are planning to come to the show. If a prominent buyer or especially buzzy retailer confirms their attendance, it's worth asking the show organizer if they have any perks you can offer them such as discount codes for ride-share services, complimentary airport pickup, etc.

Promotional opportunities: Once you've decided on a trade show, don't delay in signing up. Brands that sign up at the beginning of the show cycle (often right after the last show) and pay on time have a greater chance of being featured in promotions to buyers. Also, respond to any requests for collateral or information. Many brands don't and miss out on exposure to buyers and press. Even though you may not have your collateral (or collection!) ready for the upcoming season, it's beneficial to submit images and info whenever they are requested. You can feature core styles likely to be carried forward or items from the prior delivery when you might still have units of inventory available to sell. The point is to generate interest versus showcasing exactly what you will be showing in several weeks.

Support for emerging designers: Ask about what kind of support the show offers for emerging designers and brands that are new to the show. New brands that are not already over-distributed and heavily discounted online are appealing for buyers who are constantly in search of exciting new product. New brands may be featured in a dedicated email to buyers or other marketing collateral that highlights a specific destination on the show floor, retail development, support, etc.

Multi-channel opportunities: What are the digital components of the event? This may include an app or be a separate digital event. Being included is especially relevant in the post-COVID-19 landscape.

Sales and marketing materials: Have your collateral in order. Ensure that you have your line sheets—whether hardcopy or online—prepared with wholesale price and suggested retail price in the local currency. Ideally, this pricing should be LDP (landed duty paid) if you are showing abroad. Buyers have many options in terms of product without doing the extra work of figuring out how to import yours. If you need help calculating your pricing for various markets, there are independent retail consultants who do this work on a per-project basis. Ask your contact or the show organizer for a referral.

It's still ideal to have a beautiful lookbook—either printed or online. The production value is more important than the number of images. If a full lookbook isn't possible yet, then be sure that you have at least a couple of campaign or lifestyle images that show the product well in order to generate interest. Flat lay or ghosted images of product against a white background are also a good investment, and easy for editors and content creators to incorporate.

Networking: The trade show can be an opportunity to show your collection and take meetings with other industry people, especially if you don't have a showroom or studio space. Do check with the show organizer about press and guest policies if you are planning to invite any influencers or stylists that you have been connecting with via other channels.

Showrooms: Sales representatives and showrooms participate in trade shows with groups of brands. Look up wholesale contact information for the brands that you want to be aligned with. If they are participating in the trade show you've selected, that's another assurance that the show is relevant to your target market. Invite them to come by your booth, or meet with the showroom representatives however they can fit you in.

Market research: If the trade show is in another city, take the time before or after to visit the stores that are on your target retailer list and/or the most well-known retailers relevant to your end use customer.

AT THE SHOW

Listen to feedback: A trade show provides the opportunity to obtain more buyer feedback over the course of a few days than you would be able to seek out on your own. Though they may not buy from you during your first or second season, the feedback is valuable, and you are building a relationship.

Grow your database: Seek to obtain contact information and social handles from everyone you meet—especially buyers.

AFTER THE SHOW

Follow up: Reach out to any buyers who reviewed your collection at the show. Often, buyers take notes at a show, versus leaving the order during their appointment. This is not necessarily a bad sign, as they may need to obtain approval before confirming the order. If possible, follow up same day or the day after the show closes. Email the buyer with a copy of their notes or order to be confirmed. Some shows are aligned with online wholesale platforms that enable you to customize a line sheet to feature only the items that they were interested in. Whatever your system, include visuals and clear pricing and delivery dates for the items that were of interest. Many buyers will be traveling for a period before and/or after the show—whether to regional markets or international fashion weeks. If you don't hear back right away, follow up after a few days, after any major markets they may be shopping and of course with at least a week to spare before the production deadline to close your order.

Don't be afraid to call: After emailing twice, do follow up with a phone call. You may find that some buyers (press, stylists, etc.) have the habit of chatting via direct message on social media such as Instagram or WhatsApp. Always follow up with a confirmation regarding dates and clear payment terms via email.

Nurture the relationship: If you met with a buyer briefly and they didn't leave any notes, be sure to follow up anyway. Email them with a line sheet and to ensure that they have your contact information. If they explicitly passed on the collection, send a short note thanking them for their time and feedback—and to show your interest in meeting with them again next season!

Caution

At trade shows, you will meet buyers from stores that are unknown to you. You should require COD or credit card payment or run a credit check before you accept orders from these stores. Don't accept large orders from a new store. It's better to start small with an option to reorder. Ask questions about the store and which other designers it sells to make sure it's the right place for your line. Look it up online to be sure the image is right for you.

Don't hesitate to talk to people. Greet everyone and immediately ask where they are from. Mass manufacturers have people who walk the shows to look for ideas to copy. Your booth should be welcoming, but don't have everything out in the open, and don't just give your line sheet away before finding out where that person is from.

Overseas shows can open up entirely new markets for your business, but these shows bring greater cost and more risk and you want to make sure you are ready. If you do exhibit overseas, have someone with you who speaks the local language.

A Smart Alternative

The high price and overwhelming size of trade shows has sparked many designers to develop their own innovative ways to sell during market week. Designers band together and share the cost to rent a gallery space or hotel suite near the major shows. They pool their contacts and invite buyers to come to the space to see the lines they know and discover something new.

Partner with designers who have a similar aesthetic and price range in order to attract buyers who are potential customers for all the lines. Realize that the trade shows are time consuming and exhausting for the buyers. It's good to have food and drink and a place where the buyers can relax and charge their phones.

Who Should Sell the Line?

There are a few options for selling your collection to stores. A designer can sell it personally, hire a sales rep or showroom, or hire someone to handle sales in-house. Each approach can work. The designer must simply decide which will be the most effective at landing the desired accounts.

When starting out, sales experience is extremely valuable for a designer. Most salespeople and buyers recommend that a new designer pound the pavement and get firsthand experience selling his own line for at least the first season. Showrooms generally prefer you to come to them with a few accounts to prove the legitimacy of your business, and the selling experience will help you better manage and negotiate with an outside salesperson or showroom.

Selling Yourself

In theory, no one can sell your product as well as you. You envisioned it, chose the materials, and had it produced. Buyers love to meet the designer. It helps them understand the brand and the inspiration behind the line. But many designers simply don't want to sell or feel they don't possess the right personality or skills. It can be very difficult to pick up the phone and pitch yourself, but you should try. It gets easier with each call, and you may discover a talent for it.

By meeting directly with stores or selling at a trade show, a designer learns the sales process, develops a rapport with buyers, and better understands customer needs. The buyer feedback will reveal the limitations of your collection and help you to be more successful at future meetings.

The most important and most difficult part of selling your own line is not taking it personally. Realize the buyers know what they want and need at a particular time for a certain customer;

it doesn't mean your product isn't good. Listen to their feedback and learn from their criticism. The buyer who doesn't seem interested today might place the biggest order next season.

Showrooms and Sales Representation

A showroom offers a fixed location for several lines. Buyers come to the showroom to review multiple collections and to place their orders. For eveningwear designer Gustavo Cadile, this aspect of a showroom is key. He says, "Not only do you benefit from the showroom's connections and reputation to make sales, but it is really important to be with other designers." If a buyer came to his studio and only liked a few styles, she probably wouldn't bother to make an order, but if she goes to a showroom, she may like five of Gustavo's styles and five of someone else's, making an order worthwhile.[31] An independent sales representative presents one or several collections to the buyers and represents them at trade shows. They may travel widely to stores representing a line entirely or only in a specific territory.

While it's common for retail buyers to directly message a designer, they often prefer to work with showrooms or sales reps because they are efficient, know the language of sales, and get right to the point. Showrooms provide convenience and give buyers confidence in a brand. A buyer may be more likely to give straight feedback on a collection to a rep than to the designer, who might take the feedback or rejection personally.

Showroom and independent reps have the contacts to position you in the best stores for your brand. They have the skills and experience to negotiate terms, discounts, and markdowns and to say no to difficult demands. The stores are often more responsible about paying bills on time when you're with a showroom and the showroom has a payment history with the stores via other clients. Showrooms know who is trustworthy and will check credit for you. Many even have a blacklist of stores they won't sell to because of past payment problems or cancellations.

A salesperson can also be very helpful in development of the line. They have market expertise and a trained eye to help merchandise the line to sell it better. They can consult on financing, pricing, and production issues. A good showroom will also check on the product in the stores to see the presentation, review inventory, and strategically plan the deliveries. A showroom can be especially important when entering international markets. They have contacts and can help with price adjusting, international payment and shipping systems, and cultural norms.

While that adds up to a lot of advantages, it's not all rosy. Designers warn that you don't really know what is going on at the showroom and whether it is truly representing the line well or servicing your existing customers. If you are hanging with 15 other lines, they may not give your label any attention. Things can go wrong, and there are horror stories. One showroom with a history of selling impressive lines to good stores suddenly stopped returning calls to her designer clients, and the designers stopped receiving payment from the stores. A designer went to New

York to check in and realized the showroom owner had convinced the stores to write the checks to her, closed her showroom, and disappeared with the designer's money and samples. Another showroom sent a designer's samples to a big chain store that copied them all and sent back the copies rather than the originals. Yet another mixed up the seasons and put the designer's current samples that should have been in the showroom in her sample sale. Half of the pieces were sold before the designer discovered the error.

Finding the right representation for you. Showrooms can be set up easily with little investment, and they are just as easy to close. Lawyer Steven Hahn warns that a contract isn't worth the paper it's written on if you don't trust the person. You need to find reputable people whom you trust and who can accurately represent you.[32]

The best way to find a good sales rep is to ask experienced people in the industry. The buyers you sell to and other designers can recommend reliable people. Some designers walk the trade shows to meet the reps and observe how they present their lines. Before you commit, meet with many potential reps and showrooms—and meet with them several times. Call a few of their clients for references and try to talk to designers who have left. In the end, consider the issues below and go with your gut.

- **Business credibility.** Find out how many years the showroom or rep has been in business and research her industry reputation. A reputable showroom will help you appear more legitimate and can prescreen for the retailer.

- **Connections.** Find out which stores the showrooms or rep sells to each season and where he has the strongest relationships. Ideally, he should be working with your target stores. Michelle Smith from Milly says, "Being with a sales showroom from day one really helped to propel the line quickly into the stores. The showroom already had the contacts and relationships, whereas on my own, I would have had to start from scratch."[33] Test the rep's knowledge by mentioning a few stores to see if he knows the buyers.

- **Lines represented.** Before you meet with a showroom, find a list of its clients and think about whether you want your product displayed with these labels. The other lines should complement yours and appeal to a similar target market, price point, and quality level to attract the right buyers. Keep in mind that the stores have a different set of buyers for bags, shoes, and ready-to-wear. For a shoe designer, your aesthetic may fit perfectly into one of the most highly regarded and heavily trafficked showrooms. But if you are the only shoe line there, the buyers who actually have budget for shoes may not come.

- **Number of lines.** Big showrooms have more lines and more salespeople and attract more traffic, but a designer there may receive less attention. If you aren't one of the hot lines being pushed or attracting a lot of press, you could be left out. At a small showroom, the salespeople are able to give more attention to each line and work one-on-one with the designers. However, they are less well known and have fewer clients to attract the buyers.

- **Sales and service approach.** Try to get a sense of the personality and approach of the salespeople. The way they service customers is key to the success of your line. Aggressiveness is important to land appointments and close sales, but buyers may avoid a rep who is too pushy or rude. Find out if the rep will involve you in the sales process. Buyers still want to meet the designer, and you should have occasional meet-and-greets at your showroom. A good sales rep will handle customer service, follow up with the stores regarding deliveries, and handle sales training. Good reps can also advise you on pricing strategy, product development, and getting your line into a trade show.

- **Territory.** Ask whether the showroom has reps or another location in other cities and whether they travel, participate in trade shows, or cover foreign markets. It's good to find a showroom with worldwide contacts, but beware of road reps that insist on covering a huge, unrealistic territory. Although most buyers travel on buying trips to New York or to the trade shows, they love the convenience and one-on-one attention that comes with seeing lines in their own store. Many designers have a showroom in New York and one in Los Angeles or Europe. They may have a New York showroom and a rep that travels their line to other markets.

- **Length of agreement.** Occasionally, a showroom will offer to test your line for a season, but most require a commitment of two to three years. It takes time to build a new designer's business and get the name out to the buyers. If the rep spends a season working to build your name, he wants to be able to reap the rewards in the seasons to follow.

Getting in. It may take some effort to get into a reputable showroom. Generally, a showroom will consider a line if there are no conflicts, it has a strong identity, and the quality is good. Send the showroom a link to your portfolio, then follow up and ask for an appointment. The showroom owner will review the collection to see how it fits in with their other clients and whether it fits their needs and tastes of the buyers.

Showroom owner Denise Williamson looks at the whole presentation—the materials, the collection, and the designers themselves and their drive and willingness to work with the stores and the showroom. It's not just about the clothes; she is investing in the person. She has to believe you can deliver on time and will produce good quality. The showroom's reputation is on the line if the designer messes up.[34]

If you are new, the showroom may want to wait to pick up your line until it has a customer following and a few retail accounts or seasons selling online. Showroom owner Lynn Rosetti asks designers about their experience, whom they have worked for, and their relationships with their factories. She says, "We usually won't pick them up until they have shipped at least one store to see if they deliver on time and have good quality, but if the background is right we might make an exception."[35]

Payment and terms. Showrooms and sales reps both charge a commission on sales. Showrooms charge from 10 to 15 percent, with 12 percent being the most common. The percentage may go down as the sales volume increases. For example, for $1 million in sales or less, the commission may be 12 percent, but at $1 million to $2 million in sales, it goes down to 11 percent. Showrooms and sales reps receive their commission upon payment from the store, not when the store places the order. This prevents them from being paid on orders that are canceled or returned. Independent reps are typically paid a 10 percent commission, but many require an advance to help cover their costs until the stores pay. You will need to pay their fees for trade shows and possibly cover other expenses, such as those for travel and telephone.

A 10 or 12 percent commission may sound insignificant, but as one designer said, "What I wouldn't do to have that 12 percent back now." If you sell $300,000 in a season, 12 percent is $36,000—a lot of money for a small company. U.S. showrooms often charge a monthly *rack fee* in addition to commission. This fee can range from $500 to more than $2,000 per month. You should definitely negotiate to try and bring down this fee. If you are fortunate, it will be structured as a "draw," which is taken out of the commission when the stores pay. It is possible to negotiate different combinations of commission and monthly fee, but be sure to estimate the total end cost. A designer may negotiate a higher commission to save money on the fee, but if it's a successful season, the designer might have been better off paying the higher monthly fee. Before you sign, read your contract carefully and negotiate the clauses that don't work in your favor.

It is standard practice to relinquish all of your existing accounts to your sales showroom. This avoids confusion about who is handling which stores and makes it clear for the buyers. But again, everything is negotiable, especially if the showroom really wants your product. A hot menswear label negotiated with one of the best showrooms to pay only half the monthly rack fee and to pay it only for the two key selling months. It also negotiated to keep its existing accounts and only pay commission on new stores.

Several showrooms offer public relations services, which can result in a higher monthly fee or commission. Combining sales and PR in one place can save you money compared to hiring an additional rep for PR, but if you don't need the PR service, you should negotiate a discount.

Manage the relationship. Don't leave a showroom to handle sales and simply trust it will be okay. Despite the commission incentive, salespeople can be overwhelmed by the number of lines they represent or may focus too heavily on another line that is getting a lot of media attention and is an easy sell. Check in constantly to ask what is selling, who has been in the showroom, and what meetings are coming up each week.

Insist on hearing the feedback that the showroom receives from the buyers. They may have valuable input and suggestions. If the advice doesn't really make sense, or is given to you with bad sales results, take it with a grain of salt. If you decide to leave a showroom for any reason, be professional and try to depart on good terms. Fashion is an extremely small industry. People talk, and you may end up working with them again in the future.

In-House Sales Representative

Once you have the financial resources and are more known in the market, you may consider hiring someone to handle your sales in-house. While it can be expensive to take on a full-time employee to represent your line, bringing sales inside puts control back in the designer's hands and allows one person to understand the collection fully and be involved in merchandising and developing the line and the sales strategy. It is also easier to control your positioning in the market. If you have a $500 cashmere sweater and another label in the showroom has a $300 cashmere sweater, it's much harder to emphasize the differences in quality, design, or construction, as too often the buyer will just go on price point. Customer service can be difficult to handle through a showroom. If something in the collection changes during production, the designer needs to communicate that to the buyer, something the showroom is sometimes reluctant or can't be bothered to do. An in-house salesperson can travel to the stores to check on the merchandise, conduct sales education and training, and develop relationships with the buyers and salespeople. Hiring an experienced salesperson allows the designer to benefit from that person's past experience, contacts, and professional reputation with the buyers.

10 PUBLIC RELATIONS AND EVENTS

PR is a driving force in fashion with the power to skyrocket a designer into the spotlight and drive demand at the stores and online. Whether through influencers, print magazines, celebrity placements, or collaborations, the right exposure is vital to helping a new name compete without the mega-million advertising budget of Gucci.

PR requires a well-rounded approach to ensure your efforts work in sync with your marketing strategy to build a clear perception of your brand across all channels. The most valuable exposure depends on your brand and customer. As with every effort, stay focused on clear goals for what you want PR to do for you.

While many approach PR to build traffic and increase exposure, most designers say PR is really about credibility. As designer Bliss Lau says, "Press builds trust. When Beyoncé wore my jewelry, the queen bestowed me with trust. Every single one of my clients has mentioned it. For clients who were already following me, it's that extra push."[1]

Warning!

Exposure is a tool—the means to an end—not an end goal in itself. It's easy to get very excited seeing a celebrity with your product and be seduced by the attention it brings, but instant celebrity is not instant success and it won't keep you in business. Many of the "star" designers whose collections and lives are regularly triumphed in the media don't have the sales to back up the hype.

Sudden attention and hype can also blow someone up too quickly, putting unrealistic pressure on a new designer who doesn't have the resources and support to make it last. Success in the fashion business takes time, and even winners of shows such as *Project Runway* struggle to stay in the spotlight and achieve long-term success.

Sales First, Then PR

Designers with limited time and resources should weight their focus heavily toward sales rather than PR. Designers often tell me that press coverage really doesn't affect their sales, and many designers you may not have heard of are quietly serving their loyal customer base and getting rich. They spend their money creating great product and building strong customer relationships, and don't waste time or money on shows or chasing influencers. As one accessories designer told me, "My customers are smart, educated women who trust me, the store, and the salespeople. They just don't care about magazines or social media."

There is no denying that the right exposure can open doors. The influence of social media and celebrities on the retail business is enormous, and coverage in *Vogue* or an endorsement from Danielle Bernstein or Chrissy Rutherford can land you that first appointment with an important store. Tricia Tunstall, owner of P45 in Chicago, says that while the press doesn't sway her to buy something that isn't already of interest, it does help if she is on the fence.[2] The coverage means that someone else sees the potential in the designer, and if shoppers search for the designer because of the exposure, her store will get more sales.

Press and Media Strategy

Chasing press is very time consuming, and you need a focused strategy. The writers, journalists, producers, bloggers, and editors are inundated every day with emails, calls, and messages from brands vying for their attention. They work long hours, have tough deadlines, and have very specific missions.

With many declaring that print is dead, there are still plenty of influential fashion magazines such as *Vogue, Elle*, and *Harpers Bazaar*, along with niche print titles ranging from *The Gentlewomen* to *Fantastic Man*. Any one of these, along with dozens of online publications from *Fashionista* to *High Snobiety*, can provide exposure and cachet for your brand. But getting placements is extremely competitive. Both online and off, fashion publications are pressured to give a majority of coverage to their advertisers, so everything else must be very specific and interesting to earn a spot.

In dealing with the media, you have to be thick-skinned and realize there is no loyalty. If you consistently have an 80 percent sell-through in a department store, or you design pants with a consistently flattering fit, it's very difficult for the store or the customer to replace you. But to the media, you are entirely replaceable. Their job if to feed a relentless demand for *fresh and new* with every issue or post.

Do Your Homework

Just like researching stores, a designer should thoroughly research the media outlets and tailor her approach. *Elle, Refinery29,* and *Hypebeast* each have a different audience and target their aesthetic, opinion, and range of featured product to that readership. Spend time scrutinizing the magazines, podcasts, websites, social media feeds, and newsletters where you want your line featured. Determine whether your collection is truly relevant to each. Note the section titles or themes, the types of stories they include, and who writes them. For each target publication, determine in which specific section or column your story would best fit.

Each outlet approaches fashion differently. Some respond only if there is a celebrity angle, while others won't cover bridal or maternity. Read each outlet to understand its voice and mission. On its website, *Teen Vogue* describes itself as "the young person's guide to saving the world," so you must consider that in your approach. *Dazed,* "where pop culture meets the underground," requires a different pitch than *Kinfolk* or an industry publication such as *WWD*. If you approach a publication using its tone, there is a greater chance of being included. It's worth taking time to even customize your pitch to the individual writer's style. It will help them fit the piece in their column, especially if it saves them time and effort in writing it.

Weekly newsletters, gossip shows, and daily outlets have *short leads*, meaning the writers work very close to their deadline and you can generally approach them at any time. However, if your news relates to a specific event, such as fashion week, or you want to be considered for a regular feature, contact them at least a month in advance. Monthly publications are *long lead*, and their stories are assigned months in advance. They have editorial calendars, primarily used to entice potential advertisers, which outline topics and themes being covered over the next year. If a story on beach escapes is planned for January, targeting your swimwear pitch to that issue will greatly increase your chance of coverage. Plan ahead and contact long lead press at least four months in advance.

Don't aim solely for the obvious fashion outlets. Travel, fitness, and lifestyle media build buzz and create demand. Business magazines write about new companies, and their coverage can validate your brand with suppliers, lenders, and potential investors.

What the Media Wants

The writer or producer's job is to provide fresh, timely news; cover the trends; and keep the audience engaged with compelling, story-driven content. Think about how your story is relevant and state up front what makes you special. The media wants something original with a strong point of view. It also seeks the validation that comes if you sell at a fashion-forward store like Dover Street Market or if you used to design for Amiri or Ralph Lauren. Know your strengths and what sets you apart. Celebrity angles help but must be relevant to the outlet. You might not call *The Gentlewomen* to say that Mariah Carey just wore your dress, but you would tell them if Cate Blanchett did.

Exclusives

The fashion media is extremely competitive and wants to be first. Therefore, a website or magazine might require an exclusive, which means the designer must let them broadcast or publish the story before the designer shares it anywhere else. Be strategic with your exclusives. The most influential outlets are less likely to cover you as a new designer if you have already been covered by someone else. But you can leverage offers of coverage to try and land the publication you most want. If you really want to be in *Elle* and another magazine calls, you can inform the editors at *Elle* and offer them an exclusive if they will commit. Just be realistic and don't turn down good press in the hopes of something that might not happen.

If you have an exciting announcement or news that will be interesting to several news outlets, try to entice your first-choice publication by offering it as an exclusive. Once it prints the story, the news can be sent out to other media in hopes of further coverage. Keep in mind that stories can be delayed or cut because of space constraints or other late-breaking news. You are at the mercy of the editor or producer, and announcements can be published a week or more late because of delays.

Whom to Approach and How

The writers and editors are listed in each publication on the masthead, and online research will identify the producers and journalists most likely to cover your brand or latest news. Contact them by email or direct message with an eye-catching subject line, a product photo, and a brief, intriguing pitch explaining why are you a great fit for them. Mention any personal connections or, if possible, get someone in the industry to introduce you.

Continue to follow up with a regular relevant photo or news. Engage with their social media and share, retweet, and comment on their posts, and mention articles they've recently published or podcasts or shows they have aired. But don't harass them or clog up their inbox or feed. Ask for the opportunity to show your samples in person. If an editor responds and tells you the collection doesn't fit the publication or stories he is working on, wait to follow up again when you have new product or fresh news, such as a celebrity wearing your design. The editors have specific story outlines created by the fashion directors. If your product doesn't fit what they need at this moment, it could be perfect next season.

If you don't succeed with the features editor, you may contact the market editor to consider including you in upcoming shoots. Don't forget the junior editors who are looking for new talent. If they like your work, most likely the senior people will see it too. And always be polite, you never know who will be the next fashion director. If two people at one publication say no, then it's not going to happen that season, and you shouldn't contact anyone else.

Writers and editors are on deadline, so return calls promptly and be prepared to provide high resolution photos, samples, and accurate information quickly. It's a good idea to have a downloadable press kit or folder that lives on your website, which includes multiple high-resolution photo images with the appropriate credits, as well as a biography and a brand story. If you are pitching a time-sensitive announcement or news, provide a simple fact sheet with all the relevant information, such as dates, addresses, and people involved.

If you land an appointment or a "desk-side," be prompt and prepared with clean, pressed samples and good photos. Present the unique story of your brand to give context and emotion to the product. Point out details and explain processes and inspiration. Be professional, but let your passion and personality shine through. Answer questions, be open to feedback and criticism, and be respectful of their time.

Over time, you will build relationships with writers and editors who have shown interest in your line. They will contact you to fit specific stories and themes. Don't hesitate to ask people who like your collection to introduce you to stylists, influencers, producers, and celebrities. Editors and buyers know everyone, from each other to even finance and production contacts.

Befriend the stylists. Stylists are key to getting your clothes both into editorial photo shoots and on celebrities and influencers. They seek to pull clothes and accessories that fit into a trend story, or work for specific events, and they are extremely connected. The Rodarte designers Kate and Laura Mulleavy sent a letter to Cameron Silver, the well-known Los Angeles stylist and owner of the vintage store Decades. He reviewed the collection, liked it, and became a mentor, introducing the designers to other key people in the industry.[3] Follow the stylists you think are wonderful on social media, and keep them up to date on new product and news. Message them with an invitation to your studio.

Put It to Work

When you land press coverage or a celebrity placement, make use of that success. Send it to your customer list and retail and supply chain. Post it on social media and pay to boost it to a larger audience. Create shoppable links to purchase or pre-order featured product.

The right coverage can result in a huge response so be ready. If the *New York Times* Style section features your handbag, you need product on hand to fill orders or risk losing customers. To predict results, ask the editor or producer about the response for previously featured products that are similar to yours. Make sure you know the exact date when the show will air or the issue will hit inboxes. You can make a wholesale partner very happy by listing their website as the place to purchase, but make sure you have arranged for them to have inventory. Ultimately, it's best to underestimate the amount of product that you need. It is possible to be featured in a major news outlet and have very little response. It is better to be sold out than wallow in excess stock.

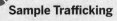

Sample Trafficking

Samples are valuable and, while you want to have them out working for you with editors and stylists, taking some precautions will help you avoid damage or loss. To borrow product, an editor or stylist will first inform you that they want to pull pieces for a particular shoot. They should email a letter of responsibility that includes the dates of the shoot or bring it when they show up to select what they want. The designer should package the samples and create a content sheet or invoice with a description of each item being borrowed, along with its dollar value. Clearly mark a due date by which the items must be returned and explain that if they are late, the borrower will be charged. Granted, you need to make sure the due date allows a reasonable amount of time to complete the shoot and return the items, especially if the editor is shooting in the Caribbean or Egypt. Include one copy of the content sheet with the samples and keep a copy for yourself. The more professional you are with this process, the fewer problems you will experience.

Saying No

Many designers are selective about which media and stylists can borrow samples. They want to keep tight control on their image or control the rate at which they are "discovered" to stay "new" longer. If you don't want to be included in a specific publication because it's not a good fit or because you are holding out for an exclusive elsewhere, be tactful in turning it down. You can tell the editor the samples are already out or are back in production, or you can be honest and say the outlet doesn't currently fall into your media strategy. Don't be offensive or rude. The outlet could become important later, or the editor could become a fashion director somewhere else.

Staying Power

Once you have been covered as a new designer by the media, it can be really challenging to land more press. New product is not enough to warrant fresh coverage, you need to offer new angles. Think about what you are doing that is unique and interesting. Designers receive coverage on their home decor, charitable involvement, work with an innovative textile, or shopping trip with a celebrity. Partnerships with other brands, influencers, and celebrities are also key to staying top of mind.

People and Partnerships

Collaborations

In addition to providing income and exposure, collaborations bring newness and energy to a brand. The right partnership can boost your image, reach a new customer, open a new market, or launch a product category. As Andy Salzer of Hiro Clark says, "It's important to be more than just a T-shirt. Collaboration gives meaning and context to an unknown brand and reflects the wearer's lifestyle." He designed T-shirts with numerous visual artists, created a bag for Bumble and Bumble, and customized shoes for Dr. Martens.[4]

Accessory and jewelry designers often collaborate with clothing designers for photo shoots, runway shows, or even a product line. Independent designers often partner to design for a mass fashion brand such as Vans x Sandy Liang, Birkenstock x Proenza Schouler, and lululemon x Robert Geller. Collaborations also extend to entertainment brands. Shoe designer Ruthie Davis partnered with Disney on the Disney x Ruthie Davis shoe collections in tandem with film releases for *Aladdin*, *Frozen 2*, and the *Mulan* live action film. Out-of-the-box collaborations extend to non-fashion categories such as TELFAR and White Castle.

Think carefully about who you partner with and the message you are trying to convey for your brand. A collaboration with a ballet company can emphasize the elegance or functionality of your designs. The collaboration between Zero Waste Daniel and the NYC Sanitation department emphasized designer Daniel Silverstein's commitment to sustainability and zero-waste design. Designer Gary Graham collaborates with fabric manufacturers including Thistle Hill Weavers and Pollack fabrics for his line Gary Graham 422. The partnerships enhance his commitment to honoring vintage materials and artisanal techniques for his narrative-driven, small-run collections.[5]

Partnering with a mass retailer, such as independent brands LoveShackFancy, Cushnie, and Lisa Marie Fernandez did for the Target Designer Dress Collection, provides national exposure to a broader audience, as well as access to production and marketing resources. When crafting a partnership agreement, make sure you understand what the project will demand in terms of your time and resources and how you will share costs and profits. Clarify each party's responsibilities in regard to design, marketing, and how you will maintain some control. Try to structure collaborations in a way that will support the time you spend on the projects. If you are doing the majority of the design work, negotiate an up-front design fee to cover those hours. Be sure to include an exit clause to explain how you are compensated and who owns the designs if the collaboration is canceled midway.

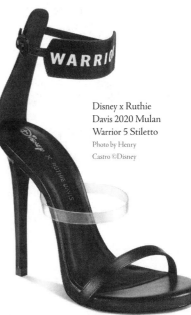

Disney x Ruthie Davis 2020 Mulan Warrior 5 Stiletto
Photo by Henry Castro ©Disney

Dressing Celebrities
by Roger Padilha, Cofounder of MAO Public Relations

Garnering press for your collection and company is one of the most important aspects in keeping your name hot and in the public eye—a necessity if you plan on building a luxury brand. How many times have you walked into a store and justified spending a lot of money on a designer's work simply because of the buzz surrounding the company? The designer world is built on dreams and the one way to sell yourself as a desirable, must-have designer is by having your collections worn by the right celebrities.

Celebrity dressing is an expensive, time-consuming chore and can often backfire, so make sure you think through your strategy. For example, if you make clothes for Upper East Side socialites, it does not make a lot of sense for your clothing to be seen on the latest sultry hip-hop star. Make sure that the people you target are men or women who inspire your customers and are people they try to emulate.

Most celebrities employ stylists who choose their clothing for red carpet events and appearances. DO NOT try sending clothing to managers, PR people, venue managers, people who say they're friends with the celeb, etc. Your clothing will most likely be regifted by these people to their friends, and the celeb will never see your designs. Celebrities pay their stylists a lot of money, trust them, and really do wear what they present. Find out who these stylists are (it's not that hard as they are constantly on TV fashion programs and credited in magazines). Send them your product images, video, and press. Be persistent but not pushy. Stylists are always interested in seeing new work, but after many years of experience in the biz, they have a very good sense of what is right for their client and what isn't. They do not want to hear your opinion on why "Ms. So and So" would look so much better in your outfit than that spring Couture Chanel the stylist recently picked out for them!

A stylist might ask you to make something special for the celebrity, which is not already included in your line. This is a great way to gain entry into that celeb's closet! But stay true to yourself. If you specialize in tailored suits and a stylist asks you to make leather hot pants, you might want to suggest that a different designer handle the project. When you do accept an assignment, listen to what the stylist needs, but feel free to put your own stamp on it.

Never, unless very specific arrangements are made prior, give your clothing away! Celebrities only wear things once and do not need to hold onto any clothing. And you need the outfit back for other important editorial placements, *especially* after it's been worn by that celebrity. I have heard horror stories of items being placed on eBAY or sold to resale by the celebrity's assistant! The only time this is acceptable is if it is for charity and you have cleared it first.

As the online influencer has gained their own celebrity status in the world, it would not be prudent to ignore them when conceiving a list of ones to dress in your label. The same rules apply as when dressing music and film celebrities; however, you must vet the legitimacy of the influencer. Many have exaggerated their reach by buying fake followers or misrepresenting themselves by publishing unwarranted placements. If possible, try to contact brands similar to yours and see if a post by the influencer actually was solicited by the company or if the influencer did it on their own to inflate their product placement list. Also, do your research and look at their other sponsored content—does your collection have a similar following? If not, a placement will not help your brand even if the influencer has millions of followers.

Influencers

Influencers and editors with large social followings can catapult a designer into the spotlight and drive thousands of dollars in sales. It's a crowded field, and you have to work to find the partnerships that will work well for you.

First, an influencer has to be a good fit for the tone and the story of your brand. The product needs to look natural on them and in their feed. Second, they have to be relevant to your specific customer. Think about the type of person you want to work with and whether they will engage your customers and attract new ones. Great influencers have deep, trusting relationships with their followers. They create fresh content and have authentic interactions with their fans. Bigger isn't necessarily better. The most popular influencers may have the biggest audiences, but there may be lesser known "micro-influencers" with very loyal followers who would be the best match for your brand.

Look to build real relationships with influencers who truly believe in your line and who will have fun working to grow your business. As designer Autumn Adeigbo says, "Working with a good, reputable influencer drives sales, but gifting blindly can be a waste. You want them to pick out what they want, but for that to happen you need to try to build a relationship via introductions from your network. If you can't do that and try to send a blind DM, do the groundwork to make sure your website and Instagram are impressive enough and you have enough social buy-in with people they respect. Then they will hopefully pay attention."[6]

Once you have contact, send them the product, invite them to events, and follow and engage with their community. Invite them to co-design an item or guest curate your website or collection. You may have to try several interactions to find the right fit. Few emerging designers can afford to pay influencers. Those with large audiences have rate cards to explain the various fees they charge for different types of exposure on different platforms—and they are expensive. If you decide to go this route, don't be afraid to negotiate.

While the right influencers can help get the word out, don't underestimate the sincerity of showing yourself with your own product. Customers may be inspired by how you mix your own product with other brands, pack for travel, or dress for events, and they will enjoy the personal approach. The best influencers might be your current customers. Encourage them to share images, and even offer them product if they will engage others to support your success.

Gifting

Product costs money, and before you give anything away you should weigh each opportunity carefully to make sure the expense is worth the potential benefit. Celebrities and influencers receive so much product and change their outfits so frequently that without a personal connection, sending anything is often pointless. The best press is people wearing your product because they *genuinely* like it. If an editor or influencer has already shown interest in your brand, offering items for them to wear at events or during fashion week—when they will be photographed—is much more effective.

What matters most is a good match of the product, the personality, and the audience. B or C list celebrities, athletes, or business leaders who authentically align with your brand, and who don't otherwise get a lot of swag, may be the most supportive ambassadors.

Placing product in gift bags at high profile events can be effective, *if* the product lands in the right hands. Opportunities such as the Oscars are difficult for a new designer to land, but there are many alternatives. Depending on your brand mission, gifting at a women's business conference or a sustainability event can position your brand in front of a targeted audience. Always confirm exactly who will receive the bags, and consider the scope of their influence with respect to your line. Be wary of unofficial gifting opportunities that attach themselves to major events, but are distributed to sponsors or volunteers. Whenever you donate to any high-profile event, be sure to publicize your involvement.

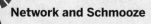

Network and Schmooze

Business is about relationships, and as an entrepreneur, it is important to meet others in the industry, among your customer base, and in your community. The more you do, the easier it will become. Attend events, introduce yourself, and ask questions. Be sincere and really listen. People like to talk about themselves, and you can learn a lot. When you do talk, focus on things that you are passionate about. You don't need to talk just about fashion and business, but don't be random or gossip. If there are influential people you want to meet, find out something about them first, introduce yourself, and learn to be brief and move on so you don't monopolize their time. After you meet someone, follow up with an email to say it was nice to meet them, and try to include a personal detail about your conversation so they can quickly recall the meeting. If you really struggle with networking, you may want to seek media training to help you in social situations. For better or worse, designers need to be able to represent their brand. Editors look for someone interesting to write about, and buyers want someone who can come into the store and charm the customers.

Competitions and Industry Awards

High-profile competitions and award programs offer independent designers a shot at money, media attention, retail partnerships, and access to production resources and business expertise. There is the LVMH Prize, the CFDA/Vogue Fashion Fund, the ANDAM Prize, the International Woolmark Prize, the Hyeres International Festival of Fashion, the Fashion Group International Rising Star Award, and others sponsored by fibers- and fashion-related organizations. Each offer a variety of prizes based on a range of criteria and entry requirements. Depending on the criteria, it can take considerable time and effort to enter—and the competition is stiff.

In speaking to dozens of designers who have been through various programs, designers tend to benefit most from access to valuable contacts and business advice. The process of explaining their vision and business strategy, and the personal feedback and mentorship that comes with some programs, is usually more valued than any financial winnings. On the flip side, there are designers who felt their mentor was a bad fit and the feedback didn't mesh with their vision and goals.

As with every opportunity, you have to decide what is right for your brand. Just because you are eligible doesn't mean it's a good fit. Don't let accolades and attention distract you from the real prize of connecting with your customer to sell your product.

Reality TV

The success of *Project Runway* has spurred a number of other broadcast fashion competitions, such as *Next in Fashion* and *Making the Cut*. Global exposure onscreen can launch a career, but it can also be distracting and take you away from the real time and effort required to build a business. It can even jeopardize your brand, making you notorious for a moment you had no control over. The success stories like Christian Siriano's are few and far between. If you do participate, have a clear strategy on how to leverage that 15 minutes of fame when the spotlight has moved on.

Who Should Handle PR?

The above information assumes that as a new designer, you are handling your own PR. Obviously, this approach will save you money, and social media makes it easy to reach out to editors and stylists directly. In fact, some designers don't work with PR agencies because they say the people who matter prefer to talk directly to the designer.

However, pitching and servicing the media is time consuming, and a PR representative with a strong reputation can open many doors. They have personal contacts with the media and stylists, they know what stories the writers and producers are working on, and their recommendations are trusted. A PR firm can develop a cohesive multi-channel strategy to pitch your story, get samples to editors and stylists, create fresh angles, target influencers and celebrities, and plan and publicize events. A press showroom can house your collection along with other labels to make it easy for editors and stylists to review and pull for shoots.

As with sales, a PR firm represents you and your brand. If your product is perfect for *Paper* magazine, don't go to a rep who is tight with *Town and Country*. Find out who represents the designers who get the coverage you desire. Interview several firms to find the one that believes in your line and understands your goals. Ask who else they represent and call some of those clients as references. Review their placements and successes and ask if they have relationships with the writers and stylists who are important for your line.

The Cost of Representation

Designers often do pay for press help when they launch to create a big initial impact and build a press book over six months or a year. After that first buzz goes away, they must decide based on their brand and customer whether it's worth the continued expense. PR firms are usually hired on a monthly retainer, which can range from $2,500 per month (at a small or generous firm) to $10,000+ per month. You can and should *always* negotiate price, especially if your line is hot and will bring cachet to the firm's existing roster. It's not unheard of for a firm to take on a new line for free just to have something new and exciting to offer the editors. PR firms usually charge for expenses on top of the retainer. Keep an eye on these and dispute anything that seems extreme.

One designer was shocked to receive a large bill for sushi and cheesecake ordered for her rep's interns.

When choosing a firm, consider whether it's better to be a small fish in a big pond versus a big fish in a small pond. One designer left a very prestigious firm where she was paying $10,000 per month for a smaller firm that cost only $4,000. While the bigger firm was well connected and brought legitimacy to her new label, her account was more important to the smaller firm, and she received more attention and service there.

Actively Communicate

When working with a PR firm, it's up to the designer to regularly communicate their goals. Listen to the rep's advice and the feedback they receive from the media to make sure the goals are realistic. If they tell you that the "exciting news" you provide isn't interesting, brainstorm together to find something else to pitch. Keep your press person up to date and check in often. It's frustrating to pay a monthly fee if you aren't getting any coverage. Ask for updates on pitches and the response. You want to give a rep enough time to build momentum for you, but if they seem inattentive or just not able to land meaningful coverage, it might be time for a change.

Events

Events enable a personal, in-depth, and interactive experience of a brand. They let you stand out from the clutter and add a human element to trigger an emotional and, therefore, memorable response. Whether online or in real life, events also generate fresh, exciting content for attendees to share, media to cover, and designers to spread across all their marketing channels.

What's the Point?

Designers stage events for many different reasons. An event can introduce new product, celebrate a store opening, allow you to connect with customers and build community, or create buzz in a new market or during fashion week. Events can be designed for branding or selling, and they can focus on industry, consumers, or both. But event production and planning requires significant time and energy and can leave you drained during the selling or production season when you need to be focused. Designers often say their fashion week event is the most stressful thing they do, and many experience a post-show letdown because of the pressure.

Behind the fun and glamour also sits the harsh reality that fashion shows and events can contribute to the financial ruin of good designers. In many cases, if the time and money spent on the show or presentation had been directed to a sales rep or paying suppliers, the brand would have survived another season.

As you plan an event, know exactly what you aim to achieve and how it benefits the brand. For some labels, it is best to stay under the radar and let buyers and editors discover you in a more organic way. It can be wise to focus on developing customer relationships online or traveling to build wholesale accounts until you have a solid customer and financial base. Solicit the opinion of your advisors, partners, and people you trust, and be wary of show producers and public relations people who may be eager for you to stage an event for their own profit. If there is not a clear purpose or outcome to an event, it's best to wait.

Leverage the Event

If you spend precious funds on an event, you want it to pay off for some time. To land pre-event coverage, alert the media in advance and highlight unique aspects of the event, influential people who are involved, or interesting facts about the collections, inspiration, or materials. Send photos and impactful statements or sketches to the media and key influencers to boost awareness. Post a series of pre-event teasers on social media channels with sneak peaks or interviews. Create livestream broadcasts or short video clips from the castings, fittings, and event preparations. Be sure to highlight and cross promote collaborations for shoes, accessories, music, and other elements.

Create as much content as possible from the actual event. Film both staged and candid moments that will create lasting buzz around your brand. Whether online or offline, find ways to keep talking about the event after the fact. Follow up with media that attended, as well as those that did not. Offer to send photos or video to be included in their coverage.

Event Formats

Events are for storytelling and allow for plenty of creativity in designing how to communicate the ambiance and message you intend. A traditional fashion week runway show is the right choice for some brands, but an intimate dinner party for influencers or a live stream styling party may be better for others.

In-Person Events

There is nothing like a live in-person event to create a lasting impression and to build community. It allows people to see the product up close and in some cases touch or interact with it in a social setting.

For many, a runway show is the epitome of fashion glamour—with models, backstage frenzy, after-parties, and celebrities. There is a collective energy of being in a show venue with others all waiting to experience the music, lights, and live visual impact at once. However, editors and buyers rarely recommend that a new designer stage a traditional runway show. In fact, Simon Doonan, former creative director of Barneys New York, has said, "The fashion system is doing a terrible disservice to students and young designers by making them think they can become the next Tom Ford by putting on a great fashion show."[7]

A creative presentation such as a dance performance or a garden party provides context and allows for more narrative than the repetitive stomp down the catwalk. A runway show also requires people to be in a specific place at a specific time, while a presentation with a three- to four-hour window allows VIPs more flexibility, greatly increasing the likelihood that they will come. Even a simple set in a gallery or photo studio, with models posing or casually interacting, can be a more effective way to show your work.

Some of the best real-world events are less about the product and instead focus on bringing the brand to life in a creative, memorable experience. To promote her range of woven bags, designer Anya Hindmarch's Weave Project installation featured playful woven nets for attendees to climb and crawl through along with an interactive workshop to learn to weave. Small community-focused events, such as the monthly "Stitch N Bitch" happy hours hosted by Knitwear designer Karelle Levy, build brand loyalty through social interaction. Partnering with like-minded brands for events can share costs and emphasize shared values.

The AW20 Love Binetti Collection runway show in Barcelona, Spain
Courtesy: Diego Binetti

A live installation during Los Angeles fashion week
Photo by Howard Wise

Designer Mandy Kordal focuses on partnerships that align with her commitment to sustainability and community. She provides clothing for events hosted by Celsious Sustainable Laundry Mat and hosts happy hours at the zero-waste restaurant Rhodora next to her store.[8]

Ultimately, you must consider how all in-person events will translate online, even if it's at a later time and for a different audience. For example, a designer could present next season's collection in-person in a small private show for buyers and long lead press, and then once the product is available in stores, stream it digitally for consumers and other media. A designer could also show next season's collection to buyers and press in-person and livestream it to a larger audience and allow consumers to pre-order or purchase select items.

Online Events

Online events are far-reaching and impactful and can be less expensive to stage than in-person events. Technology offers endless possibilities, and the global COVID-19 quarantine sparked a great deal of creativity around digital event engagements. Livestream took off, as did interactive styling and selling events, designer- and editor-led conversations, and behind-the-scenes demonstrations and workshops. When several fashion weeks had to pivot to digital formats, Shanghai Fashion Week shifted to a livestream event and partnered with the T-mall e-commerce platform to blend a traditionally industry-focused event with a consumer-focused "see now, buy now" format. Brands were able to discuss the collection with viewers in real time and let consumers purchase in-season items and pre-order others.

Live online formats allow you to share moments and interact with your audience in real time. While live can feel spontaneous, it does need to be planned in advance with attention to the camera view, templates, styling, and script. There is a lot of competing live content online, so be creative to boost participation and entice people to stay. Experiment with story lines, make it fun and include movement and strong visuals. Ask for opinions and requests, and respond to each. Be prepared to juggle unexpected questions and comments along with your planned agenda. The host should be upbeat and responsive. Consider bringing in a well-known personality to MC, or get celebrities or influencers to guest star and participate in live commentary.

The choice of platform is key to the success of your online event and depends on your content. Live music requires great sound quality, whereas a selling event requires in-app shopping. Different platforms can enable high-tech visual effects, customizable backdrops, and break-out rooms. Make sure your technology requirements are sufficient to ensure a stable and clear broadcast.

Fashion Week

Fashion week was originally designed to give editors and buyers a chance to view the collections that would be available to consumers in six months time so they could place their wholesale orders and plan coverage of the new trends. It usually refers to the weeks in September/October and in February/March when designers present collections to the industry in one of the four major fashion capitals of the world—New York, London, Milan, and Paris.

For several years, there has been growing unease about whether fashion weeks make sense. The shows are overcrowded and the schedule packed with too many events. Collections are broadcast live via social media so by the time the product is available, it's old news. Production expenses are staggering and the waste and extensive travel involved is damaging to the environment.

Nevertheless, fashion week in some form is here to stay. It's a celebration of the vast creativity of the industry and the unique viewpoint of each designer. It is an important time when buyers, editors, influencers, and business leaders get together and share notes. The format and approach of fashion week is evolving, and it is exciting to see designers experiment with new ways to show their work and include the customer.

For a new designer, the allure of fashion week is strong, but check your ego and think about what you really achieve by spending time and resources trying to compete with so many others during this particular time.

Will Anyone See It?

If the right people attend and the collection is strong, the media will cover your event, the stylists will call, buyers will be intrigued, and people will learn your name. But sadly, at most young designer fashion week events, 80 percent of the attendees are friends, family, and fashion fans. It's extremely difficult to get the right people to pay attention to a new name during such a busy time. With up to 100 events in New York each season and dozens more in other cities around the world, the schedule is extremely competitive, and many events take place at the same time. Editors must attend the events of their advertisers, and buyers have to show up to see their biggest vendors. Each show requires travel and wait time, and unknown names are the lowest priority. Staging an event at another time of year when schedules are less intense can be greatly appreciated by the industry and press.

Should Anyone See It?

Not all collections belong in the spotlight. Fashion week is for innovation and new points of view. Don't waste time and money if you can get better results at a trade show, and don't waste the press's and buyers' time on something easily introduced online or best seen in the showroom. Even many of the big brands are nixing their Resort presentations because although these collections are very profitable, they do not introduce the exciting new concepts and ideas of their Spring and Fall collections.

Who Is It For?

For designers who wholesale their collection, fashion week should be used to entice buyers to see the collection and place orders. In reality, this is best done through private appointments or at an intimate event where they can see the product close up. Renting a hotel suite near the fashion week venues for buyers and press to stop by at their convenience can have great results.

For direct-to-consumer brands, fashion week is most likely irrelevant to sales. The press would prefer an event that's held when they are less busy and need something new to talk about. However, if your customers are fashion fans and love the idea of fashion week, you can stage a consumer-facing event that doesn't even have to be on the industry radar.

Do not let the industry calendar pressure you to participate every season. It makes more sense to stage events when you have an announcement or something really special to say. A short film distributed online or a live broadcast from your showroom may be more interesting. Just because you have staged events in the past, it's okay to stop. Designers often feel their first or second show brought attention and media coverage, but after that, the results didn't justify the cost.

Alternative Fashion Weeks

Los Angeles, Toronto, Montreal, Shanghai, and India have their own fashion weeks, and many other cities, from Chicago and Nashville to Berlin and Tbilisi, have jumped on the bandwagon. Often, these fashion weeks reach out to emerging labels, inviting them to bring their collections to show. While it can be a great ego boost to be invited to Iceland, it is critical to question how the time and effort spent will advance your business goals. If you just delivered a store in Dubai, it may be worth showing your collection there. If you identify real potential to build your brand in Nashville, a show there could be a great start. But if the market doesn't make sense for your business strategy, don't waste your time.

Event Production

The Budget

When producing an event, start by creating a complete budget that takes into account each of the necessary elements outlined below. Once you know what you can afford to spend, stay within those amounts. With any type of event, it is easy for costs to escalate out of control.

Staging a runway show or presentation is extremely expensive. Keep in mind that the big-name European brands with the jaw-dropping presentations are owned by huge conglomerates with massive budgets and resources. Emerging designers generally spend a minimum of $15,000, and more often as much as $200,000, on each show. There is the cost of the space, staging, and set design; sound and lighting; securing models, hair, and makeup teams; photographers and videographers; marketing and PR; and of course producing and accessorizing an event-worthy collection.

Resourceful designers can spend as little as $5,000 by finding donated space, sponsors to cover production costs, and friends to handle PR. Creativity can help you cut costs. I've seen designers light their runway with a spotlight held by a friend on a ladder. Just keep in mind that while inventiveness is admirable, the event is a direct reflection of your brand. It does not have to look as polished as Carolina Herrera, but if it looks amateurish, it may fuel concerns about your professionalism and ability to produce high-quality product. It is better to wait to stage an event until you have the resources to do it right.

Don't forget the power of banding together with other designers or like-minded brands to stage group events. It lessens the financial burden for each designer and allows each brand to leverage the other's connections, increasing the odds that influential people will attend.

Date and Time

If you plan an event during fashion week in New York, London, Paris, and Milan, the schedules are extremely crowded, and the challenge for a new designer is finding a time slot with the least conflict. In New York, designers apply to the CFDA to arrange a time slot and list their show on the official fashion calendar. As the new kid, you have to be flexible. If you choose 5:00 P.M. on Wednesday and then Marc Jacobs books the same time, it would be wise to move. For a new label, it's often best to hold your first event outside of fashion week, when there is less competition. If the samples are ready, show the Spring collection in August or the Fall collection in late January when schedules are open and buying budgets are full.

Location and Space

Go where your audience is or where it makes sense for your product. With a focus on marketing to Hollywood, it makes sense for Tom Ford to show in Los Angeles. A tour of college towns may be a great strategy if you target the college-age consumer, or a show in a new or top performing market for local press, influencers, and customers can make the best sense for many brands.

An interesting location adds depth and intrigue, but if your event is during fashion week, the primary concern is to make it as easy as possible for the press, influencers, and others you want to attend. This is why most fashion weeks center around an official location where buyers and press can attend multiple shows without traveling. Official fashion week venues are often financially out of reach for most new designers. Alternative group show spaces created by showrooms, sponsors, or event companies are less expensive and generally offer a basic package that includes lighting, sound, and staging.

A show in an official space can feel very generic and leave out the storytelling element that a presentation in a theater, at the designer's alma mater high school, or a lush garden can provide. When you secure your own show space, just consider distance and convenience relative to the major shows. If a buyer has to travel for half an hour from an advertiser's show to get to your venue, she might not bother. But if your show follows Rodarte in the art gallery across the street, it's ideal. Warehouses, galleries, photo studios, hotels, and alleyways can all work IF they fit the overall image of your line. An edgy line could make sense in a tunnel, but a more sophisticated line is better suited to a museum.

Staging Considerations

When reviewing locations, consider the layout of the space and the staging. The cheapest route for a runway show is to have the models walk directly on the floor with three rows of chairs for attendees, plus standing room in the back. If you have more than three rows of chairs, you should either raise the models by building an elevated runway, raise the audience by putting the back rows of chairs on platforms, or use bleachers. A press area should be designated at the end of the runway where cameras can set up to get a clear, head-to-toe shot of each look. If you have a raised runway, the press needs to be on a riser at the same height. Ideally, you will work with a production company that has fashion show experience and can handle your staging, lighting, and sound needs as well as help you anticipate other concerns.

The stage backdrop will appear in all of the images and video from the event and, therefore, should be both appropriate for the collection and your brand. A plain white wall featuring the designer's logo is often used for runway because it identifies the collection in images and lets the clothing be the star. But a dramatic, visually stunning backdrop or elaborate staging can be an important element for capturing attention online. No one will soon forget the visual impact of the hot pink runway amongst the lavender fields of Provence created by designer Simon Porte-Jacquemus in 2019. Sets built for livestreaming need visual impact and can also include interactive elements to provide interest during the event.

Think through the traffic flow and the number of attendees allowed in a space. If only one small elevator goes to a seventh-floor space, it will take a long time to get everyone into the room. You want attendees to remember the clothes, not the wait. The fire code will limit the number of people allowed in the space, and if you exceed that number, you can be shut down before the event even begins. Ask the venue for a floor plan of the space or create one yourself, and use it to map out your check-in area, stage, each individual seat at the show, and the backstage. This plan will also be useful in planning for lighting, sound, and other elements of the event. Make sure you have ample space backstage to accommodate dressing, as well as hair and makeup. The more models and staff, the more space you need. Check that the power capabilities at the space can accommodate several hair dryers, makeup lights, and steamers without blowing a fuse.

Invite the Right People

Fashion events can be designed for as few as 50 guests or for more than 1,000. The size of the audience is less significant than the importance of the people who attend. It's better to show your collection to 30 of the right people than 500 who really won't influence your success. Not all editors, influencers, or customers need to be at your event. Carefully consider who is most appropriate to attend. Sometimes a factory owner, potential investor, or a showroom owner may be the person you most need to impress. An event invitation can also be a coveted reward for good clients.

The event invitation may be the first impression that many in the industry receive of you and your line. Hire a designer to create a impactful digital invite that is both memorable and representative of your brand. Make sure it clearly communicates the pertinent information concerning when, where, and what you are showing and how to RSVP. While a mailed invitation can stand out from a cluttered email box, printing is expensive and often frowned on because of its environmental impact. If you want to do something special for VIPs, consider creating something handmade and conscious of waste.

Unless there is considerable hype about your brand, up to 70 percent of industry invitees will not even respond. Of those who do, as many as 30 percent might not show. Invitations alone will not succeed in getting the target people to your event. Follow up with important people who have not responded to confirm they have the information. If they tell you they can't make it, ask if someone else from the store or media outlet could attend on their behalf. It's a good idea to confirm the RSVP of anyone important, reminding them of the date, time, and location. Offering to send a car service to VIPs helps ensure they show up.

For a runway show, a designer should overbook more people than chairs to avoid having an empty room at showtime. The RSVPs are used to create a seating chart for the show. Ideally, a publicist or PR firm that understands how to prioritize attendees should handle the chart. The most "important" people are seated in the front row, and then you work your way back. Try to keep rival publications and stores away from each other by seating them on opposite sides or placing others between them. If several people RSVP from a specific publication, such as *WWD*, call and ask which person is actually covering the show. Even if higher-ranked writers are coming, the covering writer should be in the front. It is unrealistic to expect the seats at your first show to be full of fashion directors, but realize that associate buyers have influence and editorial assistants get promoted.

Celebrities attract photographers and press, but celebrity wrangling is time consuming and there are no guarantees. It's best to try to work a connection to a celebrity who has worn your clothes or through a stylist who regularly pulls them. If you get a celebrity confirmation, send a media alert to the press and make sure they are photographed at your event.

Photography and Video

Good photographs are often the most important result of an event. They are used to create the season's lookbook, to remind media and buyers of the collection, and make up important content for your website and social media. A good photographer with fashion show or event experience is critical to getting the photographs you need. Arrange to receive high-resolution photos immediately after the show to email them out to short lead press. Some professional event photographers work closely with the media and may feed photos directly to them on your behalf. Give clear instructions to the photographer about the shots you want. Ideally, you want a head-to-toe of each look, along with close-ups that show the details of the design.

Make sure they take several photographs of the hair and makeup action backstage, as well as the VIP arrivals and people seated in your front row. You may need a second photographer just to focus on party shots and candid photos of models and attendees.

A runway photographer should take full shots of each outfit as well as close-ups of the details.
© Photos by Dan & Corina Lecca

Photos from a fashion week Vena Cava installation
© Photos by Georgia Nerheim

Clothing looks best when it moves and a good videographer is vital to capture the presentation, as well as other key components of the event. The footage can be used to create long- and short-form content for social media and to send out for television or Internet press coverage. Producers do not always have the budget to send a crew to shoot a young designer's events, but they may cover them if the designer can provide high-quality footage. Review your video and pay attention to detail, and take notes of anything that can be done better next time. Perhaps the models should pose for longer, or you should remember to take the price tags off the bottom of the shoes.

Lighting

Good lighting is critical to show the clothes clearly and to capture high-quality photos and video. There are lighting options for any budget, and Gordon Link, president of Bernhard Link Theatrical, offers the following advice on what is most important: "First, make sure your show has adequate, even, front light positioned just over the press riser, as low and/or flat as possible. What's best for your show depends on the location (indoor or outdoor), the time (daytime or night), and the designer's vision. Backlight is the second most important because front light alone makes objects appear flat and two-dimensional. Backlight looks great in pictures and allows audience members to view the back of the garment after the model has passed. Budget permitting, background or architectural lighting affects the overall look of the show. This can be achieved with color, intensity, pattern, silhouette, or special effects."[8]

When starting out, keep it simple and avoid too many effects or colors, which can distort the appearance of the clothes. It's key that you have enough light—either hung above the runway or set on goalposts at the ends and sides of the runway to flood the entire runway fully. Spotlights cast shadows that can result in dark or distorted photographs, so they should only be used as additional, not primary, lights. Test the lighting with a model and instruct the models on where to stand or walk to achieve the best results. Confirm that your location can meet the necessary power requirements to avoid leaving the audience uneasily waiting in the dark. Beware of using a shiny surface or material for your backdrop, logo, or runway, which may reflect the lights and cause a glare that distorts photos and hampers the view for the attendees.

Music

Upbeat music keeps people awake, sets the pace for the models to walk, and gives energy to the collection. While moody or esoteric music sets a dramatic tone for an intellectual collection, it can put the audience to sleep or even annoy them. For a show or performance, don't forget pre-show music to set the mood as audience enters the space and waits for the event to begin. The sound needs to fill the entire space and be clear and loud enough to cover any noise from the audience and backstage. If there is live music or a DJ during the show, the equipment needs will increase. Ideally, the space will have a sound system, and your basic needs will be included in the rental. Remember to rent headset equipment to enable the sound and lighting technicians to communicate with the producer during the event.

Models

The models you choose are key to how your collection is perceived. Of course, during fashion week, models are extremely busy, and the designers are competing to book the best. Start casting by contacting agencies and asking to speak to the runway agents. Send images and share press, social media wins, and celebrity placements to help convince them that you are a rising star worthy of their assistance. When you speak with the booker, describe the type of model you want in terms of skin tone, hair type, thin or curvy, tall or petite, muscular or lean, grungy or clean-cut. The agency will generally offer new, developmental models who need event experience and initial exposure. If there is considerable buzz about your line, it will help you book more established models who attract press and make you appear influential.

Arrange a casting time and email a call sheet with the time and location information to the booker for the models. Once you are certain that you want to book a particular model, confirm with the booker immediately, before they send the model to cast for a conflicting event. Set up a fitting time and confirm the date for your event and the backstage call time with the booker. Backstage call should be three hours before show time, but some models may come from other bookings and have only minutes to be prepped for your stage. After the casting, you may still lose models to designers with a bigger budget or better name, even on the day of your event. If this happens, stay calm and work with the booker to replace the model quickly, or work with your existing lineup to add an outfit change. If you need assistance, casting directors have connections and relationships at the agencies and can leverage their other events to help you.

Be up front with the bookers about your ability to compensate the models. Negotiate rates at the beginning or even partner with a single agency as a sponsor to receive a deal. Often, new models will walk in exchange for clothing and photos, and it can be great PR for you if the model shows up at editorial castings wearing your designs. Models can be given clothing from the current collection, or you can let them pre-order from the collection you show. Each model should receive a complete outfit or significant item such as a coat or dress. A T-shirt is not adequate compensation! Confirm the details of compensation immediately with the booker following the show. If they have to chase you down for clothes, they will hesitate to work with you again. If your clothing is extremely expensive, it may not make sense to use it as payment. It might be cheaper to hire the models at their rate or find alternative compensation. Designers have persuaded show sponsors to provide product, such as Olympus cameras, for the models. When you budget, realize that there is usually a 15 to 20 percent commission to the agency on top of the model's rate.

Fashion week is extremely stressful for models. They are running from castings to fittings to shows all day long and late into the night. People are constantly touching them, pulling on their hair, and dressing them in a multitude of uncomfortable clothes and shoes. Have some respect and patience during the casting and fitting and backstage at the event. Provide water and food and don't make the models wait long or ask them to return repeatedly for fittings. A model can become a valuable advocate for your line, agreeing to work with you for photo shoots and in future shows.

The number of models you need is based on the format of your event and the number of looks you want to show. For a runway show, the models can walk more than once in a show, so you only need one model for every two or three looks. To ensure smooth changes, recruit skilled dressers and assign one to each model. At the fittings, take a photo of the model in each outfit, complete with shoes and accessories. These photos should be attached to poster board in the order they will appear in the show and used backstage to communicate the looks to the dressers before the show.

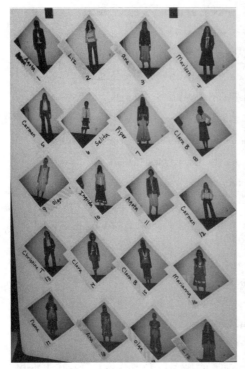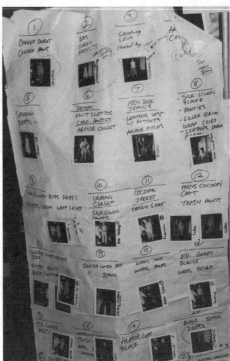

These run of show boards include photos of each outfit in the order
they should appear in the show for use by the dressers backstage.
© Photo(s) by Glenn Pasquariello (aka: 610-Glenn)

Styling and Merchandising

A new designer's presentation should be short and sweet—25 to 30 carefully edited looks
is plenty. People can see more online or in the showroom. It is wise to enlist a stylist to help
merchandise a concise show, and working with a reputable stylist can also lend cachet, draw
media attention, and help land important elements such as shoes. Partnering with a prominent
luxury line for accessories adds prestige to your collection, but the competition is great. A new
designer might love the publicity—just make sure they have enough samples. Buying shoes is
extremely expensive, but a designer can be creative with shoes from the Salvation Army. Spray
paint, glue, ribbon, or cloth can go a long way.

Hair and Makeup

There are a few options for securing hair and makeup services for your show. Hiring
professionals is one, but the more affordable route is to find hair and makeup brands that will
donate services to promote their stylists, salons, or products. If you are fortunate, they may even
provide financial support for the show.

When communicating inspiration or direction for the show, remember that hair and makeup
artists are visual people. Create mood boards with photos, sketches, and color samples. Be as
clear as possible to avoid disappointments backstage. I recommend testing the hair and makeup

looks before the show with the artist and a model to agree on the final look. Send photos of the models to the teams in advance to help them plan accordingly for each model's hair and skin. At the event, be organized and provide plenty of space, along with mirrors, lighting, and power.

Rehearsal

Before the event, conduct a full rehearsal with models, lights, and sound to make sure everyone understands their roles and the cues and to make sure that you are happy with the presentation as a whole. Give direction to the models on how you want them to walk or pose and what attitude they should project. Let them practice in their shoes.

A runway show should have consistent pacing with a continual and even spacing of models on the runway. Most shows keep at least two models on the runway at once, with a new model entering from backstage as soon as one turns at the end of the runway to walk back. If there are problems with changes during the show, the pacing can be adjusted gradually to provide more time for the activity backstage. If a model is not fully ready for the cue, send out one who is, even though the show order will be wrong. Slow pacing is boring, but there is nothing worse than an empty runway.

At the Event
Staff

If you have a few extra thousand dollars, hiring a public relations firm or production company to help organize the event will make it much easier. Before hiring either, find out whether it has other events on the same day or during the week and ensure that you will receive the attention you need. There are publicists who take on some production responsibility and producers who do PR. Clearly define responsibilities up front to make sure nothing is forgotten.

Staff at the event will need to manage arrivals, check-in, seating if applicable, red carpet photography, and troubleshooting. It takes time for people to arrive, especially if they are coming from another event. Plan carefully to make your check-in system run as quickly and smoothly as possible, and if you are staging a live presentation or show, don't start more than a half an hour late. Once 30 minutes has passed, there is no point in waiting for those VIPs who have not yet arrived.

If you have a runway show or theatrical event, you will need a producer or professional to "call" the show as well as a backstage manager. The producer will coordinate the lighting, sound, and model cues via headset to ensure that everything runs smoothly and looks professional while the backstage manager can supervise the dressers and hair and makeup teams to assure everything goes well. Most PR firms and production companies have teams with the required experience.

Materials

A *run of show* is a printed page that describes the inspiration for the collection, information on you and your brand, and a description of each look. At a runway show, the looks are listed in the order of appearance and the list is placed on every chair for use during the show. The run of show should list the models; include credits for hair, makeup, styling, shoes, public relations, production, and accessories; and thank sponsors, bookers, front and backstage staff, and anyone else who helped with the show.

Gift bags are often given to attendees at events and shows. People do love free stuff, but it's really not necessary to have a gift bag, and in fact there has been a backlash against the wastefulness of producing and distributing bags full of paper and mass-produced junk. It takes time and money to obtain bags and the contents. If a gift bag is important to your sponsor, ask them to donate the bag and the items inside. Beauty product, beverages, and food items make the most sense.

Sponsorship

A sponsor will certainly relieve some of the financial pressure of producing an event. Many companies look for opportunities to align with the glamour of fashion and position their brands as supporters of new talent.

Finding sponsors is very competitive, so start far in advance of your event. Many corporations move slowly when reviewing and approving proposals, and they often allocate their funds up to one year in advance. Do not just craft an email and then send it out to marketing departments at dozens of companies. The more targeted the outreach, the more the likelihood of success.

Think about which companies are a good match for your brand and the story you tell. The personality and values of the partner are just as important as the product category. Obvious fashion sponsors are hair and makeup companies, fashionable electronics and phones, and beverages such as Evian. Research which companies are targeting fashion audiences in their advertising. Companies with a new products or redesigns usually have large budgets to support their launch. Examine your collection and themes. If you use large quantities of a particular fiber, such as cotton or jersey, contact the fiber manufacturer or trade organization. If the collection is washable, call Woolite. The trade commission where you produce your Peruvian knits or source your Scottish wool may also have promotional funds.

Once you have a target list of companies, contact the marketing department and ask for the appropriate contact for sponsorships. Introduce yourself and send a compelling email that includes key press, intriguing photos, and an explanation of how your story enhances their brand. A company wants to believe that by aligning with you, it will receive valuable exposure, reach new potential customers, and amplify the message of its product and brand. Event producers and PR firms can often help secure sponsors.

Potential sponsors need an outline of what they receive in sponsoring your show. Generally, they want presence in exchange for their money. You can serve their champagne, water, or chocolate at the show; put items on every chair; provide signage at the entrance and mention on the invite; or even park their car in front of the venue. Try to think of fun and creative ways to integrate their brand in a meaningful way. Sometimes a designer will work with the sponsor to create a customized item. Of course, there are limits to what a designer can do without compromising integrity. Be nice when you say no, and explain how it hurts the sponsor's reputation too. Don't work with anyone in desperation.

After the show, send copies of press, a list of key attendees, and photos of both the show and their presence to the sponsor. Emphasize the success of the event and make it a good experience in hopes that they will return next season.

11 PROTECTING CREATIVITY

Having a design copied is an extremely frustrating, and unfortunately common, part of being a designer. Fast-fashion manufacturers are able to see a design on Instagram, produce it in mere days, and distribute it months before the original becomes available. Designers have had wholesale orders canceled mid-production because a store buyer saw a cheap knockoff on the market. While Diet Prada calls out hundreds of examples of blatant fashion piracy each year, the mass brands have lawyers on retainer to manage disputes and they know the small brands do not have the time or resources to fight back.

Keeping images of new designs off of social media until the product is available can help avoid the problem, but ultimately staying focused on your values and unique point of view will protect you the most. While various products can be knocked off, the story that makes your brand special cannot. Sometimes lemons can be made into lemonade. For example, a designer who recently launched her brand saw a copy of her signature jacket in the Instagram feed of a large luxury brand. She commented that it looked familiar and suggested they work together. This resulted in a high-profile collaboration and a sizable design fee for the designer.

Before we delve deeper into the issue, as a creative person keep in mind the words of the late great editor Diana Vreeland, who said, "Just go ahead. Give ideas away. Under every idea there is a new idea waiting to be born."

Fashion Designs and Intellectual Property Protection
by Olivera Medenica, Dunnington Bartholow & Miller LLP

The fashion industry is a creative industry, and intellectual property rights protect the fruits of our creative labor. But fashion design is an odd fit for intellectual property protection, and unfortunately, there is no all-encompassing right protecting fashion designs. That is because fashion is functional; it covers our body, protects our feet, keeps us warm or cool, and generally caters to our moral aesthetics and environment. Sure, there is much room for creativity in this functional purpose, but the designs we buy are largely driven by our environment and social dress code.

What Are Your Options When Seeking to Protect Fashion Designs?

This lack of protection has frustrated many and resulted in numerous debates, not to mention proposed legislative efforts before the United States Congress—all of which, to date, have been unsuccessful in changing anything for the fashion industry. Many designers invest a lot of time and money in their work only to find their creations instantly replicated in knockoff designs and sold at significantly reduced or bargain basement prices. Some argue that this cycle benefits the fashion industry as a whole and pushes the fashion cycle forward to new creations. Others argue that offering knockoffs at such a different price point does not impact a design house's income as the average consumers could not even afford the original design in the first place. Conversely, some argue that protection is long overdue, and that creativity is wasted, and revenues lost, where design piracy is left rampant and unrestricted by any design right.

This is an important debate, and there are convincing arguments to be made on each side. It is important to understand that intellectual property rights cut both ways. As much as a designer may wish for protection to prevent others from copying, so can the same designer be the unlucky recipient of an unpleasant letter accusing her of infringement. Sometimes those claims are legitimate, sometimes they are a stretch, and sometimes they are utterly baseless. Whatever the strength or weakness of the claim, the designer has to respond, and decide whether to give in or lawyer up to defend.

There are limits to each intellectual property right in fashion designs, but such rights do exist for fashion design if they are used judiciously. While you may not be able to get intellectual property protection for the entire design as a whole (for example, the shape of a dress, or a shirt), you can get protection for specific aspects of the design. So let's examine each right specifically, and how it may apply. We will be looking at copyrights, trademarks, and patents.

How Can I Use Copyright to Protect My Designs?

Copyright law protects different kinds of works of authorship including literary, dramatic, musical, and artistic works, such as poetry, novels, movies, songs, computer software, and architecture. An important point to remember is that copyright law only protects works of authorship that are "fixed"—in other words, you can see it, touch it, or hear it. So copyright does not protect facts, ideas, systems, or methods of operation. But it does protect how those things are expressed on a piece of paper or in a three-dimensional design, for example.

A work of authorship is under copyright protection the moment it is created and fixed in a tangible means of expression. There is no need to register in order to get copyright protection. However, there are substantial advantages to registration. You have to register your work if you wish to bring a lawsuit for infringement of a U.S. work. In addition, registered works may be eligible for statutory damages and attorney's fees in successful litigation.

U.S. copyright laws do not extend copyright protection to "useful articles." So, for example, that would include clothing, shoes, furniture, and dinnerware. It may, however, include pictures or sculptural works that can be identified separately from the article. So a "useful article" could have copyrightable and un-copyrightable elements. For example, the floral design on a dress or scarf could be protected by copyright, but the dress or scarf itself could not. Similarly, the three dimensional shape of buttons on a sweater could be protected by copyright, but the sweater itself could not.

In the fashion industry, we can see many examples where copyright protection is applicable. Bear in mind, however, simple logos or designs are not sufficiently original to benefit from copyright protection, it would have to be something more. For example, Louis Vuitton's well known multi-colored "LV" monogram design pattern has a copyright registration, but the mere "LV" interlocked letters would not be sufficiently original to be registered as a copyright (they are, however, registered as a trademark).

So consider how these rights apply to your own designs. You may want to design your own artwork and include it on a dress or shirt. Or you may want to consider using unique or intricate button designs, of your own creation, to incorporate into a sweater or a highly decorative heel for a shoe design. These are just some of the things to consider when creating your own designs.

To register a copyright, go to the registration portal of the U.S. Copyright Office and log in to the Electronic Copyright Office Registration System by creating an account. The Copyright Office's website is geared towards non-attorneys and includes a ton of information that is helpful to guide you through the process.

How Are Trademarks Useful to Protect My Designs?

Trademarks are probably the most valuable right a fashion company can have. Consistent use of a trademark allows consumers to recognize a brand which is appealing to them because of its price point, quality, style, or ethical choices. That is why in the absence of all-encompassing intellectual property rights, it is critical for a fashion brand to distinguish itself from others through the use of a trademark.

A trademark is generally a word, phrase, symbol, design, or a combination thereof, that identifies and distinguishes the source of the goods of one party from those of others. It is important that when you select a mark that it not be likely to be confused with any pre-existing marks. Similarities can arise when the marks sound similar, when they are similar in appearance, or when they have a similar meaning. So for example, the following marks would be considered similar:

Sound: SYMPHONICA and SIMFONIKA

Appearance: SYMPHONICA and SYMPHONICA

Meaning: BEAUTIFUL and BELLA

But the marks above would not be considered similar if they relate to completely different goods or services. SYMPHONICA for apparel would not conflict with SYMPHONICA for real estate services.

It is also important to remember that it is in your best interest to select a mark that is deemed "strong" as opposed to "weak." Some marks are easier to protect than others, and they are often referred to, in the legal sense, as "strong" marks. If a mark is "weak" then it is likely descriptive of the underlying goods or services, and others are already using it to describe their own goods or services.

"Strong" marks are thus ones that are fanciful—in other words, the mark has nothing to do with the underlying goods or services. For example, APPLE for computers, SUPREME for clothing, or SOLEIL for jewelry. Conversely, GOWN for dresses, TRINKETS for jewelry, or CHAUSSURE for shoes would not be good trademark choices. The more descriptive the mark, the less likely you will be able to prevent others from using the same mark to identify potentially competing products or services.

Moreover, registering a mark at the United States Patent and Trademark Office (USPTO) will not be possible if the mark is:

- A surname;

- Geographically descriptive of the origin of the goods/services;

- A foreign term that translates to a descriptive or generic term; or

- An individual's name or likeliness.

There are exceptions to these rules, but they are difficult to overcome. For example, it would not be possible to register the name or likeness of a living individual as a trademark, unless you obtain their permission. Similarly, it would not be possible to register a word that sounds like a last name, but it would be possible to register a first and last name together. These rules may be subject to exceptions depending upon factual circumstances. It is therefore advisable to retain an attorney to guide you through this process. That being said, understanding limitations can at least help you initially pick the right mark for your business.

Finally, it is also possible to obtain another type of trademark called a trade dress. Trade dress is a type of trademark that extends to the configuration (design and shape) of a product itself. A product's trade dress can be protected just like a trademark. A trade dress protects the total image of a product including features such as size, shape, color or color combinations, texture, or graphics. Examples of well-known trade dress include the Chanel No. 5 bottle or the Hermès Birkin bag. In some very limited circumstances, the shape, color, and arrangement of materials on a line of clothing can be protectable as a trade dress—such as, for example, the Louboutin red sole.

It is important to remember, that these rights are not available if the feature sought to be protected is functional. Thus, a brand would not be able to monopolize a handbag's handle design if the design is functional. These types of rights are difficult to obtain, and require sophisticated legal arguments by an attorney.

How you use your mark is therefore crucial in the development of your brand. You may choose to simply place your brand on a label, hidden from public view, or you may decide to visibly brand apparel by printing the mark on the textile or on an outward facing label. You may also decide to use a distinctive three-dimensional design thus creating an instantly recognizable brand. These are branding strategies that can pay off in the long term, but it is also a design choice that you must believe will appeal to your consumers. So carefully consider how these rights can be weaved into your design in the short and long term.

Trademarks, service marks, and trade dress can be registered at the USPTO. The process can be lengthy and the cost is more significant than a copyright registration. Much like the Copyright Office, the USPTO has tons of helpful information to review on getting started and on understanding trademark rights. While it is not mandatory to register a trademark, there are significant benefits to doing so, not the least of which is additional damages in certain circumstances. It also serves as a notice, and thus a deterrent, to everyone else in the world that you are using the mark in the U.S.

Generally speaking, there is no legal requirement for you to hire an attorney to file a trademark. However, if your domicile is not located in the United States or its territories, you are required to have a U.S.-licensed attorney represent you in trademark matters at the USPTO.

How Are Patents Useful to Protect My Designs?

A patent is a limited duration property right relating to an invention. There are two types of patents relevant in the fashion industry: utility patents and design patents. Utility patents cover useful inventions and discoveries. Design patents cover non-functional and ornamental designs. Both require that the invention be new and non-obvious in comparison with prior inventions. Contrary to copyrights and trademarks, in order to secure patent protection in the U.S., registration at the USPTO is mandatory.

There are many examples of utility patents in the fashion industry. For example, Nike, Inc. has a patent on a cushioning sole for use in athletic shoes. Other companies have patents for automatic lacing systems or interchangeable soles. Utility patents play an important role in preventing competitors from using functional and inventive design to gain competitive advantage.

Design patents, on the other hand, focus not on the functionality of the design, but rather its ornamental uniqueness. A design patent protects novel, ornamental designs and can be a useful tool in protecting new, non-functional, and non-obvious designs. CROCS, for example, have a design patent on their famous shoe design, as do Yves Saint Laurent, Christian Louboutin, Jimmy Choo, and Valentino on some of their heels. Similarly, Alexander Wang obtained a design patent for "bags with corners," consisting of a handbag design with metal-covered corners. Lululemon also has a number of design patents, including for bras, tops, shorts, and sleeve cuffs.

Utility and design patents are a powerful tool to deter third party infringers from using a design that is substantially the same. However, few resort to patent protection for the simple reason that it is expensive to obtain. Fashion is also highly cyclical; unless the design will be used for a long time, it is not worth the time, money, and effort to obtain a registration. Securing a patent thus means that you intend on using the invention, and profiting therefrom, for the duration of its term (usually 15 years for a design patent and 20 years for utility patents).

Evaluating Your Design: Which Intellectual Property Right to Choose?

The protection that you ultimately choose will be dependent upon your budget and goals. It is useful to view your design in the context of what common elements will be recurring throughout your creations. To be sure, your brand and trademark should be consistently used to identify your designs, but the extent to which other design elements benefit from intellectual property protection remains a careful case by case analysis. While a design as a whole may rarely benefit from protection, there are important exceptions that may apply, and they should be carefully considered. When properly used, intellectual property rights can be a designer's powerful ally in protecting and monetizing their creations.

When Should You Retain an Attorney?

You should retain an attorney when you have a specific question or specific situation that requires attention. So for example, if you see an infringing design, it is best to consult an attorney rather than taking things into your own hands. Similarly, it is best not to hurl insults and accusations over social media if you suspect infringement, as it does not help from either a PR or legal perspective.

It is important to remember that attorneys are neither therapists, trainers, nor educators. They are there to represent your interests and get the best resolutions possible to your specific problem. It is not a good idea to hire an attorney to generally educate you about the subject matter of intellectual property, or to "brainstorm" with you about an ideal trademark for your business when you have not even identified one. You should have done that work on your own.

That being said, attorneys are great resources for helping you pick the strongest possible trademark out of your favorite ones, or to strategize on how to address a potential infringer, or to respond to a cease and desist letter. They are also great at assessing your business and giving you guidance on what to protect, and how to negotiate commercial relationships. Attorneys are thus powerful allies for your business, but they are not cost effective if you have not done the work on your end.

Keep in mind that there are a number of law school clinics where students advise and represent clients with a variety of legal problems under the supervision of experienced faculty. For example, Professor Joe Forgione who is the founding director of the tech-based Fashion Law Initiative at New York Law School works with fashion designers and brands in the U.S. Patent Trademark Office Clinic program at the law school. Similarly, Cardozo law school has a Tech Startup Clinic that may be helpful to any start-up e-commerce platform. Fordham Law School also runs a number of Fashion Law Pop-Up Clinics throughout the year. This may be a good cost-effective option, and a welcome opportunity for legal experience by your local law school.

Olivera Medenica is a partner at Dunnington Bartholow & Miller LLP and chairs its Fashion and Trademark Law Practice Groups. She has almost two decades of experience advising domestic and foreign businesses in fashion, retail, media, and entertainment on transactional, litigation, and arbitration matters. She founded and chairs two annual fashion law conferences in New York and Paris (more info at www.fedbar.org). You can find her on Twitter at @omedenica and she can be reached at omedenica@dunnington.com. Disclaimer: The information contained in this article is for informational purposes only and does not constitute legal advice. Nothing provided herein should be used as a substitute for the advice of competent counsel.

12 EXPANDING THE BUSINESS

For designers with an established customer base, brand recognition, and annual sales approaching $5 million, the next step of growth can be elusive. The place between emerging and emerged is frustrating. A designer is no longer a new discovery, and may even be well known, but the business is still not firmly established. Designer Alice Roi calls it "fashion puberty" and says, "No one in this place is anywhere firm."[1]

Some believe growth just takes time, and others believe it requires a cash infusion. Increased volume causes costs to balloon as the designer must outlay more cash for production materials, as well as invest in more employees and other infrastructure and technology. It becomes harder to protect your margin as your expenses increase. This is where, if you don't have a business manager or advisor on board, you should find someone. It is critical for early-stage companies that have passed the initial start-up phase to focus on business strategy to find and evaluate opportunities and efficiencies to take the company to the next level. While many designers fear giving up control, there is too much to do alone, and bringing in business expertise is often the only way to grow.

At this stage, more than ever, a designer needs to return to their mission statement and definition of success. The key is to stay focused as you look for new opportunities in the market, stay flexible in the face of change, and adapt in a way that truly makes sense for your brand.

Growth vs. Scale

Designers often discuss *scale*, but while every business wants growth, beware of the pressure to expand too quickly or become too big. Rapid growth or scale can suffocate a company that isn't ready, and it can compromise your control over quality and vision.

Growth usually means using resources to tap into new revenue streams by expanding into new geographic markets; opening new channels such as wholesale, e-commerce, or your own store; or developing new product lines. *Scale*, on the other hand, is doing more of the same at less cost. It usually hones in on a single item or concept, finding efficiencies to cut costs and lower price, while using resources (often outside investment) to rapidly increase volume, distribution, and market share.

The first question is not how to grow or scale, but rather WHY? A goal of global expansion with exponential revenues will take you on a different path than a goal of creative satisfaction. Staying small is a viable end goal if success equals a deeper relationship with a loyal community, developing handmade product, or keeping a minimal staff. As designer Bliss Lau states, "I chose not to scale. I want to be a designer, not a people manager."[2]

Slow and steady wins the race. For small, creatively led brands, the best strategy is to build the business one step at a time, creating efficiencies before rushing to the next level. Focus on how to make the business better, not bigger.

Review and Re-examine

As you grow, it's important to take time to step back and review your business as a whole. Analyze the product and markets with the most sales and best margins. You may decide to discontinue some items to focus on others. If you launched intending to only sell direct online, it might be time to evolve and build a wholesale business as well. Greater volume could mean streamlining your supply chain or even phasing out conventional cotton to focus on organic.

Revisit your vendor and supplier relationships to renegotiate your terms and ask your best accounts for better positioning. Re-examine who is really buying the product. Your most loyal customer may not actually be who you think! This information can shape how you continue to evolve your product and customer experience.

Each growth step requires more money up front—both in terms of cash flow for increased production, as well as for investment in technology and people. Many businesses proudly fund their own growth while others explore outside investment. Fortunately, as a business becomes more established, it becomes more attractive to investors who seek brands with a good track record, a clear vision, and significant potential for growth. Chapter 3: The Money covers more on finding and securing financial investment.

Whether growth looks like breaking into a new market, partnering for distribution, or developing new product categories, you should map out each option with real steps, time lines, and numbers. This will help you effectively analyze the best- and worst-case scenarios and understand the cash flow and the potential profit or loss realities for each option.

New Revenue Streams

Licensing

Licensing is the leasing of your brand name or product to a manufacturer for a specific purpose, and for a specific length of time, in return for a royalty, or percentage of sales. Generally, a licensee manufactures and distributes product under the designer's name and handles all the costs of production and sales. Licensing can be a lucrative brand extension and not require too much work on the designer's part, but licensees look to partner with brands that already have name recognition and some success in the marketplace.

The main reason to license is to partner with someone who has expertise in an area that you do not. Licensing can extend your brand to a new product category, such as makeup, eyewear, perfume, or denim. For the early-stage designer, licensing most often means partnering for production or distribution of their designs in a new market, such as Japan or China. While a designer may be able to develop a few accounts in a new international market on her own, the differing laws, language, cultural issues, and control of the sales and distribution channels make building any sizable business difficult without a partner.

Giving up the headaches of production, sales, and cash flow sounds ideal, but the risk is losing control. It's critical that you protect your image by requiring approval on all products and places of distribution and firmly setting the quality standard. Require approval on any advertising and marketing that includes your name. An unethical licensing company could create product without your knowledge to make up its volume. In fact, a growing brand in England had a licensing agreement for high-end clothing in Japan. When traveling there, the designers stopped at a convenience store and were shocked to see water bottle holders bearing their logo. They had not approved this type of product or this type of store. It's a good idea to attach an approved distribution list to your licensing agreements.

Don't rush into a deal. When choosing a licensee, ask for references and talk to some of their clients. Make sure the financial arrangement makes sense. Typically, the designer is paid a licensing fee based on a percentage of sales, ranging from 4 to 8 percent. If you have good sales connections that will open new doors for the licensee, or if your brand is in great demand, you will be able to negotiate a higher percentage. Usually the licensor receives a guaranteed amount of royalty regardless of the product's performance.

Designers turn down deals for a multitude of reasons. Some agreements don't offer enough money, others want the designer to design a private label as part of the deal or pigeonhole the line in one specific design direction. Don't agree to anything unless it fits your brand and helps to sell your other products. Beware of companies that may have a conflict of interest. For example, if you sign a licensing agreement with a retailer, it may be less motivated to distribute the product outside its own stores.

Rental

Rental can provide an additional revenue stream and introduce new people to your brand, but it can be costly in time and maintenance and encroach on your sales. For a smaller brand, the best way to participate in rental is through a platform such as Rent the Runway or Armoire, which buy the product outright and manage the logistics. There are brands that offer rental on their own in order to keep control of the customer relationship and try to convert them to buy. Some rent on a per item basis, others charge a monthly fee for customers to choose a number of items to keep until they either return them for something new or purchase them at a discount. There are costs of cleaning the items between rentals and storing, tracking, and managing all of the shipping and returns.

Resale

Brands are working to find ways to benefit from the secondary resale market for their products. Larger brands partner with resale businesses like The RealReal and offer consignors of their product a discount on something new. Designers who find active resale communities of their products online are joining the conversation and offering these loyal fans a sneak peak on new items, private discounts, or first pick at sample sales. It's smart to find a way to reward the customers who are already engaging with your product and sharing feedback online.

Membership and Subscription Models

Membership models encourage discovery and loyalty and can even promote recycling. For a monthly fee, customers receive a number of products ranging from T-shirts to jewelry or undergarments in various silhouettes and colors. Most models ship a selection of product, and customers return what they don't want and pay for what they keep. Some offer an opportunity to return used garments to be recycled or reused for a discount or bonus item. Customers first fill out a survey to help direct the selection that will best fit their taste and needs. A brand can create their own program to send out a mix of core product or capsule collections, or designers can join styling programs such as StitchFixe or Rachel Zoe "Box of Style" to introduce their label to new consumers. Some programs focus on a specific lifestyle or category, such as fitness or socially conscious products.

Product Extensions

Many designers feel they max out the market with their signature line and can't keep growing that business exponentially. A second line at a lower price point, or in a new category, can open up another market or distribution channel. For example, Isabel Marant Étoile offers a relaxed spin on the signature Isabel Marant line. And after two seasons of shoes, Loeffler Randall expanded its product offerings to add bags. The bags were a natural extension of shoes, and buyers were asking for them from the start.[3]

A second line can take advantage of changes in the marketplace or the mindset of a customer. If a second line is created at a different quality level or focuses on a different market than your signature line, give it a different name to keep the cheaper goods from eroding the quality and image of the main collection. Fashion brand Rodarte has a huge following of fans, many of whom cannot afford to wear their exquisite signature collection. But the brand's casual line of "Radarte" sweatshirts and T-shirts allows those fans to participate and offers an alternate revenue stream to the brand.

Remember that any brand extensions need to stay authentic to your story and original product. The greater your consistency, the more easily you can reach even further into non-fashion lifestyle categories.

Consulting and Creative Direction

The popularity and hype surrounding emerging designers entices larger brands to hire them to design or consult for their brand. Marc Beckman of DMA United says, "There are opportunities in creative direction, licensing, product endorsement, sponsorship, and personal appearances."[4] His agency manages designers in a similar manner as talent agents handle actors and rock stars and helps them find alternative revenue streams.

Aside from the excitement of attaching a buzzworthy designer name to their brand, big companies realize that young designers often have close relationships with their followers because of their marketing and social media, and they understand how to appeal to their trend-setting customer base. Corporations also hire designers to tap into their technical expertise and strong merchandising sense for a particular category, such as handbags. Timberland hired British designer Christopher Raeburn as global creative director to emphasize their shared commitment to responsible design. Investment companies that buy large fashion firms often seek a new designer who has a following in the industry to renew the brand. Most of these designers continue to design their own labels while working with the larger brand (as Virgil Abloh does with Louis Vuitton and Off White).

Non-fashion partnerships and design opportunities abound as well. Designer Paul Marlow has designed uniforms for the staff at high-end restaurants including Nix in New York City. Designer Dana Buchman was commissioned to design the interior of a prototype Cadillac SRX. Other opportunities include consulting for fabric, personal electronics, and phone companies, as well as designing interiors for restaurants, hotels, and airlines.

In addition to income, a partnership expands the designer's visibility via large distribution networks and marketing budgets that highlight the designer's name in advertising and PR campaigns. Depending on the deal, compensation can be an actual salary, an annual or monthly consulting fee, or a flat design fee. Some deals include a percentage of sales. Negotiating the details is important and be specific in defining your duties. Designing a bag line could include sourcing the fabric and overseeing production or just providing sketches. The compensation should equal the time and effort put into the project, as well as the use of your name. The agreements can last for one season or one product, or include a multiyear contract for full collections or product lines.

While high-end brands bring enviable endorsement to the designer, a few designers have had their wholesale accounts drop their collections because the buyers were worried that a mass-brand partnership would cheapen the designer's name with their high-end customers. If you are a new brand with high-end accounts and are offered a mass-market partnership, you may want to limit it to one collection or to an different product category rather than gamble on whether your brand can sustain a long-term commitment at the low end.

Stand for Something

It never ceases to amaze me how generous independent designers can be. They are in tune with social movements and are ready to support the causes they believe in. Whether it's raising funds or just boosting awareness, if there is something you feel passionate about, *and it fits with your brand story*, there are great ways to get involved. Rebecca Minkoff founded the Female Founder Collective dedicated to enabling and empowering female-owned and led companies. In addition to her dedication to ecological and sustainable production, designer Maria Cornejo hosted a fundraiser for Planned Parenthood and donated 100 percent of sales of her limited-edition T-shirt to the organization. Aurora James, designer and creative director of Brother Vellies, launched the 15 Percent Pledge to challenge major retailers to dedicate more shelf space to products made by Black-owned companies. Other designers dedicate resources to materials research or residency programs for artisans. Whether you make a long-term commitment or respond to a moment in time, as so many did during the COVID-19 crises, it can be very rewarding to use your voice in an authentic way to make a difference.

ACKNOWLEDGMENTS

This book couldn't have been written if it weren't for all the designers who have taught me so much by sharing their triumphs, frustrations, and laughter during the past 20 years. There are too many to name, and while many are mentioned in this book, there are dozens more who inspire me with their vision and drive.

Thank you to the many industry experts who have shared their valuable knowledge and perspective via interviews, emails, and casual conversations. I'm particularly grateful to Alexandra D'Archangelo, Elizabeth Dunn and Mar Espanol, Manpreet Kaur Kalra, Anna McCraney, Olivera Medenica, Laura Moffat, Tim Moore, Roger Padilha, Nicholas Rozansky, and Susan Scafidi, who provided the thoughtful contributions in the book.

Thank you to Angela Tartaro, Megan Buckman, John Giordano, and the other editors and designers at Barron's/Kaplan Publishing who have worked so hard on this third edition.

Most of all, thank you to my wonderful husband, Mark Kiernan, and my patient children, for unending encouragement, insights, and so many evenings, Saturdays, and Sundays.

NOTES

Chapter 1

1. Miles Socha, "The Luxury Hangover: Designers Struggling with Harsher Reality," *WWD*, July 1, 2002.
2. https://www.sba.gov/sites/default/files/Business-Survival.pdf
3. Discussion with author, January 31, 2020.
4. Discussion with author, October 12, 2004.
5. Discussion with author, February 19, 2020.
6. Discussion with author, February 26, 2020.
7. "CFDA/Gen Art: The Business of Fashion," panel discussion, CUNY Graduate Center, New York, November 3, 2004.
8. Discussion with author, February 26, 2020.
9. Stephanie D. Smith, "Start Them Young," *WWD Global*, October 2007.
10. Discussion with author, May 8, 2020.
11. Sally Singer, "Special Talent Watch: The Fab Five," *Vogue*, December 2003.
12. Discussion with author, March 12, 2020.
13. Discussion with author, February 18, 2020.
14. Ibid.
15. Discussion with author, October 12, 2004.
16. Discussion with author, January 31, 2020.

Chapter 2

1. Discussion with author, December 22, 2004.
2. Discussion with author, November 1, 2007.
3. "CFDA/Gen Art: Business of Fashion" panel discussion, Saks Fifth Avenue, New York, August 8, 2007.
4. Discussion with author, January 29, 2020.
5. "CFDA/Gen Art: The Business of Fashion," panel discussion, CUNY Graduate Center, New York, July 13, 2004.
6. Discussion with author, February 18, 2020.
7. Discussion with author, February 26, 2020.
8. Correspondence with author, July 13, 2020.
9. Discussion with author, January 16, 2020.

Chapter 3

1. Correspondence with author, April 15, 2020.
2. Miles Socha and Marc Karimzadeh, "Backing the Boys: Valentine Group Takes Stake in Proenza Schouler," *WWD*, July 11, 2007.
3. Correspondence with author, February 26, 2020.
4. Wenlan Chia (designer, Twinkle), discussion with author, October 26, 2004.
5. Michelle Smith (designer, Milly), discussion with author, October 21, 2004.
6. Discussion with author, October 16, 2004.
7. Discussion with author, October 26, 2004.
8. Discussion with author, June 12, 2020.

9. Caroline Tell, "Eugenia Kim, Coach to Team for Hats," WWD, October 8, 2007.
10. Discussion with author, January 16, 2020.
11. Discussion with author, September 24, 2007.
12. Correspondence with author, November 24, 2007.
13. Interview with author, January 31, 2020.
14. Correspondence with author, April 15, 2020.
15. Discussion with author, August 10, 2004.
16. Discussion with author, February 10, 2020.
17. Correspondence with author, February 26, 2020.
18. Robin Givhan, "The Downfall of the House of Isaac Mizrahi," *The Washington Post*, October 3, 1998.
19. Discussion with author, May 29, 2020.

Chapter 4

1. Discussion with author, May 8, 2020.
2. Discussion with author, January 31, 2020.
3. "CFDA/Gen Art: The Business of Fashion," panel discussion, CUNY Graduate Center, New York, February 22, 2005.
4. Discussion with author, May 29, 2020.
5. Correspondence with author, July 13, 2020.
6. Discussion with author, October 19, 2007.
7. "CFDA/Gen Art: The Business of Fashion," panel discussion, CUNY Graduate Center, New York, November 3, 2004.
8. Discussion with author, March 10, 2020.
9. Maria Bobila, "How Thakoon Panichgul has adapted his fashion brand and business over the past 15 years." *Fashionista.com*, September 18, 2019.
10. Discussion with author, March 12, 2020.
11. Discussion with author, February 8, 2020.
12. Discussion with author, November 14, 2020.
13. Discussion with author, January 31, 2020.

Chapter 5

1. CGS 2019 Retail and Sustainability Survey
2. *Business of Fashion*, Drive Season 2, Episode 5: Eileen Fisher Reflects on 35 Years of Implementing Sustainable Thinking; December 13, 2019.
3. Discussion with author, January 16, 2020.
4. Discussion with author, January 15, 2020.
5. Discussion with author, May 29, 2020.
6. Worldwildlife.org, "The Impact of a Cotton T-shirt," January 16 2013.
7. https://bayouwithlove.com/pages/our-story
8. Discussion with author, January 16, 2020.
9. Discussion with author, January 5, 2020.

Chapter 6

1. Discussion with author, March 17, 2020.
2. "CFDA/Gen Art: The Business of Fashion," panel discussion, CUNY Graduate Center, New York, July 13, 2004.
3. Discussion with author, November 1, 2007.
4. Amy Larocca, "Mr. In-Between," *New York* Magazine, July 30, 2007.
5. Discussion with author, October 12, 2004.

Chapter 7

1. Discussion with author, November 14, 2019.
2. Discussion with author, February 18, 2020.
3. Discussion with author, June 26, 2020.
4. Discussion with author, November 12, 2019.
5. Discussion with author, April 14, 2020.
6. Ibid.
7. Ibid.
8. Discussion with author, November 16, 2019.
9. Correspondence with author, January 2005.
10. Correspondence with author, May 11, 2020.
11. Suzy Menkes, http://suzymenkesvogue.com/about-suzy-menkes/
12. Correspondence with author, July 8, 2020.
13. "CFDA/Gen Art: The Business of Fashion," panel discussion, CUNY Graduate Center, New York, July 13, 2004.
14. Discussion with author, February 8, 2020.
15. Discussion with author, April 14, 2020.
16. Discussion with author, March 12, 2020.
17. Discussion with author, April 14, 2020.
18. Correspondence with author, July 6, 2020.

Chapter 8

1. Discussion with author, February 13, 2020.
2. Correspondence with author, February 24, 2020.
3. Discussion with author, January 31, 2020.
4. Correspondence with author, February 24, 2020.
5. Discussion with author, June 23, 2020.
6. Correspondence with author, July 3, 2020.
7. Discussion with author, January 16, 2020.
8. Discussion with author, February 10, 2020.
9. Correspondence with author, July 13, 2020.
10. Discussion with author, June 23, 2020.
11. Discussion with author, January 31, 2020.
12. Discussion with author, January 29, 2020.
13. Discussion with author, February 8, 2020.
14. Discussion with author, February 18, 2020.
15. Discussion with author, February 13, 2020.

Chapter 9

1. Discussion with author, January 31, 2020.
2. Discussion with author, June 12, 2020.
3. Discussion with author, February 8, 2020.
4. Discussion with author, January 31, 2020.
5. Discussion with author, June 12, 2020.
6. Marc Karimzadeh, "Rolling the Dice," *WWD*, November 14, 2007.
7. Discussion with author, February 27, 2020.
8. Discussion with author, February 10, 2020.
9. Discussion with author, February 14, 2020.
10. Discussion with author, October 16, 2019.
11. Correspondence with author, April 14, 2020.
12. Discussion with author, January 31, 2020.
13. Discussion with author, February 5, 2020.
14. Discussion with author, March 10, 2020.
15. Discussion with author, December 22, 2004.

16. Discussion with author, October 12, 2005.
17. "CFDA/Gen Art: The Future of Fashion," panel discussion, CUNY Graduate Center, New York, March 25, 2003.
18. Discussion with author, September 24, 2004.
19. "CFDA/Gen Art: The Business of Fashion," panel discussion, CUNY Graduate Center, New York, November 3, 2004.
20. Correspondence with author, May 8, 2020.
21. "CFDA/Gen Art: The Business of Fashion," panel discussion, CUNY Graduate Center, New York, November 3, 2004.
22. Discussion with author, November 4, 2007.
23. Discussion with author, October 21, 2004.
24. Discussion with author, January 2005.
25. Discussion with author, October 26, 2004.
26. Discussion with author, January 29, 2020.
27. "CFDA/Gen Art: The Business of Fashion," panel discussion, CUNY Graduate Center, New York, November 3, 2004.
28. Bonnie Bing, "Designers Sometimes Play Well Together," *The Wichita Eagle*, June 16, 2003.
29. Discussion with author, March 12, 2020.
30. Discussion with author, February 5, 2020.
31. Discussion with author, October 17, 2007.
32. Discussion with author, August 10, 2004.
33. Discussion with author, October 21, 2004.
34. "CFDA/Gen Art: The Business of Fashion," panel discussion, CUNY Graduate Center, New York, November 3, 2004.
35. Discussion with author, December 7, 2004.

Chapter 10

1. Discussion with the author, January 16, 2020.
2. Discussion with author, October 2004.
3. "The Next Big Names in Fashion," The ShowBuzz, June 5, 2006.
4. Correspondence with author, April 15, 2020.
5. Correspondence with the author, June 20, 2020.
6. Discussion with author, June 23, 2020.
7. David Lipke, "If I Only Knew Then What I Know Now," *DNR*, January 6, 2003.
8. Discussion with author, March 12, 2020.

Chapter 12

1. Discussion with author, November 30, 2004.
2. Discussion with author, January 16, 2020.
3. Discussion with author, October 24, 2004.
4. Correspondence with author, June 30, 2020.

RESOURCES

Find more extensive and updated resources at www. fashiondesignersurvivalguide.com.

General Business Resources

· Art of Citizenry (www.artofcitizenry.com) Coaches conscious businesses to maximize their impact through business development, branding, and strategic marketing.

· Athena International Powerlink Program (www.athenainternational.org) Women's business mentoring program.

· The Business of Fashion (www.businessoffashion.com) A leading source of fashion industry news and reporting.

· Centre for Fashion Enterprise (CFE) (https://fashion-enterprise.com/) The CFE at London College of Fashion supports new high-fashion companies in London.

· Columbia University Small Business Consulting Program (SBCP) (www. columbiasbcp.com) Founded by MBA students to provide pro bono consulting services to entrepreneurs.

· DMA United (www.dmaunited.com) Talent representation services for luxury fashion designers, including creative director placement, licensing, co-branding, sponsorships of shows and events, and product endorsements.

· Entrepreneur's BizStartUp (www.entrepreneur.com/bizstartups) Covers all aspects of starting a business, from business plan and financing to market research and legal issues.

· Fashion Capital (www.fashioncapital.co.uk) London-based online resource for comprehensive insight into the world of fashion, manufacturing, and business.

· Hello Alice (www.helloalice.com) Matches small business owners to personalized opportunities and resources.

· Launch Collective (www.launchcollective.com) Boutique consulting firm that provides business expertise to creative businesses in design and retail.

· My Own Business (www.myownbusiness.org) Offers a free online course for starting a business.

· National Federation of Business and Professional Women's Clubs (www.nfbpwc.org)

· Service Corps of Retired Executives (www.score.org) Free business mentoring and education from retired business executives.

· Small Business Administration (www.sba.gov)

· Tory Burch Foundation (www.toryburchfoundation.org) Capital, education, and digital resources to support women entrepreneurs in the United States.

Fabric and Materials Sourcing

· B&J Fabrics (www.bandjfabrics.com) High-end novelty fabrics and trims.

· C&J Textiles Inc. (www.cjtextile.com) Importers of fine fabrics.

· CFDA Sustainability Resource Guide (https://cfda.com/resources/sustainability-resources) Materials sourcing index and the very informative CFDA Guide to Sustainable Strategies.

· Cotec (www.cotec-epo.com) Sells eco-friendly fabric, including PVC-free handbag linings.

· Digifair (www.digifair.com) is a free app that connects fashion designers with suppliers who match their needs with no minimum order quantity requirements.

· The Ethical Making Resource (www.ethicalmaking.org) Practical information for jewelers and silversmiths to improve environmental and social sustainability.

· Fab Scrap (www.fabscrap.org) Recycles unused textiles in NYC and makes them available for reuse.

· Fashiondex (www.fashiondex.com) Publishes guides for sourcing and production including the The Small Design Company's Guide to Wholesale Fabrics.

· Jasco Fabrics (www.jascofabrics.com) High-end jersey with low minimums.

· Los Angeles Fashion District (www.fashiondistrict.org) Guide to suppliers and contractors in Los Angeles, California.

· Mood Fabrics (www.moodfabrics.com) Extensive selection of fabric, trims, and notions in both New York and Los Angeles.

· Natural dye resources: Earthues (http://earthues.com/), BotanicalColors.com (https://botanicalcolors.com), and Maiwa (https://maiwa.com)

· Queen of Raw (www.queenofraw.com) A marketplace to quickly and easily buy unused fabrics online.

· Re:Source library (www.study-ny.com/consulting) A library of up-to-date sustainable sourcing options along with consulting and education such as Textile Tuesday presentations and workshops.

· Responsible Jewelry Council (www.responsiblejewellery.com) Organization helping to transform supply chains to be more responsible and sustainable.

· Robert Kaufman Fabrics, Los Angeles, California (www.robertkaufman.com)

· Swatch On (www.swatchon.com) A global online fabric supplier to help emerging designers source with more efficiency through a large selection of fabrics and no minimum order quantity.

· SynZenBe (www.synzenbe.com) High-quality fabric resource with low MOQ, dedicated to reducing waste.

· Textile Exchange (www.textileexchange.org) Sets multiple standards for raw materials and fibers such as the Responsible Down Standard (RDS) and the Responsible Wool Standard (RWS).

· Vartest (www.vartest.com) NY-based textile laboratory for testing for fabric content.

· WeConnectFashion (www.weconnectfashion.com) Sourcing, production, and other industry resources for designers.

Fashion Organizations

· Accessories Council (www.accessoriescouncil.org)

· British Fashion Council (www.londonfashionweek.co.uk)

· Chicago Apparel Industry Board (www.aibi.com)

· Council of Fashion Designers of America (CFDA) (www.cfda.com)

· The Emerging Designer (https://theemergingdesigner.com) A platform for emerging designers and creative professionals focused on business-building content, consulting, and providing opportunities for designers.

· Fashion Group International (www.fgi.org) National organization for fashion professionals with chapters in multiple U.S. cities.

· Fashion Revolution (www.fashionrevolution.org) A global fashion movement to conserve and restore the environment and value people over growth and profit.

· Fashion Scholarship Fund (www.fashionscholarshipfund.org) Supports the careers of promising fashion students from all backgrounds with financial scholarships, internships, and career opportunities.

· FIT Design Entrepreneurs (www.designentrepreneursnyc.com) Provides NYC businesses an opportunity to participate in a free "mini-MBA" program. Each business is paired with a mentor to create a business plan and to competively "pitch" for a financial prize.

· Modem (www.modemonline.com/fashion) International reference lists of fashion showrooms, PR offices, and trade shows.

Finance

· Accion New York (us.accion.org) Provides micro-loans to local micro-enterprise owners, mostly minorities and women.

· Dun and Bradstreet (D&B) (www.dnb.com) Credit-checking service.

· Hilldun Corporation (www.hilldun.com) Offers accounts receivable, financing, and factoring services specializing in the needs of small fashion businesses.

· The Pace Small Business Development Center in NYC (www.pacesbdc.org) Free one-to-one assistance for entrepreneurs, as well as workshops and events in financing, marketing, staffing/operations, and accounting procedures.

· Pursuit Lending (https://pursuitlending.com) Affordable loans and resources for small business in NY.

· Prosper (www.prosper.com) America's first people-to-people lending marketplace—list and bid on loans using an online auction platform.

· Seed Co. Loans (www.seedco.org) National nonprofit organization works with local partners to create economic opportunities for entrepreneurs in select cities and states.

Incubators

· Chicago Fashion Incubator at Macys (www.chicagofashionincubator.org)

· Denver Design Incubator (DDI) (www.denverdesignincubator.com)

· Detroit Garment Group (DGG) (www.detroitgarmentgroup.org)

· London Fashion East (www.fashioneast.co.uk)

- Not Just A Label (www.notjustalabel.com) Online platform offers young brands easy access to e-commerce via the NJAL online store and tools for marketing.

- Philadelphia Fashion Incubator (www.philadelphiafashionincubator.com)

- Portland Fashion Week (www.portlandfashionweek.net)

- St Louis Fashion Fund (www.saintlouisfashionfund.org)

- San Francisco Fashion Incubator (www.fashionincubatorsf.org)

- The Market NYC (www.themarketnyc.com)

- Toronto Fashion Incubator (www.fashionincubator.com)

Job Resources

- 24 Seven (www.24seventalent.com)

- Business of Fashion Careers (www.businessoffashion.com/careers/)

- Fashion Career Expo (WWD) (www.fashioncareerexpo.com)

- Fashion Internships (www.freefashioninternships.com)

- Style Careers (www.stylecareers.com)

- The Fashion Network (www.thefashionetwork.com)

- Vault (www.vault.com)

Legal Services

- Fashion Law Initiative at New York Law School (https://www.nyls.edu/academics/specialty-areas/centers-and-institutes/innovation-center-for-law-and-technology/fashion-law-initiative/)

- Nicholas Rozansky, Brutzkus Gubner (www.bg.law)

- Olivera Medenica, Dunnington Bartholow & Miller LLP (www.dunnington.com/olivera-medenica-2)

- Tech Startup Clinic at Cardozo Law School (https://cardozo.yu.edu/tech-startup-clinic) For start-up e-commerce platforms.

- The Fashion Law Institute (www.fashionlawinstitute.com) Provides educational programming, free legal resources, and consultations. Their Fashion Law Pop-Up Clinics match designers with volunteer attorneys with fashion expertise.

- Volunteer Lawyers for the Arts (www.vlany.org)

Patternmaking and Development

- Blank Canvas Development (www.blankcanvasdevelopment.com)

- LC Workshop (www.lc-workshop.com) Patternmaking, production, and development for small labels.

- Patternmakers (www.tukaweb.com)

- Pattern Design (www.pattern-design.com) Sally Beers.

- Privy Label (www.privylabel.com/about) Development and production.

- Sepia NY (www.sepiany.com) Handbag development.

· Shoe Girls Studio (www.shoegirlsstudio.com) Workshops and consultation for shoe development and production.

· StitchLuxe (www.stitchluxenyc.com) Luxury apparel development with top-quality patternmaking, sampling, and full production management services.

Production

· Apparel Search (www.apparelsearch.com) Directory lists CMT factories and contractors.

· Bergen Logistics (www.bergenlogistics.com) Leading warehouse and fulfillment center for the apparel industry.

· ByHand Consulting (http://byhandconsulting.com) Consulting and networking to source socially responsible artisan-made product.

· CFDA Production Directory (https://cfda.com/resources) Directory of production and development resources.

· Ethical Fashion Initiative (www.ethicalfashioninitiative.org) Connects marginalized artisan communities in remote locations with global lifestyle brands.

· The Evans Group (TEG) (http://evansgroupinternational.com) Development and production house for high-end independent designers with locations in Los Angeles and San Francisco.

· Garment Contractors Association of Southern California (www.garmentcontractors.org) Lists services, minimums, and specialties.

· Made in NYC (www.madeinnyfashion.nyc) NYC initiative to fortify fashion design, manufacturing, and educational sectors.

· Makers Row (https://makersrow.com) Extensive resources for all production services and suppliers.

· NY Garment District (www.garmentdistrict.nyc) Lists of fashion factories, fabrics, and services, as well as seminars and workshops for designers.

· Opportunity Threads (www.opportunitythreads.com) Worker-owned cooperative in North Carolina. Provides sampling, upcycling, and small and large batch production.

· Source My Garment (www.sourcemygarment.com)

· Style Source (www.style-source.com) Production and materials resource includes specific information geared to small companies.

· Wing Son Garments Limited (www.wsandcompany.com) One of Canada's leading manufacturers of high-quality activewear.

Trade Shows

There are hundreds of trade shows around the world, including those in Australia, Canada, China, Denmark, Hong Kong, Korea, Poland, Russia, and Sweden. Many shows focus on categories such as bridal, childrenswear, shoes, jewelry, and lingerie. Below is just a small selection.

Textile and Sourcing

· Apparel Sourcing USA (www.apparel-sourcing-usa.us.messefrankfurt.com/new-york/en.html)

· Future Fabrics Expo (www.futurefabricsvirtualexpo.com) London-based show produced by The Sustainable Angle, dedicated to sustainably and responsibly produced fabrics and materials.

· FIT's CitySource (https://citysource.fitnyc.edu) Meet NY-based factory and sourcing representatives in person.

· Kingpin Sourcing and Textile Show focused on premium denim. (www.kingpinsshow.com) Created by New York–based fabric agent Olah Inc.

· Linea Pelle, Italy (www.lineapelle-fair.it) Leather and components for footwear, bags, and other leather goods.

· Los Angeles International Textile Show (www.californiamarketcenter.com/latextile)

· Première Vision Paris and New York (www.premierevision.fr)

· Sourcing at Magic, Las Vegas (www.magicfashionevents.com/en/shows/sourcingmagic.html)

· Spin Expo NY (www.spinexpo.com/) Focus on yarns and knits.

· Texworld (https://texworld-usa.us.messefrankfurt.com/new-york/en.html) Large sourcing show in New York and Paris.

Product Wholesale

United States

· Accessories Circuit, New York (www.nywomensfashionevents.com)

· Accessories the Show, New York and Las Vegas (www.accessoriestheshow.com)

· Capsule, New York (https://libertyfairs.com/) Menswear, Accessories

· Cabana Show Miami (www.cabanashow.com)

· Coterie, New York (www.coteriefashionevents.com/en/home.html)

· Curve, New York (www.curve-newyork.com/) Lingerie

· Designers and Agents, New York and Los Angeles (www.designersandagents.com) Womenswear, Accessories

· Magic, Las Vegas (www.magicfashionevents.com) Huge show focused more on the contemporary market for menswear, womenswear, and accessories.

· Man/Woman, Paris, New York, Tokyo (www.manwomanshows.com)

· NY Now (www.nynow.com)

· Pool, Las Vegas (www.pooltradeshow.com)

· Reassembled Show (www.brandassembly.com/reassembled-show)

· Shoppe Object (https://shoppeobject.com/the-show)

· Sole Commerce, New York (www.coteriefashionevents.com/en/show/sole-commerce.html) Shoes

· Swim Show Miami (www.swimshow.com)

China
· On Time Show (www.ontimeshow.com)

France
· Man/Woman (www.manwomanshows.com) Menswear, Womenswear

· Premiere Classe (www.premiere-classe.com) Accessories

· Tranoi (www.tranoi.com) Menswear, Womenswear

· Who's Next (www.whosnext.com) Ready to wear, Accessories

Great Britain
· Jacket Required (www.jacket-required.com) Menswear, Accessories

· Scoop (www.scoop-international.com) Womenswear

Italy
· Mipel (www.mipel.com) Leather, Accessories

· Pitti Immagine and Pitti Uomo, Florence (www.pittimmagine.com) Menswear

· White, Milan (www.whiteshow.com) Womenswear, Accessories

Japan
· Project Tokyo (www.project-tokyo.com) Womenswear, Menswear, Accessories

· Rooms (www.roomsroom.com) Womenswear, Menswear, Accessories

Wholesale Showrooms

· CD Network, New York (www.cdnetworkny.com)

· Denise Williamson, New York (@williamsonpr)

· EM Productions, New York and Los Angeles (www.emprds.com)

· Findings, New York and Los Angeles (www.findingsinc.com)

· Fiftytwo (www.fiftytwoshowroom.com)

· Franklin Street Showroom (www.franklinstshowroom.com/designers)

· Greg Mills, New York (www.gregmillsshowroom.com/index.html)

· Mint Showroom (www.mintshowroom.com)

· The News, New York and Los Angeles (www.495news.com)

· Peoples Revolution, New York and Los Angeles (www.peoplesrevolution.com)

· Seedhouse New York (www.seedinc.net)

· Showroom Seven New York (@showroomseven)

· Simon Showroom, New York (www.simonshowroom.com)

· Summer Somewhere (www.summersomewhere.com) Multiline showroom catering to the contemporary and resortwear markets.

· W29 Showroom, New York (@w29showroom)

Check Out the Designers in This Book

- Adiff (www.adiff.com)
- Alabama Chanin (www.alabamachanin.com)
- Alice Roi (www.aliceroi.com)
- Ashya (www.ashya.co)
- Autumn Adeigbo (www.autumnadeigbo.com)
- Bell by Alicia Bell (www.aliciabell.com)
- Bliss Lau (www.blisslau.com)
- Brother Vellies (www.brothervellies.com)
- Built by Wendy (www.builtbywendy.com)
- Canava (www.canava.co)
- Christian Siriano (www.christiansiriano.com)
- Christine Alcalay (www.christinealcalay.com)
- Duckie Brown (www.duckiebrown.com)
- Eugenia Kim (www.eugeniakim.com)
- Flora Obscura (www.floraobscura.nyc)
- Gary Graham (www.garygraham422.com)
- Grammar (www.grammarnyc.com)
- Gustavo Cadile (www.gustavocadile.com)
- Hfredriksson (www.hfredriksson.com)
- Hiro Clark (www.hiroclark.com)
- Keanan Duffty (www.keananduffty.com)
- Kirrin Finch (www.kirrinfinch.com)
- Kordal studio (www.kordalstudio.com)
- Krelwear (www.krelwear.com)
- Labucq (www.labucq.com)
- Lewis Cho (www.lewischo.com)
- Lindsey Thornburg (www.lindseythornburg.com)
- Loeffler Randall (www.loefflerrandall.com)
- Lost Art (www.lostart.com)
- Love Binetti (www.diegobinetti.com)
- Lulu Frost (www.lulufrost.com)
- Malia Mills (www.maliamills.com)
- Milotricot (www.milotricot.com)
- Naadam (www.naadam.co)
- Paige Novick (www.paigenovick.com)
- Patch NYC (www.patchnyc.com)
- Paul Marlow (www.paul-marlow.com)
- Rafe (www.rafe.com)
- Rebecca Taylor (www.rebeccataylor.com)
- Robert Geller (www.robertgellerstore.com)

- Rodarte (www.rodarte.net)
- Ruthie Davis (www.ruthiedavis.com)
- Subversive Jewelry (www.subversivejewelry.com)
- Study NY (www.study-ny.com)
- Thakoon (www.thakoon.com)
- Thea Grant (www.theagrant.com)
- Twinkle (www.twinklebywenlan.com)
- Yarborough (www.yarboroughjewelry.com)
- Zero Waste Daniel (www.zerowastedaniel.com)

INDEX